ENVIRONMENTAL RIGHTS

Law, Litigation & Access to Justice

ENVIRONMENTAL RIGHTS

Law, Litigation & Access to Justice

edited by

Sven Deimann & Bernard Dyssli

CAMERON MAY
LONDON

Published 1995 by Cameron May Ltd.

ISBN 1 874698 11 2

Printed by Watkiss Studios Ltd

CONTENTS

ENVIRONMENTAL RIGHTS

Law, Litigation & Access to Justice

Preface

The 1994 ELNI conference, hosted in cooperation with the Société Française pour le Droit de l'Environnement in Strasbourg, concentrated on the issue of the right to a healthy environment as a fundamental human right and what NGOs can do to further it, even in the absence of its constitutional recognition in most countries.

Contributions in the first section focused on environmental rights as a (quasi-)constitutional issue. Sandra Walker provides an interesting overview of recent developments in Ontario where the Ontario Environmental Bill of Rights had come into force only a short time before the conference. While the style and purpose of Ontario's legislation has constitutional implications, Sandra Walker notes the mostly political nature of the EBR which did not entrench a right to a healthful environment but rather seeks to empower Ontario's citizens to hold their political leaders politically accountable for respecting what the legislation still terms a right to a healthful environment. Two speakers from Eastern Europe, Y.S. Shemshuchenko from the Ukraine and Zurab Nogaideli from the Republic of Georgia, provided the conference participants with valuable information on the role that the environment plays as an issue in the current drafting of new constitutions in the republics of the former Soviet Union. Their contributions make clear the limits to environmental rights and environmental law in general in a culture where independent courts and judicial proceedings have played only a minute role in resolving social issues.

The following sections all deal with the more practical aspects to environmental litigation and NGO involvement in enforcing environmental provisions. The papers in section II focus in particular on standing for NGOs to bring suits in national and supra-national courts. Papers from Carol Hatton, James Cameron, Todd True, and Yves Corriveau highlight the possibilities for NGO litigation before the European, English, American and Canadian courts. This section was completed with a paper from Thomas Ormond who presented the network's Access to Justice study to the conference. Contributions in section III centre on the practical aspects of transfrontier environmental litigation and cooperation. Moreover Gerrit Betlem's paper canvasses the possibilities for adapting recent innovations in other areas of the law - in particular international intellectual property law - to an environmental law context. Section IV deals with the role of criminal and civil liability law in NGO strategies for the enforcement of environmental law. The conference concluded with a section on regulatory negotiation and voluntary agreements as part of NGO strategies for a healthful environment.

In focusing again in part on issues such as standing for NGOs, the 1994 ELNI conference revisited some of the topics that were already discussed at the network's first conference in 1990. Regrettably then, one might say, some of the contributions in this volume still dwell on the importance of citizen suits and open standing provisions as an efficient and effective means of enforcement. At least at the European level, things do not seem to have moved beyond the Access to Justice study commissioned by DG XI of the EC Commission.

On the other hand, the papers in sections II-V taken together do provide a refreshing reminder of the possibilities that are open to NGOs on the basis of the existing environmental law in many countries. While constitutional recognition of a right to a healthy environment should not be underrated, in particular with respect to its educational effects, the papers in this volume demonstrate the practical importance of the law below the constitution. This is where real progress will have to be made if environmental law is to be more rigorously enforced in future.

As editors we would like to thank the Commission of the European Community, the Gesellschaft für Politische Ökologie and the Öko-Institut e.V. for their generous financial support without which the conference could not have taken place. Special thanks also to Elisabeth Brand and the volunteers of the Société Française pour le Droit de l'Environnement who had to bear the brunt of organizing the conference on the spot in Strasbourg. We would also like to express our gratitude to our new publishers Cameron May Ltd. who have done a superb job in publishing the proceedings in a very short time indeed.

Finally we are particularly indebted to Heike Unruh and Betty Gebers at the Öko-Institute's ELNI coordination bureau. Without their unswerving support and dedication through many long hours of work this publication would not have been possible.

Darmstadt/Strasburg May 1995

Bernard Dyssli/Sven Deimann

Citizen Rights and Litigation in Environmental Law
Annual Conference of the Environmental Law Network International
Strasburg, 13-15 October 1994
Summary of Discussions

by Sven Deimann

Wednesday October 13, 1994

The 1994 annual elni board meeting was opened by Elisabeth Brand of the Société Française pour le Droit de l'Environnement - Section Régionale Est as host to this year's elni conference on Wednesday, October 13 at 7 p.m.

Present at this meeting were representatives from various environmental NGOs throughout Western, Central, and Eastern Europe as well as from Canada, the USA and Australia. The debate at this meeting focused mainly on two issues: the topic and venue for the 1995 annual elni conference and a suitable subject for a research project that members of the network could work on to generate funding on a more permanent basis for the network's year-round activities. The possibility of organizing a separate North-American chapter was also considered in a number of comments from the floor.

As for a possible research project, a general consensus emerged fairly soon that in the face of multifarious pressures from industry and governments to deregulate vast sectors of the economy deregulation and its effects on environmental law and public participation in licensing procedures should be taken up as issues which would merit further research.

Friday October 14, 1994

The conference was officially opened by Professor Alexandre Kiss of the Société Française pour le Droit de l'Environnement - Section Régionale Est and Strasburg's Robert Schuman University.

Following papers by Sandra Walker, Prof. Shemshuchenko, Zurab Nogaideli and Ludwig Krämer, Professor Michel Prieur as chairman during session I took a few questions from the floor. In the ensuing discussion, most speakers concentrated on the nature and objectives of greater public participation in environmentally relevant administrative or other legal procedures.

Speakers from Eastern and Central Europe - notably Zurab Nogaideli and Konrad Nowacki - drew attention to the fact that any form of bureaucratic, state-led procedure, however open it might be to public participation, met with considerable suspicion in the general population due to negative experiences with the rhetoric of popular participation under communist rule. Konrad Nowacki in particular stressed that some form of an actio popularis had been fairly wide-spread in many communist countries. This type of action had been retained under the revised Polish Constitution, although it had been rarely used under the previous régime. At the time, it had been perceived by many as a waste of time and resources.

Other comments focused on the role that the courts could play in an environmental law system which emphasized public participation. Gerhard Roller reminded participants of the necessity to link participation rights to substantive standards. Courts should not be overburdened. Zurab Nogaideli agreed that access to the courts should only be available where certain standards which had previously been officially laid down were being violated.

While Prof. Shemshuchenko again noted the reservations many people in Eastern Europe harboured against the courts, Ludwig Krämer expressed his confidence in the courts as institutions which had the potential to change society. He questioned how social behaviour could be transformed without institutions such as courts. Hence, he concluded that access to the courts had to be ameliorated in order to improve the state of the environment. He saw a role for NGOs in giving direction to the courts where improvements are possible and necessary. Furthermore, through citizen suit action, NGOs could also demonstrate that in some instances court action could lead to concrete results.

Referring to the situation in Australia, Paul Stein of the New South Wales Land and Environment Court agreed that court procedures could be cumbersome and bureaucratic and hence, for some people, a deterrent. He argued, however, that they do not necessarily have to be. Attempts by the Land and Environment Court in New South Wales to be more readily accessible, for example, had been very popular with the public in N.S.W. For instance, the court had adopted very open standing procedures which did not require the applicant to show that his or her personal rights had been infringed when alleging a breach of environmental regulations. Similarly, there was no requirement of an undertaking as to damages in interim procedures. Nevertheless, easing some of the procedural requirements and making courts more easily accessible did not necessarily mean that the number of frivolous suits would rise. Litigation still imposed enormous burdens on a potential plaintiff and hence, nobody in his right mind would take his case to court light-heartedly.

Concluding this round of discussion, Gerhard Roller agreed with Zurab Nogaideli that the role of the courts would have to be a different one in Western and Eastern Europe because of the different history.

Several questions concerning the nature of the EC Commission's procedures to investigate infringements of the EC Treaty by the Member States were taken after Ludwig Krämer's overview of the Commission's enforcement activities.

Replying to a question from the floor whether the Commission was under a formal obligation to process a complaint brought under the Commission's complaint procedure under art. 155 EC Treaty, Ludwig Krämer noted that the Commission had always viewed the processing of complaints as a matter over which it could exercise discretion. The Commission's position had never been formally challenged.

Peter Pagh of the University of Copenhagen criticized the Commission's public relations policy in the Oresund case. Instead of addressing a reasoned opinion to Greenpeace, a press release was issued which was subsequently treated as an authoritative statement by the Danish government.

In response Ludwig Krämer argued that nobody had asked

for access. There was no per se incentive for the Commission to publish reasoned opinions and, thus, to share its powers with other actors in the field.

As for procedures to challenge a decision by the Commission not to bring infringement proceedings under art. 169 of the EC Treaty - a possibility raised by Carol Hatton -, Ludwig Krämer maintained that no-one had ever tried to do so. Concerning public access to letters of formal notice and reasoned opinions, he drew attention to the practice of some of the German Länder which have started making public letters of formal notice received under the art. 169 EC Treaty procedures. Ludwig Krämer also claimed that answers by the Commission to questions from Members of the European Parliament were sometimes treated like "acts of God."

Marga Robesin insisted that there was nonetheless an information and communication gap to be closed by the Commission itself.

To this Krämer replied that the Commission simply lacked the necessary resources and man-power to keep complainants informed about the state of the complaint procedure they had commenced. In the particular case Marga Robesin had raised the Commission could not write the complainant earlier because the Dutch government had taken a very long time to respond.

In response to a question from Jerzy Jendroska Ludwig Krämer explained that the DG XI monitoring activities did not extend compliance with association agreements or the agreement on the European Economic Space. Likewise, compliance with the Berne Convention was not subject to the EC Commission's monitoring activities, as not all the Member States had signed the convention.

Following Carol Hatton's paper on the WWF, U.K./An Taisce v. Commission of the EC Case there was some discussion on the application of the Community's environmental policy to other areas of Community legislation and activity. Carol Hatton stressed the need for more transparent decision-making procedures inside the Commission. She also called for NGOs to be given access to justice at a European level. This she felt was all the more important as it was very difficult to hold a commissioner otherwise accountable for the activities of his or her directorate-general.

Nicolas de Sadeleer argued that the problem in the structural fund-cases such as the one brought by WWF, U.K./An Taisce was that the plaintiffs did not seek annulment of a specific decision within the meaning of art. 189 of the EC Treaty.

Ludwig Krämer drew a parallel to two-tier decision-making procedures in national law. Referring to the now abandoned plans for a waste incineration plant in Kehl on the eastern bank of the Rhine, he noted that under national law it was sometimes equally difficult to identify the proper decision against which to mount a legal challenge. Thus German law does not distinguish between planning permissions and subsequent permits which allow a facility to operate and to discharge emissions.

James Cameron then drew a parallel to similar difficulties under U.K. law when it came to defining a "project" within the meaning of the EIA directive. The legal measures adopted under the Town and Country Planning Act to implement the EIA directive appeared to suggest that an environmental impact assessment was necessary only in relation to planning procedures.

Saturday October 15, 1994

Environmental Impact Assessment was also the subject of a short round of floor discussion with which the conference was resumed on Saturday, October 15. Todd True's presentation of the Sierra Club's litigation in the north-western United States to protect the spotted owl - an endangered and rare species dependent on a certain forest habitat - sparked a number of comments on the nature of environmental impact assessment. While in the United States the Sierra Club was able to base a legal challenge to logging and other permits on purely procedural grounds - e.g. non-compliance with environmental impact assessment requirements, a number of speakers from Europe noted that the situation in Europe under the EIA directive was less clear.

Betty Gebers, for instance, explained that under German law violation of procedural requirements alone - such as the EIA provisions in the specific legislation of 1990 which sought to implement the EIA directive - was not sufficient to obtain a court order setting aside official permits and licences. A plaintiff had to demonstrate in addition that the alleged breach of procedural requirements had been material to the concrete decision taken and that it had in fact affected its substance.

Other speakers pointed out the difficulty of characterizing the nature of environmental impact assessment procedures under the EIA directive. A number of Member State governments had taken the position that the directive did not concern the substance of planning or licensing procedures and decisions. They rather viewed EIA procedures as a purely procedural device.

The conference next focused on issues of trans-frontier cooperation in environmental law.

In his presentation Mr. Jean-Michel Augé, an official with the Strasbourg Préfecture, outlined the institutional mechanisms that had been set up since the mid-1970s to allow for trans-frontier cooperation in the Alsace-Baden/Palatinate region. He explained that under a 1975 inter-governmental agreement different institutional levels of cooperation had been set up. Among them was the Conference of the Upper Rhine Valley at which officials from France (préfets), the Federal Republic (Land (State) officials) and several Swiss Cantons (elected Canton officials) participate. At the level below the Conference, specialized working groups coordinated cooperation with respect to specific subject matters such as, for instance, the environment. The working group in the field of the environment, then, was comprised of five expert groups which dealt with such matters as water quality, technological risks or generally speaking ecological problems. Within this institutional framework, official and informal meetings between French and German officials were quite frequent and M. Augé concluded by noting that generally speaking official relations in the Alsace-Baden region were marked by a high degree of exchange and intensive cooperation.

M. Augé cautioned, however, that against this background of intensive trans-frontier cooperation certain problems persisted that, in his view, could be put down to the fact that different legal systems and concepts applied in relation to the environment in France and in the Federal Republic. One particular problem concerned the concept of zoning or planning procedures in the Federal Republic on the one hand and in France on the other. While in the Federal Republic the licencing of a number of projects - such as waste incinerators of the type that was to be constructed at one point across the Rhine in Kehl - requires one form or another of a planning procedure, in France the concept of planning or zoning was somewhat different. Zoning was primarily an economic concept which sought to balance conflicting economic interests. M. Augé believed that different concepts as to the purpose and function of planning procedures had lain at the heart of a number of misunderstandings. He referred in particular again to the formerly planned waste incinerator in Kehl. In this particular instance, the French opponents of the project did not understand the nature of the German planning procedures. Conversely, many Germans have difficulty in understanding that planning procedures do not feature as prominently in the French system of environmental regulation as in the Federal Republic.

A further difference consisted in the way construction permits were granted in France. M. Augé explained that in granting such a permit, the competent authority was under no obligation to ensure that the applicant's project would comply with provisions under the French legislation on so-called "classified installations". Different procedures existed to ensure compliance with these provisions, and hence it was quite possible under French law that a construction permit would be granted while a permit to operate a "classified installation" could be refused. This situation, as a rule, does not arise under German law, M. Augé explained.

As for air pollution control, the French system relied primarily on emission limit values while the German system used both ambient air quality standards and emission limit values.

M. Augé concluded by canvassing some of the solutions that

had been found to grapple with the problems arising from the above-mentioned differences in environmental regulation. Some of the solutions were not exclusively of a local nature but comprised elements of EC law as well. The legal instruments used to consist mostly of recommendations adopted by the Conference of the Upper Rhine Valley. Thus two recommendations of 1982 and 1983 lay down rules for the mutual information concerning polluting industries and emergencies. M. Augé drew the conference's attention in particular to the recent practice of exchanging officials in order to improve the mutual understanding of the other side's culture, regulatory practices and law. Moreover, in Kehl a European Institute for the common training of officials had been established a few years ago.

M. Augé concluded by saying that the quality of cooperation had been improving because public opinion in both regions seemed to understand each other better these days.

The conference was closed with a short debate of voluntary agreements following Bernard Dyssli's paper on the Mackolsheim voluntary agreement.

Martin Führ expressed concern over the enforcement of such agreements with industry. He himself had concluded one with one of Germany's big chemical corporations - the BASTA agreement. Following a change of government in 1987 the company no longer felt any necessity to abide by the agreement, once the political pressure to stick to it had evaporated.

Commenting on the situation in Australia, Paul Stein was more optimistic about the possibility for enforcing voluntary or "mediated" agreements. In Australia, when litigation is first commenced, a polluter is offered "mediation". If a company agrees to a mediation procedure, the court can then in the end make a mediation order which is binding on the parties.

David Robinson added that this had helped in the case of a Bayer subsidiary in Sydney which had failed to carry out an Environmental Impact Assessment. Under a mediation order issued by a court the company in the end agreed to carry out an EIA and pay costs.

Ludwig Krämer, on the other hand, questioned the use of voluntary agreements. Referring to the Mackolsheim case he wondered whether the partial logging of the ancient river bank forest had not actually been a defeat for the environmentalists.

Bernard Dyssli nevertheless defended the agreement. At the time it was reached a factory had already been built on cleared land. The agreement, however, allowed the local NGO to secure very stringent protection measures for the remaining forest.

Sanford Lewis identified several means for achieving enforceability of negotiated or mediated solutions. Thus agreements could contain provisions for continued community rights of inspection of facilities. Agreements to reduce pollution could also be inserted into collective bargaining agreements thus lending them more strength.

Chapter 1

The Ontario Environmental Bill of Rights

by Sandra Walker

1. Background

On February 15, 1994, the Ontario Government pro claimed the Environmental Bill of Rights[1] (the "EBR" or the "Act"), legislation long-awaited by environmentalists in Ontario, Canada's most populous province. The purpose of the EBR is to promote environmental protection and a healthful environment through a democratization and opening up of government decision-making that affects the environment.[2] The gestation process for the EBR in Ontario was long and tortuous. Earlier bills were introduced by opposition parties in the Ontario Legislature, but until 1993 no bill had been introduced by a government in power. The most recent predecessor to the current EBR was a bill, Bill 12, introduced by the current governing party in 1989 when this party was in opposition. Bill 12 was not enacted.

In 1991, the Minister of the Environment charged a Task Force composed of three business representatives, two environmentalists, an independent legal advisor, and three government representatives with creating an environmental bill of rights for Ontario. After nine months of deliberations during which time each member of the Task Force consulted with a network of organizations and associations, a draft bill was crafted and recommended to the Minister of the Environment. Following public release of the draft bill, the draft was subject to extensive public debate as well as consideration within government ministries. This consultative process resulted in a significant number of revisions to the original bill. The EBR came into force on February 15, 1994 and is to be phased in over a period of five years.

Section 2(3) of the Act sets out the objectives of the Act: to enhance public participation in government decision-making affecting the environment[3], increase government accountability for its environmental decisions, improve access to the courts for Ontario residents seeking to protect the environment, and expand protections for employees who are penalized by their employers for taking action to protect the environment[4]. The Act differs significantly from its predecessor, Bill 12. Bill 12 would have granted to the people of Ontario the right to a healthy and sustainable environment, and made the Ontario Government the trustee of the environment for the benefit of present and future generations. To enforce their environmental rights, individuals were permitted under Bill 12 to commence legal action in the courts against persons responsible for contamination or degradation of the environment, the tolerable level of harm to be decided by the court.

In contrast, the EBR focuses on participation "rights": the public is given the means to participate in government decisions that affect the environment and to hold government accountable for such decisions. Recourse to the courts is seen as the last resort. Even where such recourse is had, as discussed more fully below, the judiciary is not given wide latitude to define the content of those rights. The approach taken in the EBR is that greater emphasis should be placed on making environmentally sound governmental decisions in the first place. Legal action taken once environmental damage has occurred is not sufficient. At the same time, the necessity for an environmental law regime to provide for private legal action to prevent harm to public resources and for restoration once environmental damage has been suffered is not ignored in the EBR.

As will become apparent in the following analysis of the EBR, this Act does not guarantee public participation in all decisions affecting the environment nor does it ensure that legal action to protect the environment will always be taken where necessary. The Act is clearly the product of compromise - the work of a committee of environmentalists, government and business - with the result that the Act has been somewhat attenuated for the sake of achieving a consensus among the Task Force members.

This paper focuses on and critically examines the three principal features of the EBR:

1. public participation in environmental decision-making;
2. access to the courts; and
3. government accountability for the environment.

2. Public Participation

2.1 Prospective Environmental Decision-Making

Part II of the EBR "sets out minimum levels of public participation that must be met before the Government of Ontario makes decisions on certain kinds of environmentally significant proposals for policies, Acts, regulations and instruments",[5] while expressly preserving rights of participation in environmental decision-making set out in other environmental legislation (for example, environmental assessment legislation). The EBR applies to 14 government ministries which are considered to make decisions affecting the environment.[6] While the government might be criticized for pre-emptively restricting the number of ministries which are considered to make decisions which affect the environment, the government did recognize the wide gamut of ministries that make decisions affecting the environment, from ministries responsible for areas customarily perceived as being irrelevant to the environment, for example, Economic Development and Trade, Finance, Labour, and Consumer and Commercial Relations to those ministries more traditionally found within the "environmental" fold: Environment and Energy, Natural Resources, and the Agriculture, Food and Rural Affairs.

Subject to certain qualifications discussed below, the 14 ministries are obliged to notify the public of proposals for environmentally significant decisions. This general requirement to give notice of potentially environmentally significant proposals did not exist prior to the EBR. The scope of the government's obligation to notify is limited to "decisions". While the word "decision" is not defined in the Act, the EBR expressly mandates the prescribed ministries to notify policies, acts, regulations under prescribed statutes, and prescribed "instruments". An "instrument" is defined to mean "any document of legal effect issued under an Act and includes a permit, licence, approval, authorization, direction or order issued under an Act"[7].

The minister of each prescribed ministry must notify those decisions in each category (for example, a policy) which are "environmentally significant". While the Act does not define "environmental significance" as such, it establishes four criteria for assessing significance: (a) the extent and nature of measures that might be required to mitigate or prevent any harm that could result from a decision whether or not to implement the proposal; (b) the geographic extent (local, regional or provincial) of any environmental harm that could result from a decision; (c) the nature of the private and public (including governmental) interests involved in the decision; and (d) any other matter considered relevant by the minister[8]. For policies and acts, the minister's discretion to notify also depends on whether the minister considers that the public should have the opportunity to comment[9].

Notice of environmental policies, acts and regulations is to be given for a minimum period of 30 days. This period can be extended "to permit more informed public consultation on the proposal"[10]. For instruments, the EBR has created a hierarchy of public participation from Class I instruments (with the least public participation) to Class III (where a formal hearing is required). For Class II instruments, the minister is specifically mandated to consider lengthening the time for public comment and enhancing the means for public involvement from opportunities for oral representations to the minister or his/her representative to public meetings and mediation between different interests involved in the decision-making process. The minister is also required to give additional notice to the public of Class II instruments by a variety of means, including actual notice to community leaders[11].

The primary means for giving notice of proposals under the EBR is an electronic registry (the "Registry"). This "electronic bulletin board" is one of the most innovative aspects of the Act and has the merit of being environmentally progressive (less paper will be used), and of providing widespread, simultaneous notification through existing computer networks. Members of the public are able to gain access to the registry at public libraries around the province or from a personal computer and modem at no charge. The Registry was designed to use language accessible to the general public. Members of the public wishing to comment on a new policy, statute, regulation or instrument may obtain additional information by contacting ministry officials listed on the Registry, and may provide written comments on the proposal. The government ministry must consider the comments submitted in its decision[12] and then provide notice to the public of the final decision, again through the Registry.

Whether the EBR will open up environmental decision-making to the extent touted by its proponents may be debated. The public participation rights of the EBR are subject to a number of criticisms (some justified, others not). For example, the EBR leaves the power of making environmental decisions with the government and does not, in general, require decision-making by consensus. Two responses can be levelled at this criticism. First, the Act requires ministers to "take every reasonable step to ensure that all comments relevant to the proposal ... are considered"[13]. Second, the EBR should heighten awareness of environmental decisions and thus generate public pressure for the government to take community concerns into account. A second criticism is that the EBR notification provisions give the minister an excessive degree of latitude in deciding whether to notify policies and acts. If a policy is considered environmentally significant, it is questionable how the minister could then conclude that the public should not have the opportunity to comment. This is a potentially gaping hole in the structure of the Act which could be exploited by environmentally indifferent governments (depending on the success of the government accountability measures discussed below). Finally, since the majority of instruments fall within the Class I designation, the EBR can be criticized for providing insufficient minimum (30 days) notice of most decisions. Whether this criticism is valid may be debated. The 30 days is a minimum and additional time may be granted. In addition, the EBR does provide that Class I instruments may be treated as Class II instruments (i.e., bumped up) if the minister considers that additional notice and time for comment are necessary[14].

2.2 Review of Past Decisions

The process described above relates to the development of new acts, policies, regulations, and instruments. The Act also applies retrospectively in that residents of Ontario may apply for reviews of decisions that were made in the past.[15] While such applications could have been made before the EBR, ministers are now legally obliged to consider a number of criteria in determining whether or not to conduct the review and to notify applicants within certain time limits as to whether a review will be conducted. If a review is performed, the minister must given notice of the outcome of the review to the applicant, among others. Interestingly, the application for review provision has been the subject of interest from both business and environmentalists as a mechanism to challenge existing environmental policies, acts, regulations, or instruments.

The application for review procedure is deficient on several grounds. First, the review only applies to those laws that are prescribed under the Bill. Since there is discretion to determine what is prescribed, this provision is correspondingly attenuated. Second, the Minister retains wide discretion to determine whether or not to conduct a review[16]:

67(2) In determining whether the public interest warrants a review, the minister may consider,

a) the ministry statement of environmental values;

b) the potential for harm to the environment if the review applied for is not undertaken;

c) the fact that matters sought to be reviewed are otherwise subject to periodic review;

d) any social, economic, scientific or other evidence that the minister considers relevant;

e) any submission from a person who received a notice under section 66;

f) the resources required to conduct the review; and

g) any other matter that the minister considers relevant.

While a consideration such as the resources available to

conduct the review is certainly understandable at a time of severe government budgetary deficits, it does offer governments which are not committed to environmental protection a ready excuse for inaction.

Third, decisions which were made within the preceding five years must *not* be reviewed if there was public participation at the time the decision was originally made unless new social, economic, scientific or other evidence indicates that a failure to review could result in significant harm to the environment[17]. This "presumption of immunity" for recent decisions clearly gives ministries significant discretion not to review. While the government cannot continuously review past decisions, this provision seems unnecessarily pre-emptive of the review possibility. Moreover, the list set out in section 67(2) already provides an extensive range of factors which the minister may consider when deciding whether to conduct a review; an arbitrary five year cut-off should not preclude a review when these factors indicate that a review is necessary.

3. Access to the Courts

Beyond opening up the government's environmental decision-making, the EBR creates a new right of action by which members of the public can sue polluters who have caused significant environmental harm to a public resource. Public resources include air, water, public lands, and any associated plant life, animal life or ecological system[18]. Before the EBR, Ontario residents could sue for environmental harm in civil proceedings only where they had suffered personal injury, property damage, or direct economic loss.

Unlike its predecessor, Bill 12, the EBR does not grant Ontario residents a substantive right to a healthy environment; residents do not have the right to sue for any harm to the environment. Indeed, there are three prerequisites to a successful suit. First, the plaintiff must have made an EBR application to the government for an investigation of the environmentally harmful activity and must have received a government response that is "not reasonable" or not within a "reasonable time". As there is little guidance in the Act as to what constitutes a "reasonable response", it will fall to the courts to determine what such a response is. Second, the plaintiff must establish that the alleged polluter has violated one of the environmental laws, regulations or instruments prescribed by regulation under the Act. As the standard of proof is on "balance of probabilities", a less stringent standard than that employed in criminal prosecutions is applicable. Third, the plaintiff must demonstrate that there has been "significant" harm to the environment, a level of harm to be determined by the courts.

Where the court finds in favour of the defendant, there are two principal remedies: an injunction to stop the environmentally harmful activity, and/or an order to the parties to negotiate a "restoration plan". No damage awards may be made, although the normal rules of civil procedure apply; that is the court may order the losing defendant to pay the plaintiff's legal costs. The reverse is also true. An unsuccessful plaintiff may have to pay the defendant's legal costs.

Other jurisdictions have approached citizen-initiated environmental suits from a different perspective. For example, the 1970 *Michigan Environmental Protection Act*[19] (MEPA) authorizes citizen suits against the state or any person, including corporations, "for the protection of the air, water and other natural resources and the public trust" from "pollution, impairment or destruction". Unlike the Ontario legislation, the Michigan right to sue provision does not require the plaintiff to show a contravention of environmental statutes. Instead, the courts are left the task of determining the threshold of environmental harm at which a defendant will be found liable. As noted above, Ontario's EBR leaves such determinations to the legislators. This represents a fundamental difference between the Michigan and Ontario citizen suits. One implication of applying the Michigan approach in Ontario would be that a company operating its facilities "legally" (that is, with a permit, licence, approval or other instrument under Ontario's statutory regime) could be held liable in a civil proceeding for violating a different, judicial standard for environmental harm.

Another feature distinguishing Michigan's statute from Ontario's EBR is MEPA's reference to the "public trust". The significance of this phrase is that government is the trustee of those natural resources and can therefore be sued for failure to take action to protect the environment. Under the Ontario statute, the government can be sued under the EBR, but only for environmentally harmful actions which it undertakes and not in its capacity as a government (for example, enforcing laws or issuing licences).

The main limitation of this new cause of action is that environmental groups who will likely be the main users of this action could be saddled with significant legal costs if they lose a suit and are forced to pay the defendants' legal costs as well as their own. This may prove to be a significant constraint on use of the new right of action. Ironically, members of the business community have voiced the opposite concern - that the new right to sue will result in a flood of litigation. This fear has not materialized in Michigan where the right to sue is framed more broadly than in the Ontario EBR. Second, some consider it a weakness of the EBR that the government *qua* legislator/ enforcer itself is not subject to suit under the EBR. In response, it may be argued that the mere possibility that the government could be named as a third party in suits against polluters (e.g., the failure by the government to enforce the laws strictly could, it is argued, lull the polluter into believing its polluting activity is legal) will lead to greater vigilance and enforcement activity on the part of government ministries.

4. Government Accountability

The Act's effectiveness in increasing environmental protection will depend to a large extent upon how ministers exercise the discretion which is liberally conferred upon them throughout the Act. As all governments cannot be counted upon to be equally diligent in protecting the environment, the drafters of the EBR decided that there had to be some constraint on the exercise of discretion by public officials and politicians. Judicial review of ministerial action or inaction is limited under the EBR to instances where the minister has "failed in a fundamental way to comply with the requirements of Part II respecting a proposal for an instrument[20]. Even if this privative clause were held to be ineffective, the circumstances in which judicial review would be available are limited.

The instrument of accountability the EBR relies on instead is the Office of the Environmental Commissioner. This independent office acts as the government watchdog and is responsible for monitoring the implementation of the Act. In particular, the Environmental Commissioner is empowered to review the exercise of ministers' discretion under the EBR by, for example, noting if a minister has failed to place a proposal for an environmentally significant policy on the Registry.

To ensure the Environmental Commissioner has a high profile, the Commissioner is required by law to report annually to the Legislature on ministries' compliance with the Bill's provisions. In addition, the Commissioner may make special reports where deemed necessary. The potential political embarrassment resulting from such a report is calculated to ensure ministry compliance with the EBR.

The second mechanism by which the EBR seeks to improve government accountability is the requirement for the 14 prescribed ministries to prepare "statements of environmental values" or SEVs. These statements are to explain how each ministry incorporates the EBR objectives of environmental protection, sustainability and a healthful environment into its decision-making process. These documents constitute a public commitment by each ministry to take the environment into account. As such, they may be used by the public and the Environmental Commissioner to rate a ministry's environmental performance. Draft SEVs were placed on the Registry in May, 1994 and following a public comment period, the SEVs were finalized and placed on the Registry in November, 1994. The SEVs have been subject to the criticism that they are too couched in generalities to be useful and there is a concern that they may not be implemented. It will be the Environmental Commissioner's mandate to monitor and publicize ministries' compliance (or failure to comply) with their SEVs.

5. Conclusion

The EBR aims to democratize environmental decision-making by increasing public knowledge of and participation in decisions that affect the environment, and to increase access to the courts where government has failed to take the necessary enforcement measures. The Act's primary focus is the establishment of participatory decision-making to protect the environment. Since the EBR puts less emphasis on judicial determinations of acceptable and unacceptable levels of environmental harm than other environmental bills of rights, it does not take any direct steps towards establishing higher thresholds of intolerance to environmental harm. Nevertheless, more environmentally stringent standards may result from greater public awareness and participation in environmental decisions. Furthermore, greater access to the courts to protect public resources should improve the government's enforcement record. Thus, while the EBR has not satisfied all constituents, this Act represents a welcome advance in environmental legislation in the Province of Ontario.

Notes

[1] Chapter 28, Statutes of Ontario, 1993.

[2] Section 2(1) states that: "The purposes of this Act are, (a) to protect, conserve and, where reasonable, restore the integrity of the environment by the means provided in this Act; (b) to provide sustainability of the environment by the mans provided in this Act; (c) to protect the right to as healthful environment by the means provided in this Act."

[3] The "environment" is defined as "the air, land, water, plant life, animal life and ecological systems of Ontario" (section 1(1), EBR). Note, the "environment" does not include the indoor environment.

[4] The EBR expands protection for employees who are disciplined or dismissed by their employers because such employees have taken action to protect the environment by, for example, seeking the enforcement of an environmental law or providing information to the government to be used in an investigation of the employer. (Such employees are said to "blow the whistle" on their employer and hence are called "whistleblowers".) The EBR expands existing whistleblower protection for actions to enforce environmental laws from five statutes to twenty-one, including the EBR. Where an employee has suffered reprisals, he or she may file a complaint with the Ontario Labour

Relations Board which may authorize an investigation. If the matter cannot be settled, the Board may order an enquiry. The employer has the onus of proving that he or she did not take reprisals on a prohibited ground. If the employer is found to have taken such reprisals, the Board may order the employer to cease the prohibited acts, to rectify the acts, or to reinstate or compensate the employee. This provision has been criticized as not overcoming the significant disincentive employees may have to blowing the whistle on their employers.

[5] Section 3, EBR.

[6] The 14 ministries are: Ministry of Agriculture, Food and Rural Affairs, Ministry of Consumer and Commercial Relations; Ministry of Culture, Tourism and Recreation; Ministry of Economic Development and Trade; Ministry of Environment and Energy; Ministry of Finance; Ministry of Health; Ministry of Housing; Ministry of Labour; Management Board Secretariat; Ministry of Municipal Affairs; Ministry of Natural Resources; Ministry of Northern Development and Mines; Ministry of Transportation.

[7] Section 1(1), EBR.

[8] Section 14, EBR.

[9] Section 15(1), EBR.

[10] Section 17, EBR.

[11] Section 28, EBR.

[12] Section 35, EBR.

[13] Ibid.

[14] Section 26, EBR.

[15] The EBR provisions on applications for review also permit Ontario residents to request a review of the need for a new policy, Act or regulation.

[16] Section 67(2), EBR.

[17] Section 68, EBR.

[18] Section 82, EBR.

[19] Environmental Protection Act of 1970, MICH.COMP.LAWS ss 691.1201.1207 (West Supp.1984).

[20] Section 118(2), EBR.

Chapter 2

Human Rights in the Field of Environmental Protection in the Draft of the New Constitution of the Ukraine

by Y. Shemshuchenko

Before discussing this problem it is necessary to outline the history of the development of this draft. As you may know, in August 1991 the Ukraine officially declared its independence. However, already in October 1990 the Parliament of the Ukraine formed a Constitutional Commission to prepare a draft for a new Constitution of the Ukraine. I was a member of this Commission. The Commission had two co-chairmen: the President of the Ukraine and the Chairman of the Supreme Council (or Parliament) of the Ukraine. The Commission prepared several draft versions of the new Constitution of the Ukraine. The final version was approved by the Commission in October 1993 and was submitted to the Parliament. However, the powers of the former Parliament were to expire shortly and the Parliament was hesitating and did not take the responsibility to review the draft. Due to the elections of the new President and of Parliament at the end of last year, the process of adopting the Constitution was actually suspended for more than half a year. By that time, new Constitutions have been adopted in almost all independent states, i.e. the former republics of the Soviet Union. The Ukraine, however, still lives with the Constitution of 1978. It contains a large number of amendments and additions.

Recently, the new political leaders of the Ukraine declared that the process of drafting a new Constituion would be renewed. A new Constitutional Commission will be formed soon. The Commission's aim is to accelerate the work on a new draft of the constitution which should be based on the draft prepared in 1993.

Now let me turn to the problems of reflecting ecological rights of individuals and citizens in the draft Constitution of the Ukraine of 1993.

1. The Problem of the Human Right to a Safe and Healthy Environment.

The right to a healthy environment is mentioned neither in the Universal Declaration of Human Rights, nor in the International Pacts on Economic, Social and Cultural Rights, or the European Convention on Human Rights. To a small extent this right was reflected only in the documents of the 1972 Stockholm Conference of the United Nations on the Environment and the UN Conference on the Environment and Development, held in Rio in 1992. For example, Principle I of the Declaration of the latter Conference provides: that human well-being people is a central point in the efforts aimed at ensuring sustainable development. People have a right to a healthy and fruitful life in harmony with nature.

The point here is not the quality of the environment, but the quality of the individual's life which, naturally, may not be limited to ecological factors. Secondly, although the definition "life in harmony with the nature" indicates the appropriate relationship between the individual and nature, this is not sufficient from the point of view of a qualitative characteristic of the environment.

To a certain extent, the caution shown at the international level with respect to ensuring the human right to a safe environment does slow down and restrict the process of incorporating this right in domestic legislation. In the Ukraine this problem gave rise to an extensive theoretical discussion. Eventually, the position in favour of an official recognition of this right has prevailed. For the first time, this right was officially stated in 1991, in the Law of the Ukraine on the Protection of the Environment. Today, this right is included in the draft of the new Constitution of the Ukraine. The draft provides that "everyone shall have the right to the environment that is ecologically safe for life and health."

The problem was resolved in the same manner in a number of new Constitutions of other states. The right to a safe environment is stated, for example, in the Constitution of the Russian Federation (Article 42), the Constitution of the Republic of Belarus (Article 46), the Constitution of the

Republic of Kazakhstan (Article 26). However, the new constitutions of some other states do not mention this right.

Different approaches to the resolution of this problem at the Constitutional level are determined in my opinion by the insufficient theoretical development of the notion of the right to a safe environment. Usually, the quality of the environment is defined by the standards of the contamination of water, air and soil which are provided for in the legislation. Compliance of environmental conditions with these standards would be evidence that the environment is safe for a human being, and non-compliance - that the environment creates hazards for human life and health. Therefore, the human right to a healthyl environment is actually the right of an individual to demand the maintaining of ecological standards, set up by law.

Sometimes some observers say that the so-called "positive rights" (to work, education, health protection) which include the right to a safe environment are not the rights in the full meaning of this term but are, rather, social intentions. This position stems from the fact that these rights may not be guaranteed to the full extent, in particular, through the courts.

It is difficult, however, to agree with such arguments. While it is true that no absolute guarantees exist, this fact may not be an obstacle to constitutionally securing the human right to a safe environment. It is clear that such a right does not simply determine the type and scope of the permitted behaviour of the holder of this right. The same concerns the right to life. But there are no disputes about its rights as to the existence of this right. The concept of the human right to the healthy environment is better reflected today in domestic legislation than in international law. A national legislator in this respect has actually nothing to implement as regards the Universal Declaration of Human Rights or the European Convention on Human Rights. In view of the development towards internationally recognised values, the absence of an international legal recognition of this right objectively slows down the process of securing the human right to a healthy environment in national legislation and leads to the unjustified divergence as regards the understanding and interpretation of the right. That is why it would be proper to add to the European Convention on Human Rights a special Protocol regarding the right of an individual to the healthy environment. It has also become necessary to secure this right in other documents which are of worldwide importance.

2. The Problem of the Title to Natural Resources

According to the current Constitution of the Ukraine, all natural resources fall within the scope of exclusive competence of the state. These resources may be given to the citizens only for purposes of usufruct, not ownership. In recent years, however, we experienced a substantial reassessment of the problem of title to natural resources in favour of private ownership. This fact has been reflected in the draft of the new Constitution. The draft provides for two types of ownership: public and private.

Unfortunately, the draft does not contain any detailed provisions with respect to the right to private ownership of natural resources. The draft only provides that the right for private ownership of land shall be granted only to citizens of the Ukraine in accordance with applicable legislation.

What do other new Ukrainian laws say about this problem? According to the Law on the Protection of the Natural Environment, the title to all natural resources of the Ukraine belongs to its people. The right to dispose of these resources on behalf of the people is vested with the Supreme Council of the Ukraine (Article 5). However, the 1993 Law of the Ukraine on Wildlife governs the issue of title to fauna in a different manner. Under the Law, the title does not belong to the people of the Ukraine as a whole, but to the state, public collectives and individuals (Articles 5, 6).

Of special interest is the regulation of the issue of land title in the Land Code of the Ukraine, adopted in 1992, which differs from land-title regulations in the Law on the Protection of the Natural Environment. In particular, the Code provides for three forms of ownership for land: state, collective and private.

All these forms have equal legal standing. At the same time, however, the Code sets up maximum limits of the size of land lots which may be transferred to citizens and prohibits to sell such land lots for six years following the date of acquisition of the title to the land lot. This situation was partially changed by a Decree of the Ukrainian Government "on the Privatisation of Land Lots" (December, 1992). The Decree allows citizens to sell land lots which have been transferred to the citizens free of charge. This provision applies to land lots used for a villager's or farmer's individual needs (the size of the land lot may not exceed 0.6 hectares); for constructing and maintaining a residential house (up to 0.25 hectares); for building individual cottages (or "dachas" - up to 10.1 hectares). All other land lots may not be sold. In addition, the Law prohibits foreign ownership of land in the Ukraine. As we can see, the Ukrainian legislation governing land issues is more conservative than the respective legislation in Russia which at the moment allows the purchase and sale of all types of land lots owned by citizens without any restrictions.

Now a few words about the perspectives for possible future developments in the area of natural resources law and title to them. It is more likely that the new Constitution of the Ukraine will incorporate the general rule that natural resources of the Ukraine constitute a heritage of its people. Not the property, but the heritage received for use from the preceding generations. As regards land, land lots will still be transferred to private ownership of citizens. The size and order of granting such land lots must be governed by the special law. It is obvious that the Constitution should contain a provision ensuring the right of citizens of the Ukraine to use freely all other natural resources in compliance with the legal requirements.

3. The Right to Information on the Environment

The issue of granting constitutionally this right assumed particular importance after the catastrophe at the Chernobyl nuclear power station. Following the accident, many persons suffered heavy losses due to the lack of reliable information on the character of the disaster. That's why the draft of the New Constitution of the Ukraine contains the provision that the state guarantees to every person the right to a free access to information about the state of the environment and the quality of food-stuffs as well as the right to the dissemination of such information. There is also the draft provision that the hiding and distortion of such information by officials is punishable according to the order established by the law.

4. The Problem of the Protection of the Ecological Human Rights and the Solution of Disputes Connected with the Realisation of these Rights

According to the new draft of the Constitution, the solution of this problem is incumbent on the state. The state's ecological policy is aimed at ensuring the safety of the environment and a rational use of natural resources. The state establishes ecological rules and requirements and ensures compliance with minium ecological standards when carrying out construction projects.

At the same time the state recognises the priority of ecological interests over economic interests. But today the above mentioned provisions are only good intentions, because there is a gap between legal norms and reality. Under the conditions of the deep economic crisis the budgetary fundings for environmental protection are cut back year by year. For example, in 1993 only 0.2 percent of the national gross product was assigned to these purposes from the state budget of the Ukraine. Five years ago this index was more than one percent. In other countries it reaches more than three or four percent. Such a situation is aggravated by the fact that the density of pollution per one square kilometre in the Ukraine is more than six and a half times higher than in the United States and more than 3.2 times higher than in the EC Member States.

The environmental control is not effective and there is no due responsibility for violations of ecological norms. According to the data compiled by sociologists, only one in ten violations of ecological legislation is discovered. In spite of the increase in the number of environmental offences, the courts nowadays bring criminal charges against law-breakers 4 times less than 10 years ago. The costs of environmental damage reach huge sums of money which are not recovered from polluters and hence do not flow into the national budget. Consequently one of the most important sources of financing environmental clean up measures is not used.

There are serious problems concerning the solution of ecological disputes. The law of the Ukraine on environmental protection has granted the citizens and public organisations the right to sue in the courts the enterprises which polluted the environment. Many countries have such experience. But in our country such cases are very rare. There are two main reasons for that. First, there are no reliable methods for calculating damages resulting from environmental pollution. Second, the individuals often do not want to be involved in court procedures. Polls have shown that only slightly more than 11 percent of all the persons asked trust the courts. We need further reforms of the judicial system.

According to the draft of the Constitution the judicial system will include the courts of general competence and arbitration courts. But now some new models have appeared. In particular, there are projects of the creation of criminal, civil, administrative, financial and other courts. In my opinion, there is also a place for environmental courts in these models. But all this may be done in the remote future. Today there is an urgent need to prepare highly qualified judges (in our country the quantity of judges per 100 thousand inhabitants is two or three times lower than in England, Germany, France and other countries). We must also draft new laws, build new premises for courts and so on. Until our judicial power builds up the necessary strength, many environmental disputes will continue to be settled by administrative methods. Moreover, these disputes often are resolved at the highest level. For example, the Odessa District Council recently prohibited the construction of an oil terminal at the sea coast near Odessa to prevent environmental damage. This issue was submitted to our Parliament for consideration. Here the economic interests of the Government came into conflicts with ecological interests of the Odessa region. The Government insisted on the construction of the terminal which was to supply the Ukraine with overseas oil. Unfortunately, neither the current Constitution nor the new Constitution's draft made a precise distinction between the competence of central and regional authorities. Experience has shown that under these circumstances the central authority is often the highest judge. The Constitutional Court has not yet been established. For this reason, one-sided environmental decision-making cannot be ruled out in the near future, either.

The general conclusion is: The environmental human rights are reflected in the new Constitution's draft. But adequate guarantees for the realisation of these rights have not yet been created. This is why the main attention of the society and state must be paid to the creation of such guarantees. It is furthermore necessary, in my view, to consider more fully the right to a clean and healthy environment in other constitutions.

Chapter 3

The Citizens Role in Georgian Legislation

by Zurab Nogaideli

Before speaking about our future plans let us say a few words on current public participation regulations together with some examples and procedures for appealing to the Court.

1. According to the new Georgian law on public organisations, which was passed by the Parliament on June 14 1994, the public organisations have the right to conduct meetings and demonstrations, to represent and defend interests and rights of their members in the State and other public organisations. This also includes going to the Court, but the problem is that NGOs may represent only interests of the organisation itself and not general public interests as we wish.

2. Despite the fact that there has been no formal regulation of public participation in the decision-making process we have a lot of examples of stopping environmentally damaging projects due to public demand. In 1987 a series of high dam hydro power stations were to be built on the Enguri river in one of the most beautiful places in Georgia - the Svaneti Mountains. No environmental impact assessment was conducted (It was not required that time). The Enguri Valley and its flora and fauna was in danger. The Georgia Greens Movement campaigned by public demand against this project. Certainly no regulations for public participation existed at that time, but nevertheless public pressure was successful and the project was stopped. Another very important achievement was, that after this public activity everyone, even very technocratic energy people, agreed on the necessity of environmental impact assessments of dangerous projects.

The next successful story regarding public participation was the Trans Caucasian tunnel. Its building was also stopped due to public demand. On three occasions the Greens stopped different projects importing hazardous wastes to Georgia and utilising them and land filling. But everything was illegal. Georgian Government officials were afraid of "public opinion" and were passing decisions in accordance with that opinion. Now many people, who are afraid of difficulties that Georgia faces today, would like to take a decision in a small group of higher officials and so-called specialists. Now our task is to provide legal procedures for investment decision making and public participation with clearly defined rights for the investor, government and public.

We see public participation not only as a very important basis for making correct decisions, but also a very important step towards building a democratic society in Georgia.

3. We have a very complicated system of litigation. As you probably know, in the ex-USSR the role of the Court was neglected and we are at the beginning of the process of reforming this system. We have three different codes regarding responsibility for violation of the laws: civil, administrative and criminal. A citizen has the right to appeal directly to the Court only in a case of violation according to the Civil Code, e.g. divorce etc. Most of the cases of violation of environmental legislation are considered under the Administrative and Criminal Codes. The procedure for appealing to the Court here is very complicated. Only the public prosecutor has the right to take the decision to pass the case to the Court. The Court only defines the guilt of a person. Public organisations and citizens can not directly appeal to the Court, but should apply in written form to the public prosecutor and he has the right (as it was mentioned earlier) to pass the case to the Court.

So public organisations and citizens in Georgia can not hire lawyers and solve problems in the Court. Another problem is that even this very weak role of the Court in regulating disputes were neglected in our country. For instance if someone cuts trees illegally, a Georgian citizen would normally appeal to the local government, to the Parliament, most of all to the Greens, but never to the Court. It is vital, that public organisations obtain the right to litigate and consequently defend public interests in the Court.

4. Georgia is working now on the draft Constitution which should be presented to the Parliament next year. Two possibilities are now discussed: the first leaves the procedure almost the same, with the public prosecutor and so on; the second gives the Court more rights and allows us to avoid the public prosecutor.

5. The role of the public in environmental protection and especially in public awareness is essential. The draft Environment Protection Act sets only general principles of public participation in the decision-making process and of appealing to the Court but we see it as the first important step towards an increasing role of citizens, an increasing role of the Court for the regulation of disputes and establishing a democratic society in Georgia. The draft Environment Protection Act of Georgia states:

"Citizens have the right to obtain full, timely and truthful information on the state of environment."

"Citizens have the right to take part in investment decision making processes and to provide control on implementation of decisions in the field of environmental protection and utilisation of natural resources, especially if their vital interests are concerned."

"Citizens have the right to unite in environmental non governmental organisations. ... Environmental NGOs have the right: ... to organise meetings, demonstrations, petitions and to come up with a proposition to conduct a referendum."

"Environmental NGOs and citizens have the right to appeal to the Court in the case of violation against this Act and other environment laws".

As mentioned above, the Draft Environment Protection Act sets very general principles and many changes in the Georgian legislation need to be made in order to achieve implementation of them. For Georgia, it is not enough only to state that environmental NGOs have the right to appeal to the Court. The procedure for the application to the Court should be changed in a way that allows citizens and public organisations to appeal directly and not through the attorney's office. This would be revolution in the Georgian litigation system.

The next step would be to increase the role of the Court in the regulation of disputes. Today citizens prefer to appeal with their problems to anybody except the Court. Normally citizens appeal to the local governments, to the central government, to the Greens, but never to the Court. Nobody sees the Court as a place where disputes or other problems can be solved. This goal cannot be achieved by changes only in the legislation; but we also need a kind of psychological adaptation and time which will bring new traditions.

Then we should identify the NGOs which can be named environmental and which will have the right to obtain information, to take part in decision-making processes and to appeal to the Court in the case of violation of environment laws, which should also be identified.

Chapter 4

The Relationships between Environmental Rights and Property Rights in the Environmental Legislative Process in Romania: The Danube Delta Case

by Dumitra Popescu

1. The Development of Environmental Legislation in Romania

The environmental legislative process in Romania is taking place in the context of economic reform and democratic changes. A significant part of this reform and change is the process of privatisation, especially of land, forests, as well as immobile facilities.

In September 1994, the Chamber of the Deputies of the Romanian Parliament adopted the draft environmental framework Law. The draft is waiting to be discussed and adopted by the Senate. Therefore Romania will soon have a new Environmental Framework Law covering important legal measures and tools following the newest developments of environmental law in western countries such as principles and rights, environmental impact assessment, protection of natural resources, a regime of hazardous substances and wastes, responsibilities and sanctions, according to the newest developments.

The relationships between environmental rights and property rights are to be found in a number of different laws such as the fundamental law, which is the Romanian Constitution of 1991, the Land Law no 18/1991, Law no 29/1990 on Administrative Contentions, Law no 50/1991 on Constructions, Law no 11/1993 on Protection of Consumers, the Law no 33/1994 on expropriation on grounds of public utility as well as in a number of governmental decisions and ministerial orders. Of these, examples are: their ministerial order of 1992 on environmental impact assessment, the governmental decision no 127/1994 on sanctioning violations of environmental laws and decision no 138 1994 sanctioning violations against water laws.

Obviously, the Civil Code of 1864 as well as the Penal Code of 1968 reveal relationships between environmental rights and property rights, since the Civil Code defines the property and property rights, the mode of its acquisition and its limits etc. and the criminal Code provides the tools for defending the property. However, the Civil Code does not include specific provisions on environmental matters.

There have been new developments in the relationships between environmental rights and property rights, including the duties that are provided for in the draft Environmental Framework Law, as well as in the specific drafts or new specific laws on forests and water, which were adopted by the Government and may soon enter Parliamentary discussions. Of such laws, governmental decisions and ministerial orders, we will refer to the most significant ones and will deal specifically with the Law on the Danube Delta.

2. Environmental Rights

Chapter II of the Romanian Constitution of 1991 concerns fundamental rights and freedoms. A number of these apply to the environmental field.

Among such rights are: the freedom of expression, of thoughts, opinions, including the freedom of the press (Article 30), and the right to information, meaning that a person's right of access to any information of public interest cannot be restricted and that the public authorities shall be bound to provide correct information to citizens (Article 31).

The Constitution does not expressly provide a right to a healthy environment. However, it is linked to the right to health and to the State's obligation to secure environmental protection.

Accordingly Article 33 of the Constitution states that:

1) The right to the protection of health is guaranteed. The State shall be bound to take measures to ensure public hygiene and health.

2) This right is ensured by the organisation of the medical care and social security system.

Also Article 134 provides that

1) the State must secure environmental protection and recover as well as preserve the ecological balance.

2) the State must ensure the creation of all necessary conditions so as to increase the quality of life.

Other rights provided for in the Constitution and Law on Administrative Contentions are free access to justice, the right of petition, the right of a person aggrieved by a public authority and the institution of Ombudsmen who may represent individuals in their complaints against governmental action or inaction.

New developments are introduced by the draft Environmental Framework Law which provides that everyone shall have a right to a healthy environment (Article 5).

It also stipulates the following rights:

a) the access to information on environmental quality

b) the right to associate in order to set up NGOs for environmental protection

c) the right of public participation in environmental decision-making

d) the right to sue, directly or through NGOs, before the administrative authorities or courts for the recovery of damages.

Up until now the NGOs in the field of consumer protection have been the only ones having the right to bring cases before the courts in order to defend rights and interests of their members, and such cases are tax exempt (Article 34 of the Law no 11/1993).

3. Property Rights

As regards property, first of all, we mention Article 135 of the Constitution which provides that the State shall protect property and that property can be public and private. Public property belongs to the State or its territorial administrative units.

Article 135 (4) identifies the object of State property as such: sub-soil riches of any nature, means of communication, air space, water with hydropower potential and which can be used for the public interest, beaches, territorial waters, natural resources of the economic zone and the continental shelf, as well as other assets established by law. All this shall be exclusively public property. Public owned assets shall be inalienable. They may be taken over for administration or may be leased or granted in concession, in accordance with law (Article 135, 5).

Private property shall be, in accordance with the law, inviolable. In the chapter of fundamental rights and freedoms, Article 41 provides:

1) The rights of property as well as the debts incurring on the State are guaranteed. The content and limitations of these rights shall be established by law.

2) Private property shall be equally protected by the law, irrespective of its owner.

The most significant point is that Article 41 (6) states:

"The right of property compels one to observe the duties relating to environmental protection and and the assurance of good neighbourliness, as well as of other duties incumbent upon the owner in accordance with the law or custom. Such duties are provided for in the Civil Code, where Article 588 in the chapter on easements states that the law obliges the owners to observe various obligations they have to another, even in the absence of any agreement between them".

Moreover, in the Civil Code chapter on easements, Article 610, specifies that any person erecting a building or depositing wastes shall comply with distance laws and carry out all the necessary works to avoid damage to his neighbour.

In this context, Articles 53 and 58 of the Land Law no 17/1991 mentions all owners of agricultural land (holders) must ensure cultivation of the land and soil protection against degradation and pollution. Article 3 of the Land Law makes it clear that a holder of land means: a holder of title to the property, of other real rights over land, such as a right of use, an easement, a right of occupation, or those who, according to civil law, have possession rights.

Therefore the holders of land, regardless of their title, are under an obligation to carry out the environmental protection.

Such obligations and specific protection measures should also be carried out by proprietors and other holders of forest land according to the land law and the provisions of the Forest Code.

In conformity with Article 47 of the draft environmental law the measures for protection of soil, subsoil and terrestrial ecosystems are obligatory for all holders regardless of their title. Article 51 states that in order to ensure soil protection, holders, regardless of their title, have the same obligations i.e.:

a) to prevent the degradation of soil quality,

b) to comply with any conditions set out in the authori sation to construct in respect of location, erection of any kind of buildings or in respect of land utilisation.

In addition, the holders of forests and wood vegetation outside the limits of forest have the same obligations regardless of their title. Article 26 (1) of the draft Water Law, taking account of Civil Code provisions on easements,(i.e. Article 578) specifies that the holders of land down stream are obliged to receive the water naturally flowing from upper land areas. However, a problem may arise in the case of acid rain or even in the case of water quality. To what extent should the neighbours tolerate each other in respect of water quality? In protected areas, the holders of terrestrial or water areas which are near to protected areas or to nature monuments must comply with the regime of those areas. The expenses generated by the implementation of the protected regime are compensated by the Environmental National Fund as regards zones of private property. As regards the nature of water as property the draft Environmental Law makes no provision. However, Article 39 (a) specifies that a drilled well of up to 50m in depth for household needs does not require authorisation.

The water law draft makes clear the conditions in which water might be the object of private property. Article 3 (2) provides that a minor river bed of up to 5 km and with a hydrographic basin of up to 10 km2 belongs to the holders of land on which they are formed or through which it flows. Underground water may be used by a proprietor under certain conditions. Such conditions are provided for in Article 8 of the draft, which states:

1) The right to use surface waters and ground-waters shall be provided for in the authorisation of water management.

2) The surface and ground water may be used freely for household needs in compliance with sanitary and protection standards, on the condition that for such purposes the equipment used for water abstraction draws no more than 0,2 litre per second.

Therefore regardless of its owner the water must be used in compliance with required standards and no one is allowed to discharge pollutants or wastes on its land or into waters.

In the draft of Environmental Law, the Water Law draft, and the Forest Code draft there are other provisions revealing the relationships between environmental rights and property rights such as:

a) the Ministry of Water, Forests and Environmental Protection can ask for information from other ministries, local public authorities, legal and natural persons

b) the environmental inspectors, in carrying out their tasks, may at any time enter a facility generating a negative impact to the environment.

In this context a significant provision is included in Law no 33/1994 on expropriation for grounds of public utility. According to Article 5 of this law, work by the installations for environmental protection (including work against soil erosion), and by its installations for protection of national parks and reserves and nature monuments is considered work of public utility and, if necessary, in order to carry it out, the owners can be expropriated, in conformity with the law and on the basis of compensation.

All such limits and restrictions are based on the premise that as regards the environment, all legal and natural persons have both rights and obligations. In this respect the draft Environmental Law specifies in Article 78 that: "The protection of the environment constitutes an obligation belonging to all natural and legal persons".

4. The Danube Delta Case

The Law no 82/1993 established the Biosphere Reservation "Danube Delta", determined its territorial limits, the zones of integral protection other zones, as well as economic zones in which traditional economic activities can be carried out.

For the management of the natural heritage of the public domain which is of national interest, the Administration of Reservation has been created, having a number of powers and functions.

In conformity with article 10 (3) of Law 82/19093 the proprietors (legal or natural persons) of the land within the reservation limits are obliged to manage it in compliance with permitted ecological techniques (i.e. traditionally practised by them or recommended by the scientific authorities).

This law contains 34 sanctions against violations to its provisions. Three of the violations are:

1) The use on Delta land (in agriculture and silviculture activities), of chemical products and equipment that are not authorised by the Administration of Reservation or are not in compliance with conditions provided for in authorisation, regardless of the owner.

2) The cutting or deterioration of trees declared to be nature monuments or trees from those zones having a regime of integral ecological protection, the leaving of equipment or devices on non-organised space, regardless of the land owner.

3) The grazing within the limits of zones having a regime of integrated ecological protection.

Such kind of violations are considered as contravention and are sanctioned with fines.

As concluding remarks we point out firstly that between environmental rights and property rights there exist a number of relationships the interference of which should be taken account of in the environmental legislative process and secondly they may impact upon litigation in the environmental field.

Chapter 5

Rights of Complaint and Access to Information at the Commission of the EC

by Ludwig Krämer[1]

1. Right of Complaint

1.1 Citizens Rights under the EC Treaty to Bring an Action

The European Community (EC) was set up in 1958. According to the long-established legal interpretation given to the EC Treaty by the EC Court of Justice, the EC constitutes a new legal order of international law for the benefit of which the Member States have limited their own rights; the subjects of this legal order are not only the Member States but also their nationals[2]. EC law - either the law of the EC Treaty itself or the secondary Community law, which is based on the EC Treaty - is thus autonomous from national law and must be understood and interpreted independently. It may impose obligations on individuals and confer rights on them.

Where a citizen is directly and individually affected by a decision of EC institutions against that citizen, he is entitled to institute proceedings before the EC Court of Justice, under Article 173(4), against the responsible institution. Where an institution has failed to address to a citizen a decision, the citizen may, under Article 175(3) EC Treaty and according to the conditions laid down in that Article, complain to the EC Court of Justice.

The citizen cannot, however, tackle the validity or interpretation of a provision of a directive or a regulation before the EC Court of Justice, since, normally, he is not directly and individually concerned by them. This right is limited, under Article 173(1), (2) and (3) EC Treaty, to the Council, the Commission, Member States and, under certain conditions, to the European Parliament and the European Central Bank. Whether a citizen may challenge the validity and interpretation of EC directives or regulations before a national court depends on the national legal order of Member States.

1.2 The Commission's Function to Control Complete and Correct Transposal of Directives into National Law

Under Article 155 EC Treaty, the Commission shall "ensure that the provisions of this Treaty and the measures taken by the institutions pursuant thereto are applied". This Commission function is often described as that of a "guardian of the Treaty": the Commission has to ensure that EC regulations and directives are actually complied with in Member States. Regulations, under Article 189, are directly applicable in all Member States. Directives, in contrast to that, are addressed to Member States and require them to reach a specific result, while leaving to Member States the ways and means how to achieve this result.

As the first part of its surveillance function under Article 155(3), the Commission therefore examines, whether Member States have transposed the requirements of a directive into their national legal order. This examination is facilitated by the fact that all directives, including all environmental directives, require Member States to inform the Commission of the national legislation which they adopted in order to transpose the directive into national law. Since the early nineties, the different directives even require national legislation , when it transposes a directive, to contain a reference to the transposed directive.

The second step in the Commission's examination of the situation in Member States is, whether the national legislation completely or correctly transposes the requirements of Community law into national law. This examination is mainly a comparative task, since national, regional or, where this is relevant, even local legislation is in the hands of the Commission. Even then, though, the examination of the interdependency of different rules, the subsequent amendments of legislation and the interplay between general and specific environmental rules, central and regional provisions, parliamentary acts, decrees and administrative circulars make comparisons between EC directives and national legislation sometimes rather complicated. It is true that the Commission regularly asks Member States to provide it with tables which list, for each individual article or sub-paragraphe, the relevant national transposing provisions; however, only a minority of Member States and only for a minority of directives actually transmits this kind of transposal tables.

1.3 Monitoring Actual Compliance with EC Environmental Rules

The third level of the Commission's examination under Article 155 pertains to the problem, whether the EC directive in question is actually complied with. This examination is of particular difficulty in environmental matters. Indeed, compared, for instance, to food law or motor vehicles legislation, environmental law has some specific features. Where one of the some 60 directives on motor vehicles is in question, this directive addresses - economically or technically - the more or less two dozen car manufacturers or importers and requests them, as of a specific date, to change the technical specificities of the product which they intend to put on the market; quite similar is the situation as regards food law rules, only that the number of professionals is considerably higher. Compliance with the "new" EC standards is then ensured through national surveillance bodies such as police, certification or inspection bodies etc. There are, certainly, a number of cases, where EC requirements are not respected - and in food law certainly more than in motor vehicles law -, however, the intensity of local, regional or national pre-marketing and post-marketing controls ensures relatively large compliance with those rules, and the more the policing functions are taken seriously at national, regional or local level and sanctions are applied in the case of non-respect, the greater is the actual compliance probability.

Environmental law is different, since, normally, environmental contamination and pollution normally stems from emissions, discharges etc., which are authorised by local, regional or national authorities. Thus, typically, public authorities authorise the emissions into the environment and these emissions are diffuse, i.e. less visible, perceptible and measurable. Also, since the problems of environmental degradation, contamination and pollution are of recent date - they have been perceived as problems for about a quarter of a century - police, surveillance bodies and control mechanisms exist to a much lesser degree, with very considerable differences between the different EC

Member States; even the analysis methods, sampling rules and the frequency of measuring emissions or discharges vary largely within the EC, since the EC - under subsidiarity rules and the soft pressure from economic interests - has gradually abandoned the fixing of common or equivalent control rules in Member States.

This leads to the situation that the discrepancy between the legislative standards that are fixed at EC level - probably also at national level, but this is not the subject of this contribution - and actual compliance is considerably higher than in other sectors of EC law.

The EC Commission does not have any inspection mechanism, laboratories, mobile analysis possibilities or other mechanisms to monitor compliance of local, regional or national situations with EC environmental law. This kind of mechanism exists in a number of areas of EC law, such as competition, fishery, veterinary rules, EC financial aids etc. Each time, this mechanism was set up by a specific Council rule.

This situation has as a consequence, for instance, that where the Commission is informed of a company having concluded, in disregard of Article 85 EC Treaty, a cartel with another company in order to increase prices artificially, the Commission may send inspectors to that company, search the rooms, seize documents and take all necessary steps in order to find out about the facts. Where the Commission is informed that the same company discharges waste water into a river, in breach of EC environmental directives, the Commission is obliged to write to the Member State's embassy and ask to be informed about the discharge in question.

1.4 The Environmental Complaint

In view of this specific situation, the complaint procedure in Community law has gained a specific importance in the environmental sector. The complaint procedure is not fixed by the EC Treaty, but has gradually been developed by the Commission. In the late sixties, the Commission wished to ensure the establishment and the functioning of the common market, in particular the free circulation of goods. It thus addressed traders and importers and encouraged them to write to the Commission whenever they met difficulties at Member States' borders as regards documents, fees, charges or other administrative or financial problems; the Commission indicated that it would intervene with national authorities in order to eliminate, whenever possible, the different barriers to trade. In order to facilitate this complaint system, the Commission developed a form which was to be used by complainants.

In 1982, a charge of some 40 barrels of toxic waste disappeared on its way between Italy and France, which raised considerable concern in some Member States. The European Parliament instituted, for the first time in its history, an inquiry committee which was very critical of Member States' compliance with EC environmental law, but which also severely critized the Commission for not fulfilling its role as guardian of the Treaty with respect of environmental law[4]. In order to meet this criticism, the Commission decided to systematically apply the complaint rules to the environmental sector.

At present, a complaint is any written application to the Commission, by alleging non-compliance with EC environmental law is raised and asking for intervention of the Commission, in order to remedy this situation. The complainant may use the complaint form which the Commission finally published in 1989[5], but is not obliged to do so; thus the complaint on the quality of bathing water in Blackpool(United Kingdom), which led to a judgment of the Court of Justice in 1993[6], originated in a simple postcard to the Commission, where the facts were presented and an intervention by the Commission was requested, in order to "save our shorelines".

It is not required that the complainant's allegations should be substantiated, or that specific provisions or directives should be cited or that formalities should be otherwise observed. But the allegations must be sufficiently specific to enable an investigation to be made. General claims, such as "the air in the city of X is polluted" or "bathing at beach Y is an unpleasant experience", are not dealt with as complaints as they are too vague.

The complainant need not to have taken any action before the authorities of an individual Member State or sought legal redress under the relevant national procedural law before he can institute a complaint. Such prior action can of course be useful for achieving the cessation of the environmental impairment, but prior recourse to national remedies cannot be a condition for the admissibility of a complaint. It is also irrelevant whether the breach of Community law raised in the complaint took place in the complainant's State or in another Member State. Indeed, the Commission is dealing with numerous cases where the complainant objects to impairment that takes place in another Member State. In environmental matters such complaints are of particular significance because levels of environmental awareness differ strongly as between Member States.

Every complaint is entered into a central register kept by the Commission and receives a specific complaint number. Entry in the register has the consequence that the complaint is considered not by one particular service of the Commission, but by the full body of all Commission members, which is intended to reduce arbitrary administrative decisions.

The complainant is given an acknowledgment of receipt, in which he is informed of the number allocated to it. It is left to the complainant what he does with this information. These last years, complainants have more frequently informed the public and the media of the existence of the complaint in order to alert the public of the case of environmental impairment, win support and induce the local, regional or national administration, if possible, to stop going ahead with an authorisation or the realisation of a project or to check itself whether the argued breach of rules exists. Experience shows that public discussion of environmental problems is one of the most efficient safeguards against pollution or breaches of environmental protection rules.

1.5 The Instruction of the Complaint

Once a complaint received and registered, the Commission services investigate the complaint, trying in particular to clarify the factual situation. Since, as stated, there are no inspectors, the main source of information on the actual application of a provision of a directive are the complainant and, even more, the Member State in question. Under Article 5 EC Treaty, Member States are obliged to answer questions posed by the Commission, as the Court of Justice expressly confirmed in an environmental case against Italy[7]. The name of the complainant and other details that would enable him to be identified are not communicated to the Member States. In rare cases a study is made or a place is visited by Commission officials in order to ascertain more complex facts.

The Commission proceedings on a complaint are not public. The Commission publishes no detailed information on the complaints made and registered. The request formulated recently by members of the Committee of the Regions that the Commission should publish an annual report on environmental complaints (and on petitions addressed to the European Parliament) and their investigation, has not yet received any follow-up.

At the end of the instruction of the complaint there is a decision by the Commission, which is generally made within one year from the registration of the complaint. Where no breach of Community law can be established, the case is filed. Where the Commission finds that Community law has not been respected, it normally opens proceedings under Article 169 EC Treaty[8]. In either case the complainant is informed of the decision. There is no procedure for complaining about the decision to terminate the proceedings and the Commission cannot be compelled by a complainant to take action under Article 169 against a Member State. The complainant may of course put forward contrary views, new facts or arguments, which could lead to the reopening of the procedure. As an example, a case may be quoted, where the Commission, upon a complaint, had seized the Court of Justice, because local Spanish authorities had allowed the discharge of waste water containing HCH levels in excess of Directive 84/491[9] and had not prevented the discharge of dangerous waste from a specific installation at unauthorised places. When the installation was closed and Spain undertook to remedy the situation, the Commission withdrew its application to the Court. However, when, several months later, it was informed by the complainants that the dangerous waste had not yet been taken care of, it started a new investigation of the case.

1.6 The Publicity of the Procedure under Article 169 EC Treaty

The complaint-based infringement procedure against a Member State under Article 169 EC Treaty which consists of three parts - letter of formal notice, reasoned opinion, application to the Court of Justice - is not any different from procedures under Article 169 which are started at the initiative of the Commission only. Therefore, some remarks which are particularly relevant to environmental complaints may suffice.

The Commission's decision to start infringement proceedings against a Member State is not published; nor is the letter of formal notice. This is not based on the wording of Article 169 or any other Treaty provision, but is administrative practice of the Commission and of Member States. It seems that at present only the Netherlands publish the letters of formal notice and the correspondence between national and Community authorities. Of course, the complainant cannot be prevented from making public the fact that proceedings have started against a Member State; however, he has available, at best, only a short summary of the arguments on which the Commission decision was based.

The administrative practice of the Commission and of Member States as regards publicity shows clearly how the procedural law of Article 169 et seq. derived from the classic rules of public international law, which relate solely to relations between sovereign states or international organisations. Dispute settlement in public international law is still argely influenced by diplomatic discussions, governmental secrecy and the absence of international courts which take binding decisions; the very slow emergence of an international legal order, also and even in particular in environmental law, has not really changed this state of affairs.

By contrast, Community law assigns a totally different status to individuals from that under international law. Community legal acts are binding upon Member States and, unlike international treaties, do not require prior ratification by the legislatures of the individual Member States. The constitutional and human rights of the individual are part of the

Community legal order and, therefore, do not have to be conferred on him first. Furthermore, numerous Community regulations and directives expressly or implicitly give rights to individuals and impose obligations on them, which is practically not the case with international treaties. Finally, one of the Community's institutions which participates in its legislative procedures and the formulation of its political will, namely the European Parliament, is elected by the free and direct vote of the citizens of the Community.

All these circumstances argue for an extensive assimilation of the procedural rules of Article 169 to those of ordinary procedural law in the Member States, and thus for the publication of procedural decisions, thus in particular the letters of formal notice and the reasoned opinions. Indeed, in both cases, there is a formal decision by the college of the Commission, which is carefully prepared by a series of internal preparatory meetings. There is no reason to keep these formalised documents, where every word is several times checked internally, away from public discussion. Transparency, public awareness and public interest in the preservation, protection and improvement of the environment are so desperately needed that the interests of the administrations, to keep possible breaches away from public discussion do not deserve priority consideration.

1.7 The Complaints Procedure in Practice

The following figures show the evolution in environmental complaints with regard to all complaints[10]:

1982	10 out of 352	1988	216 out of 1137
1983	8 out of 399	1989	465 out of 1195
1984	9 out of 476	1990	480 out of 1252
1985	37 out of 585	1991	353 out of 1052
1986	165 out of 791	1992	587 out of 1545
1987	50 out of 850	1993	383 out of 1340

The greatest number of complaints concern habitat protection of birds and other species of fauna or flora, the omission to make an environmental impact assessment prior to the granting of planning permission, the pollution of bathing or drinking water and bird protection in general. Complaints are introduced not only by citizens and environmental organisations, but also by professional associations, industrial companies, traders, local or regional authorities, regional national or European MEPs, ambassadors, chambers of commerce etc.; even the Danish and the Belgian ministers for environmental affairs have introduced complaints to the Commission.

There are, in particular in the framework of the ongoing discussion on renationalising EC issues, also attempts to reduce the possibility to introduce complaints with the EC Commission, for instance by requiring that national remedies must have been sought first. The outcome of this discussion is uncertain.

The complaint procedure is entirely free of cost. This certainly creates an incentive for citizens to file complaints, since national remedies - provided they exist at all, which is far from being the case in all sectors of environmental law - are sometimes very expensive, in particular in British law.

A considerable advantage of the procedure is that, almost for the first time, planning permissions by local authorities in all Member States are checked by a neutral body - the Commission - as to their compatibility with EC environmental law. This is very new to numerous local or regional bodies which, in the past, were used to their decisions not being challenged or put into question and will, without doubt, have a long-term positive impact on environmental requirements being integrated in planning decisions within Member States.

A disincentive to file complaints is on the one hand the absence of transparency, which was already discussed earlier. There is little communication with the complainant, who is left in the dark about the outcome of his complaint, sometimes for more than a year. Another disincentive is the length of the procedure: between the filing of a complaint and a decision by the Court of Justice, more than six years pass on average and there is no possibility for the Commission to take interim measures against a Member State, such a right being reserved to the Court of Justice and for cases, which are already pending before the Court.

This rather suggests that citizens, for breaches of Community environmental law, should also look for remedies under national law, where such remedies exist and are efficient. As a matter of fact, complaints from Dutch and Danish sources, where national systems to remedy breaches of (national and) Community environmental law exist, are markedly lower in number than from other Member States.

1.8 Perspectives

As regards the perspective of the complaint procedure, much will depend on the political determination of EC institutions and Member States to push environmental protection. It would without doubt be useful, be it only for legal certainty and in order to reduce political interference in complaint cases and infringement procedures, if there were a legally fixed complaint procedure. Neither the complaint procedure nor the handling of petitions is at present equipped with legal certainty of procedures. And the Commission might well be capable of handling 500 or even 700 complaints per year: once citizens really start complaining about breaches of EC environmental law more or less systematically, it will become impossible to manage the then numerous cases at EC level only, which could easily run up to several thousands. Since such breaches first of all occur at local level, a decentralised system of complaint handling will sooner or later become imperative, if one really wishes to monitor actual compliance.

Article 20 of Regulation 1210/90 on the European Environmental Agency provides that the Council shall, within two years after the setting up of the Agency, decide whether the Agency shall become involved in the monitoring of application of EC law[11]. This provision is rather general. In fact, it was inserted into Article 20 at the insistence of the European Parliament which wanted to see the Agency establish the facts of the individual complaints, in particular by visits "sur place". It remains to be seen how the review discussion of Article 20 evolves; the 1995 working program of the Commission does not provide for a proposal to review Regulation 1210/90.

2. Access to Information Held by Community Institutions

2.1 Directive 90/313 on Access to Information on the Environment

In 1990, the Council adopted Directive 90/313 on the freedom of access to information on the environment[12]. This Directive gives every citizen - be he EC citizen or not - a right of access to information on the environment held by public authorities.

The Directive is addressed to Member States and thus does not apply to Community institutions and bodies. When the Commission submitted its proposal to the Council, it announced for this reason that it would take other initiatives with the object of applying the principle to the Community bodies[13]. When the Directive was adopted by the Council, the Commission repeated this declaration.

The discussion on transparency and better participation of citizens at Community decisions was reanimated by the conclusion of the Maastricht Treaty on European Union and subsequent discussions at several European Councils. It was generally accepted that greater transparency of decision-making at EC level was necessary.

2.2 Council and Commission Decisions on Access to Documents

On 6 December 1993, the Council and the Commission jointly agreed a code of conduct on the access of the public to Council and Commission documents[14]. This Code was followed, on 20 December 1993, by Council decision 93/731 on the access of the public to Council documents[15] and by decision 94/90 of 8 February 1994 on public access to Commission documents[16]. The Commission decision provides for the "adoption" of the Code of Conduct of 6 December 1993 and for some rules in order to give effect to that Code[17].

The Code provides that the "public will have the widest possible access to documents held by the Commission and the Council". A document is any written text, whatever its medium, which contains existing data. The Decision 94/90 does not contain any enumeration on grounds on which the application may be refused. Such a list is, however, to be found in the Code which lists the following grounds:

- protection of public interests (public security, international relations, monetary stability, court proceedings, inspections and investigations);

- protection of the individual and of privacy;

- protection of industrial and commercial interests;

- protection of the Community's financial interests;

- the confidential character of a document, where this was asked for by the person who made the information available or where national provisions so provide.

Furthermore, access to documents may be refused in order to ensure the secrecy of deliberations of the Commission.

It should be noted that all the grounds which oblige the Commission to refuse access to a document are general, objective grounds which lie outside the interests of the Commission itself. Thus, except in order to protect the secrecy of deliberations, no internal reasons may be invoked to refuse access to documents.

Applications to the Commission must be precise and be made in writing. Where the document was written by a natural or a legal person, a Member State, another Community institution or body or another national or international body, the application must be sent direct to the author.

Of particular interest, in particular as regards the application of Directive 90/313 in some Member States, is the problem of fees. In that respect, the Code states:

"The applicant will have access to documents either by

consulting them on the spot or by having a copy sent at his own expense; the fee will not exceed a reasonable sum".

Commission Decision 94/90 takes up this point by stating:

> "A fee of ECU 10, plus ECU 0,036 per sheet of paper, shall be charged for copies of printed documents exceeding thirty pages..."

Thus, it can be concluded that the Community notion of "reasonable costs" is, according to the Commission's understanding, ten ECU per thirty pages. Since Article 5 of Directive 90/313 also contains the notion of "reasonable costs" and since EC law has to be interpreted independently from national notions and interpretations, the understanding of Article 5 of Directive 90/313 by the Commission cannot really be considerably different.

The appeals procedure set up by Decision 94/90 and the Code is also of some interest. The Decision provides that a request for access to a document must be addressed to the relevant Directorate-General of the Commission. The applicant must be informed, within one month, whether the application is granted or whether it is intended to refuse access; failure to reply within one month of application being made constitutes an intention to refuse. The applicant is then informed of this intention and of his possibility to make, within one month a confirmatory application "for that position to be reconsidered". If then the confirmatory application is refused by the Commission - the decision on it, which must again intervene within one month, is no longer made by the relevant Directorate-General, but by a central body, the Secretariat General - the applicant is informed in writing of the refusal, of the grounds for the refusal and "indicate the means of redress that are available, i.e. judicial proceedings and complaints to the Ombudsman under the conditions specified in, respectively, Articles 173 and 138e of the Treaty".

Thus, Council and Commission consider themselves that the decision to refuse access to a document may constitute a legal measure which may harm the interests of the applicant. These interests can be no other than that of having access to documents, which thus constitutes a "right" of the applicant. Despite the somehow unusual and legally rather unclear construction of a code of conduct and a Commission decision, the instruments as such do grant individual rights of access to information that is available with the Commission.

2.3 Commission Decision 94/90 in Practice

In September 1994, the Commission published a small report on the experience gained with the new mechanism, as between 15 February and 15 September 1994. 91 applications were made, 25 by academics (professors, students, research institutes), 21 by attorneys, 16 by lobbyists, 10 by industries, 8 by public authorities, 5 by citizens, 4 by journalists, and 2 by MEPs. 11 applications were made in the environmental sector (Directorate-General XI), which is the biggest number for all Directorate-Generals. One application out of four (25.6%) was refused, among them 19.8 percent as inadmissible: either the document had already been published, or it did not come from the Commission, the application was not precise enough or the document did not exist. The other grounds for refusal were the confidentiality of deliberations (7.4%), Committee documents whose activities are confidential (5.8%), public security (4.9%), cases with several grounds (3.3%), confidentiality asked by person or Member State (2.5%) and commercial and industrial secrecy (1.7%).

Nine confirmatory applications were introduced; six refusals were confirmed, in one case the applicant was asked to specify his application and two cases were still under consideration, when the report was made public. No refusal seems to have been tackled before the Court of Justice.

2.4 Differences between Decision 94/90 and Directive 90/313

If one looks at the access to information available with the Commission and the Council, it is obvious that there are marked differences between Directive 90/313; among those, the following seem of particular relevance:

- legal form: Directive 90/313 gives a right to access to information which may only be refused in specific, expressly enumerated circumstances.

Decision 94/90 and the Code are everything but clear in their legal construction. The intention was most probably to establish some sort of self-commitment by the Commission and the Council. Whether there is not, in fact, some legal right which is given to EC citizens, will in the last instance, have to be decided by the Court of Justice: in the meantime, legal certainty is not improved by the construction of a Decision/Code.

- bodies covered: Directive 90/313 tries to cover all authorities which are "public" and to give the widest possible access to information on the environment.

The Decision/Code does not refer to all bodies. First, other Community institutions, such as the Economic and Social Committee, the Committee of Regions, the European Parliament (in its non-legislative activity) are not included. Second, it is unclear, whether Community bodies, such as the European Environmental Agency, the Trade Mark Office, the Foundation on the improvement of live and working conditions etc. are covered. Also, the situation of scientific, technical, advisory and regulatory committees and their documents is not clear at all.

- the form of information: Directive 90/313 grants access to information which is available; Decision 94/90 and the Code give access to "documents", which is considerably narrower than access to "information". This narrow interpretation cannot be better demonstrated than by the Council declaration which accompanied the publication of the Code and where the Council stated that the Code and the subsequent decisions did not mean a change of existing practices.

- environment: Directive 90/313 is limited on access to information on the environment. Decision 94/90 and the Code refer to any information and are thus considerably broader.

2.5 Perspectives

The Code provides that Council and Commission will review the Code by end 1995, based on experience reports submitted by the two institutions. The Commission announced, in its legislative proposal for 1994, that it would submit a proposal on a legal instrument on access to environmental information held by Community institutions[18]. Since no such proposal was made in 1994, the Commission's work program 1995 repeats this intention. Thus, the discussion on transparency, access to information on the environment which is held by Community institutions and citizens rights to a clean environment are bound to continue in 1995.

Notes

[1] The author expresses his own view, not that of the EC Commission.

[2] Court of Justice, case 26/62 *van Gend en Loos v. Netherlands Administratie*, ECR 1963, p.1.

[3] See Commission, Eighth annual report to the European Parliament on Commission monitoring of the application of Community law - 1990, Official Journal of the European Communities 1991, no.C 338, p.1 (p.204 et seq. which describe in detail the monitoring procedure in environmental law).

[4] European Parliament

[5] Official Journal EC 1989, no.C 26 p.6.

[6] Court of Justice, case 56/90 *Commission v. United Kingdom,* ECR 1993, p.I-4109.

[7] Court of Justice, case C-33/90, *Commission v. Italy*, ECR 1991, p.I-5987.

[8] Article 169 EC Treaty: "If the Commission considers that a Member State has failed to fulfil an obligation under this Treaty, it shall deliver a reasoned opinion on the matter after giving the State concerned the opportunity to submit its observations.

If the State concerned does not comply with the opinion within the period laid down by the Commission, the latter may bring the matter before the Court of Justice".

[9] Directive 84/491 on limit values and quality objectives for discharges of hexachlorocyclohexane, Official Journal EC 1984, no.L 274, p.11.

[10] Figures based on the Commission reports on the monitoring of applications of EC law which the Commission publishes since 1973; last report(11th report) on 1993 in Official Journal 1994, no.C 154 p.1. The figures from 1992 onwards include presumed infringements which are based on other sources than complaints and are thus not really comparable.

[11] Regulation 1210/90, Official Journal 1990, no.L 120,p.1, Article 20: "No later than two years after the entry into force of this Regulation ... the Council shall ...decide on further tasks of the Agency in particular in the following areas:

associating in the monitoring of the implementation of Community environmental legislation, in cooperation with the Commission and existing competent bodies in the Member States...."

[13] Directive 90/313 on the freedom of access to information on the environment, Official Journal EC 1990, no.L 158, p.56.

[14] Code of conduct concerning public access to Council and Commission documents, Official Journal EC 1993, no.L 340, p.41.

[15] Decision 93/731, Official Journal EC 1993, no.L 340, p.43.

[16] Commission decision 94/90, Official Journal 1994, no.L 46, p.58.

[17] Subsequently, only the Commission, not the Council decision will be discussed.

[18] Commission, COM(93) 588 final, of 24 November 1993.

Chapter 6

"Access to Justice" for Environmental NGOs in the European Union

by Thomas Ormond

Introduction

This morning we have heard about environmental rights in general and about several - in my opinion quite promising - new initiatives towards establishing these rights in national legislation, in Bills of Rights, in constitutions - all examples from outside the European Union as it stands.[1] This afternoon, the conference programme will focus more specifically on the role of environmental NGOs and of litigation in administrative law. In this context, it is more and more common to speak of "access to justice", but the term also has a specific meaning explaining the quotation marks in the title of my paper: It is under this heading that in 1992 the Öko-Institut (Darmstadt) and the Foundation for International Environmental Law and Development (FIELD, London) presented a proposal to the European Commission for a Community directive on the legal standing of environmental associations in the EC Member States. As the text and the explanatory memorandum of this proposal have been published[2], I will not give a full summary of its contents but rather make a brief survey of the situation in the EU Member States that gave rise to the draft proposal and then concentrate on some important aspects and problems of this "European" approach to remedy the situation.

No Access to Justice? - The Situation in the Member States of the European Union

The idea of a European directive was based on the diagnosis that the limitations imposed in the Member States of the EU on persons and organisations working for the defence of the environment in their access to the courts of law represent one of the major obstacles to an effective protection of the environment, and especially to the effective implementation of existing environmental laws in Europe. It is perhaps no accident that this point has particularly involved German and British members of ELNI and driven them to action. It is these two countries, Germany and Britain, who today seem to be the most backward, the least developed as concerns the law of standing for environmental NGOs, i.e. the formal side of "access to justice".

Germany is moving only slowly, state by state, towards allowing a very limited measure of participation and litigation by officially recognised environmental associations. Since my last summary in 1990[3], 2 more *Länder* in Western Germany and 4 of the 5 newly acceded East German states have adopted legislation granting access to the courts to NGOs in certain matters of environmental law. This has raised the total number of "*Verbandsklage*" states to 11 of 16; among the others which still flatly refuse to allow public interest litigation in this field are three of the largest and most populous states (Bavaria, Baden-Württemberg, North Rhine-Westphalia). Besides, most of the states that did grant legal standing to associations have done so only against a very small body of administrative decisions. A notable exception to this rule is Lower Saxony, a *Land* that for some years was ruled by a coalition government of Social Democrats and Greens, including a former Greenpeace executive as minister of the environment. However, even Lower Saxony and Hesse (another "red-green" state which has just amended its nature conservation statute) have not opted for wide general clauses, otherwise the standard instrument in Germany's post-war administrative jurisdiction, but rather for enumerations that delimit the right of standing in a grotesquely complicated and eventually half-hearted way.[4] Apart from restricting judicial review to certain types of planning permissions and licences, the new legislation has laid down the rule that an environmental association may appeal only on those points of fact which it has put forward in earlier administrative proceedings.

In Britain, the development of the rules of standing, as formulated by the Supreme Court Act and by case-law[5], appears to be similarly cumbersome, even though *THORP* and other recent cases may now give some reason for hope. James Cameron will give details on this in his presentation later on.[6] In any case, there are many more impediments to environmental lawsuits in Britain, among them particularly the high cost of litigation against a powerful opposing party.[7]

In the other Member States of the European Union, the formal prerequisite of standing to sue does not seem to constitute a big hurdle any more. Some countries, such as Ireland, Spain or Greece have liberal standing rules anyway, permitting virtually any citizen to bring an action against at least certain environmentally harmful decisions of authorities.[8] Other European states have introduced specific legislation on the right of environmental NGOs to avail themselves of administrative and judicial remedies, starting with France in 1976 and the Netherlands in 1979, continuing with Denmark in 1982, Italy in 1986 and Portugal in 1987[9], and most recently ending up with Luxembourg in 1992 and Belgium in 1993 amending and extending their respective provisions on environmental litigation.[10]

Access to the courts in some states - France, the Netherlands, Belgium, Italy - does not only mean the right to attack administrative decisions that effect the environment. It also may enable an environmental organisation to take part in criminal proceedings as a "partie civile" - as it is called in France - and/or to bring directly an action against a private person or company urging the defendant to stop ongoing pollution or claiming damages from him for past activities.[11] On the other hand, the relevant statutes in Ireland, while allowing any citizen or organisation to sue a private investor, rule out any action against most projects of the public sector.[12]

The formal openness of a court system to environmental public interest litigation does not mean, of course, that its remedies are necessarily effective. Spanish observers, for instance, complain about the sheer length of administrative and judicial proceedings in their country and the lack of quick interim relief especially in cases of illicit building or pollution.[13] French procedural law, due to its very strict adherence to the separation of powers, enables the plaintiff in general only to demand the nullification of an administrative act, and excludes mandatory injunctions against administrative authorities.[14] More important still is the deterrent effect of the high costs (or the cost risk) of litigation in some countries, where the plaintiff has to pay even extravagantly high fees of defence counsels or experts of the other side if he or she loses the case.

There are of course many more examples for the shortcomings of national procedural laws when seen from the perspective of an effective defence of the environment. But the proposal for an "Access to Justice" directive concentrates on what we as the authors have seen as the three crucial elements: 1) legal standing, 2) effective remedies, and 3) reasonable costs.

The Articles 3-6 of the draft proposal are meant to establish legal standing for environmental NGOs in the courts and in administrative complaint facilities independently of the violation of individual rights or legal interests. This guarantee should, however, not prejudice existing standing rules which are more liberal insofar as they allow any citizen to bring an action for environmental reasons.

We found it important to make sure that the scope of judicial review is not limited to administrative acts, but also comprises sub-statutory rules, such as by laws and development plans, which often have far more serious consequences on the environment than a simple licence or building permit. We were careful to stop short of interfering with the powers of national or regional parliaments, since the constitutions of some EU Member States do not in any way allow for the judicial review of parliamentary decisions. Still, the suggestion in Art. 4 para. 3 of our proposal that courts shall have the power to compel administrative authorities to positive action might seem quite offensive to French lawyers who are committed to the idea of judicial restraint in the face of administrative discretion. Here it is perhaps that the directive as proposed would cut deepest into national legal traditions, and it is here where the question has to be asked particularly in how far European law can order a Member State to alter traditional procedural and organisational structures if they have proved to hamper the effective implementation of that law.

The basic answer which I would give to this question is that with the Internal Market destroying a great deal of national traditions and creating many additional dangers to the environment, and with Article 130r of the EC Treaty promising in principle to all Community citizens a high level of protection for the environment, Member States may be asked to adjust their laws to the common objectives also in this field. The more the implementation and enforcement of existing rules are seen as the key to a high level of environmental protection, the more they will be able to override the objections based on a conservative view of the principle of subsidiarity. In a broader and more dynamic perspective, the principle of subsidiarity in fact supports the "Access to Justice" proposal because that instrument decentralises the enforcement of environmental law by strengthening the position of Community citizens and national courts, and thus obviates the establishment of a powerful central executive. The last of the Commission's Action Programmes on the environment and sustainable development have increasingly emphasised this point.[15]

While it is of central importance to make administrative activities in the environmental field subject to judicial review, this does not solve the problem of administrative failure to act against illegal practices of private persons and enterprises. In some of these cases it may be sufficient and also easier to sue directly the responsible party rather than to bring a mandatory action against the supervising authority. The respective Article 6 of our proposal, which we modelled to some extent on citizen suit provisions in U.S. legislation, will prove to be effective especially if it is combined with rules on environmental liability and on sizeable damages to be awarded to a successful plaintiff.

Among the remedies which should be guaranteed by the EU Member States is particularly important a functioning system of interim relief in urgent cases for the time pending judgment. Because of its crucial role for the practice of environmental enforcement we have drafted a separate article - Art. 7 - for this purpose.

Apart from standing and effective remedies the question of costs is the most likely to determine the practicability of an "Access to Justice". High counsel's, expert and court fees, security deposits and especially the risk that damages and all expenses, even the extravagant ones, of the other side will have to be paid eventually in case of defeat, can virtually suppress litigation except for extreme cases where a wealthy sponsor, a powerful organisation or a broad coalition of well-to-do residents come to the aid of environmental interests. The British experience in this field has led to the formula which you will find in Article 8 of the draft directive, namely that court fees and the costs of other parties - it should be added: their reasonable costs - should be borne by state funds, if the action, though unsuccessful, had been brought on the basis of an arguable case and in good faith.

The cost rules as proposed here do not completely remove the financial risk for environmental NGOs. In my opinion, this makes sense, as it forces environmental groups to take matters seriously and prepare their case carefully before going to court. But the limitation of the cost risk acknowledges that a legal action aiming at the implementation of environmental laws is in the public interest and should be treated differently from lawsuits started purely in order to defend individual interests.

There are of course alternatives to this formula, e.g. a system whereby NGOs are subsidised out of public funds either for their activities in general or for certain legal actions in particular. To me the concept fixed in Article 8 of the draft directive seems preferable because it does not constitute a potential threat to the independence of these organisations.

Conclusion

Since the proposal was made, in 1992, environmental policy in the European Union and its Member States has largely come to a standstill or even had to retreat in the face of economic pressure to free capitalism from its social responsibilities. This momentary trend and, more particularly, pressure from the German government have so far prevented the European Commission from pursuing further the idea of "Access to Justice" in environmental matters. It is, however, doubtful whether the opponents of effective environmental protection will manage to shelve the issue much longer. The ecological crisis has not abated, quite on the contrary. The mounting financial difficulties of many states, on the other hand, have promoted the development towards "lean government" and tend to weaken the capacity of administrative authorities to "command and control" in the interest of environmental protection. In the context of this development, in which Europe's social and legal structures will become more and more similar to that of the United States of America, the only realistic way to compensate for the growing enforcement deficit is to enable the "general public" or, more precisely, its affected and concerned members and specialised organisations in particular, to represent the public interest effectively and thus redress the impaired balance.

Appendix: Draft Proposal for a Council Directive Concerning Access to Justice in Environmental Matters

Preamble

The Council of the European Communities,

Having regard to the Treaty establishing the European Economic Community, and in particular Article 130s thereof,

Having regard to the proposal from the Commission,

Having regard to the opinion of the European Parliament,

Having regard to the opinion of the Economic and Social Committee,

Whereas the Community's environment policy, as set out in the Treaty and detailed in the European Communities' Action Programmes on the Environment, aims at a high level of protection;

Whereas, in particular, the Fourth Community Action Programme on the Environment emphasises the primary importance of an effective implementation of Community legislation by all Member States;

Whereas the Council declared, in its resolution of February 1993 concerning the Fifth Action Programme "Towards Sustainability", that involvement of all levels of society in a spirit of shared responsibility will require a deepening and broadening of the range of instruments to complement normative legislation;

Whereas the Fifth Action Programme stresses the crucial role of the general public and of non-governmental organisations in environmental protection; whereas it particularly calls for an accessible and efficient complaints facility to be devel-oped at local, regional and national level, as well as practicable access to the courts for individuals and public interest groups;

Whereas the Council adopted, on 7 June 1990, a Directive on the freedom of access to information on the environment;

Whereas an accessible and efficient complaints facility in environmental matters will improve confidence between the general public, the competent authorities and industrial and business establishments;

Whereas a practicable access to the courts for citizens and public interest groups will ensure that their legitimate interests are protected and that prescribed environmental measures are effectively enforced and illegal practices stopped;

Whereas, in view of the principle of subsidiarity laid down in Article 130r (4) of the Treaty, it is desirable that the control of the implementation of Community environmental law should be decentralised as far as possible, the proceedings in national courts and administrative complaints facilities being an effective control mechanism of this kind;

Whereas the disparities between the laws in force in the Member States concerning administrative and judicial review in environmental matters can create inequality within the Community as regards the standard of environmental protection and the conditions of economic competition;

Whereas a specific guarantee of the access to justice for environmental public interest groups corresponds best to the legal traditions of the Member States and takes into account the prominent role of these associations in the practice of environmental protection;

Whereas it is necessary to grant to environmental associations practicable access to the courts and administrative complaints facilities, whenever administrative acts violate a rule of environmental law or a public authority refuses or fails to act against environmentally harmful activities, and does so in breach of its duties;

Whereas it must be possible for public authorities to investigate the matter, and for persons allegedly responsible for environmentally harmful activities to answer to the accusation, and it may therefore be justified to require prior participation in administrative proceedings and a certain waiting period before legal actions may be commenced;

Whereas the successful defence of environmental interests in court requires an effective system of interim relief;

Whereas the overriding public interest in the correct implementation of environmental law justifies a considerable reduction of the plaintiff's cost risk and a partial bearing of the costs by public funds in such environmental lawsuits;

Whereas the positive experience made in some Member States with citizen suit provisions in environmental law demands that the choice of such a legal concept should not be impeded in any way;

Whereas the operation of this Directive should be subject to a review in the light of the experience gained;

HAS ADOPTED THIS DIRECTIVE:

Article 1 - Objective

The object of this Directive is to ensure practicable access to the courts and to administrative complaints facilities for public interest groups in environmental matters.

Article 2 - Definitions

For the purposes of this Directive:

(a) "environmental association" shall mean any non-governmental organisation which

(i) has as its primary objective the protection of the environment, of human health or of the cultural heritage, or the prudent and rational utilisation of natural resources, and

(ii) allows any person to join who supports the objectives of the association;

(b) "environmental law" shall mean the law of the Community and the Member States relating to the protection of the environment, human health or the cultural heritage, or to the utilisation of land or natural resources;

(c) "administrative act" shall mean any positive action of other than legislative or judicial character, taken by a public authority with external effect, including the authority's refusal to act;

(d) "sub-statutory rule" shall mean any decree, ordinance, order, bye-law or other binding norm of environmental law below the level of legislation enacted by a national or regional parliament, including, inter alia, land-use plans, limit values for emissions, and quality standards;

(e) "court" shall mean any institution exercising jurisdiction by force of law, composed of independent judges, and empowered to settle disputes by binding and enforceable judgements;

(f) "environmentally harmful" or "harmful to the environment" shall mean causing actual or potential damage to the health of man or any other living organism, reducing the quality of air, water, or soil, interfering with ecological systems, or impairing the aesthetic appearance of the landscape or of natural or cultural monuments.

Article 3 - Administrative review

Any environmental association is entitled to make use of existing extra-judicial complaints procedures against an administrative act that it considers to be in breach of a rule of environmental law, without having to show an impairment of its own interests.

Article 4 - Judicial review of administrative acts and omissions

(1) An environmental association which considers an adminis-

trative act to be in breach of a rule of environmental law may bring an action in the courts for the annulment or alteration of that act without having to show an impairment of its own interests.

(2) Member States may make the legal standing of the plaintiff dependent on prior participation in administrative proceedings only if that participation could reasonably be expected.

(3) If the competent authority, in breach of a duty under environmental law, has refused or failed to act, the association may bring an action in the courts for the enforcement of the law. The courts shall have the power to compel the authority to fulfil its duty.

(4) In the case that the authority has failed to act as requested by an environmental association, Member States may prescribe a waiting period of up to 60 days after the request has been made before the plaintiff may commence the action.

Article 5 - Judicial review of sub-statutory rules

(1) An environmental association which considers a sub-statutory rule to be in breach of higher-ranking environmental law may bring an action in the courts for the annulment or alteration of that rule without having to show an impairment of its own interests.

(2) If a public authority is under a duty to draft a sub-statutory rule of environmental law and has failed to do so, an environmental association may, under the same conditions, bring an action in the courts for the enforcement of that duty. Member States may prescribe a waiting period of up to one year after the request before the plaintiff may commence the action.

Article 6 - Judicial remedies against environmentally harmful activities

(1) An environmental association may bring an action in the courts against any person whom it considers to carry out an environmentally harmful activity in breach of environmental law, without having to show an impairment of its own interests,

if the competent public authority has refused or failed to act or if the action taken is obviously insufficient. The plaintiff association shall be entitled to all remedies that will effectively stop the harmful activity and enforce the measures required by environmental law. Besides, subject to the provisions of Community law on environmental liability, it may claim damages or restoration of the environment.

(2) Member States may prescribe a waiting period of up to 60 days after notice of the alleged infringement has been given to the public authority and the prospective defendant, before the plaintiff may commence the action.

Article 7 - Interim relief

(1) Member States shall take the necessary steps to ensure that the access to court under Articles 4, 5 and 6 includes effective interim relief in urgent cases and for the time pending judgment. The time limits mentioned in Articles 4 (4) and 6 (2) shall not apply.

(2) In cases where a person or an authority act obviously in breach of a rule of environmental law, the plaintiff is entitled to demand the immediate suspension of this activity.

Article 8 - Costs

(1) Member States shall take the necessary steps to ensure that the cost of administrative and judicial proceedings under Articles 3 to 7, including lawyers' and experts' fees and possible security deposits, shall not cause a barrier to the commencement or continuation of such proceedings. In particular they shall ensure that the plaintiff in case of success obtains recovery of all costs reasonably incurred, either from the defendant or from state funds. If the action is unsuccessful but has been brought on the basis of an arguable case and in good faith, the plaintiff shall not be required to pay court fees or the costs of other parties, and these costs shall be borne by state funds. Exceptions may be made for unnecessary expenses caused by the conduct of the plaintiff.

(2) The court shall decide at an early stage of the proceedings

on whether the association brought the action in good faith and has an arguable case. If the answer is positive, the plaintiff shall not be required to deposit securities for the indemnification of other parties.

Article 9 - Option for "citizen suit" provisions

Nothing in this Directive shall prevent Member States from retaining or introducing legislation that gives any person the right to institute administrative or legal proceedings in environmental matters.

Article 10 - Report

Four years after the date referred to in Article 11 (1), the Member States shall report to the Commission on the experience gained, in the light of which the Commission shall make a report to the European Parliament and the Council together with any proposal for revision which it may consider appropriate.

Article 11 - Entry into force

(1) The Member States shall bring into force the laws and regulations necessary to comply with this Directive by ‹18 months after the decision of the Council›

(2) The Member States shall immediately inform the Commission of all laws and regulations adopted in implementation of this Directive.

Article 12 - Addressee

This Directive is addressed to the Member States.

Done at ..., date

For the Council
The President

Notes

[1] This presentation was given before the accession of Austria, Finland, and Sweden to the EU on January 1st, 1995. Initiatives for the extension of the rights of environmental organisations are to be found also in these countries; see e.g. Phillips, C., The Proposed Swedish Environmental Code (Miljöbalken), in: (1993) 2 ELNI Newsletter 9, at p.11-13.

[2] Abridged version in: (1994) 1 ELNI Newsletter 3, and (1994) 4 Review of European Community & International Environmental Law (RECIEL) 261; full text with later amendments and annotations now in: Robinson, D. and Dunkley, J., Public Interest Perspectives in Environmental Law, 1995, p.71-108.

[3] Ormond, T., Environmental Group Actions in West Germany, in: Führ, M./ Roller, G. (eds.), Participation and Litigation Rights of Environmental Associations in Europe, 1991, p.77-92. Cf. also Berger, M., The Right of Environmental Organisations in Germany to Bring Suits and the Environmental Legal Assistance Fund eV, in: Robinson/Dunkley, op. cit., p.109-116; Wolf, R., Zur Entwicklung der Verbandsklage im Umweltrecht, in: (1994) 1 Zeitschrift für Umweltrecht (ZUR) 1.

[4] Cf. ss. 60a-60c of the Lower Saxon Nature Conservation Act (Niedersächsi-sches Naturschutzgesetz), as amended by Act of October 18th, 1993, (1993) Niedersächsisches Gesetz- und Verordnungsblatt 444, and ss. 35 and 36 of the Hessisches Naturschutzgesetz, as amended by the Act of December 19th, 1994, (1994) Gesetz- und Verordnungsblatt für das Land Hessen 775. The Lower Saxon law e.g. grants access to administrative proceedings and judicial review as against permissions for the discharge of effluents of 8 cubic metres or more per day, or for the abstraction of ground water amounting to 10,000m^3 or more per year. Hesse, on the other hand, does not allow environmental organisations to challenge discharge permits at all; in the case of water abstraction, the access to justice is opened only against certain types of permissions, a quantitative limit is set at 500,000m^3.

[5] For details see especially Grosz, S., "Access to Environmental Justice in Public Law", in: Robinson/Dunkley, op. cit., p.194-207.

[6] Cameron, J., Judicial Review of Government Decisions: The *Thorp* Litigation in the U.K., in this book, cf. Grosz, op. cit. at p.199-200; Sands, P., Access to Environmental Justice in the European Community: Principles, Practice and Proposals, in: (1994) 4 RECIEL 206 at p.210-1.

[7] Grosz, op. cit. at p.203-7.

[8] For all three states see the articles by Scannell, Y., Borrego-Cabezas, C., and Karakostas, I., in: Winkelmann, C., Untersuchung der Verbandsklage im Umweltrecht im internationalen Vergleich (Report 101 06 031 for the German Environmental Protection Agency - Umweltbundesamt), 1992, at p.207, 210-1, and p.270-1; for Ireland also Scannell, Environmental Law in Ireland, 1993, for Greece Kallia, A., Participation Rights of Environmental Associations in Greece, in: Führ/Roller, op. cit. (n. 3 supra) at p.66-76.

[9] Cf. the articles by Dyssli, B., Robesin, M., Rehling, D., Carrubba, C., and Lemos, P., in: Führ/Roller, op. cit. (n. 3 supra), and by Littmann, M.-J., Nespor, S., and Boerema, L. in this book; for the Netherlands also Betlem, G., Environmental Locus Standi in the Netherlands, in: (1994) 4 RECIEL 238.

[10] Cf. de Sadeleer, N., La Loi du 12 janvier 1993 concernant un droit d'action en matière de protection de l'environnement, in: (1994) 1 ELNI Newsletter 54, also referring to the Luxembourg Act of 10th August 1992 concerning the legal standing of conservationist or environmental associations.

[11] See for instance Littmann, M.-J., Criminal Law and Intervenor Action in France, and Nespor, S., Liability Litigation in Italy, both in this book.

[12] ss. 4 (1) and 84 Local Government (Planning and Development) Act 1963; Scannell, in: Winkelmann, op. cit. (n. 8 supra) at p.267-8.

[13] Borrego-Cabezas/Winkelmann, op. cit. (n. 8 supra) at p.208; Alvarez Baquarizo, C., Civic Participation in the Implementation of Environmental Legislation, in: Führ/Roller, op. cit. (n. 3 supra) at p.36-37.

[14] Cf. Winkelmann, op. cit. (n. 8 supra) at p.158-168.

[15] Cf. Fourth Environment Action Programme (Commission draft, COM (86) 485 final), OJ No. C 70, 18.3.1987, at p.9-10; Towards Sustainability. Fifth Environment Action Programme, OJ No. C 138, 17.5.1993, at p.80-82.

Chapter 7

WWF UK, An Taisce and the Burren The Standing of Environmental Groups before the European Courts

by Carol Hatton

Introduction

The aim of this paper is to inform you about our joint case with An Taisce against the European Commission, with particular reference to our standing before the European Court. Many of you, however, will be aware that the Court ruled our Application inadmissible on 23 September 1994. Unfortunately, this ruling was not based on our standing, but on the technicality of whether there had been a challengeable decision as to whether the Commission had decided not to withhold or suspend funding for the project. In that respect, the judgement is of little value to those keen to see case law established in this area. I would like to state here that WWF UK is very disappointed with the judgement of the Court of First Instance and we are currently considering whether to appeal.

This paper is in four main parts. First, I would like to provide an introduction to the Burren and take you through the events that lead WWF UK and An Taisce to lodge an Action against the European Commission in December 1992. Secondly, I will examine the issue of *locus* before the Court. Thirdly, I would like to refer to the recent judgement of the Court of First Instance and discuss its implications for the standing of other groups. Fourthly, I should like to briefly explore the role of the Commission in the enforcement of European law and end with some brief remarks.

1. A Background to the Burren

The Burren in County Clare, Western Ireland is the largest expanse of limestone pavement in Western Europe. It is a place of history, beauty and mystery. The grey landscape is devoid of trees, save only dwarfed hazel and hawthorn shrubs stunted and shaped by the harsh winter winds. However, if one looks between the grey slabs, a dazzling mixture of plants can be found thriving in the thin soils. It is a botanists haven. Calcareous and acid loving species grow side by side - bloody cranesbill, wild thyme and orchids jostle for space with tormentil heather. Arctic-alpine plants grow at sea level - mountain avens and rock rose can be found in profusion along the narrow, twisting lanes. Its unspoilt lakes or turloughs are a law unto themselves - being interconnected by a subterranean network of channels, changes in the water levels can cause entire lakes to disappear and reappear within days or even hours.

It is no surprise, perhaps, that environmental groups within Ireland and in the UK welcomed plans for designation of part of the Burren as a National Park in April 1991. Less welcome, however, were proposals for a major visitor centre at Mullaghmore, an area many consider to be the "quiet heart of the Burren". The proposed centre, which the Irish Government predict will cater for approximately 60,000 people a year, was to be funded by the Commission with a 75% grant of £2.7 million from Structural Funds.

WWF UK and An Taisce believe that the chosen site will endanger many species and habitats protected by International Conventions and European Law. Several species found on and around the site of the proposed centre are listed in the Convention on the Conservation of European Wildlife and Natural Habitats (the Bern Convention) including the otter, the marsh fritillary butterfly and the pine marten. Limestone pavements, karstic grasslands and turloughs are all listed as priority habitats for protection in Annex I of Council Directive 92/43/EEC on the Conservation of Natural Habitats and of Wild Fauna and Flora (the Habitats Directive). Much of the Burren will qualify for designation as a Special Area of Conservation (SAC) in accordance with the Directive. The Burren also supports species listed on Annex II and IV(a) including the otter, the marsh fritillary butterfly and the rare fen moss *Drepanocladus vernicosus*.

Shortly after the proposals were announced, WWF UK

submitted a complaint to DG XI (Environment, Nuclear Safety and Civil Protection) because of the Irish Government's failure to comply with Council Directive 85/337/EEC on the Assessment of the Effects of Certain Private and Public Projects on the Environment (the EIA Directive). The Commission responded in writing to WWF UK on 23 August 1991 stating that funding „will only be approved if it is satisfactorily demonstrated that there are no significant adverse effects".

On 7 October 1992, the Commission issued a press release announcing that they would not be initiating Article 169 proceedings against the Irish Government (in respect of the EIA Directive and the Council Directive on Groundwater 80/68/EEC) and that the file was closed. The day after this announcement, the Irish Government let the contract for the construction of the centre.

1.1 The Basis for a Case against the Commission

Article 7(1) of Structural Fund Regulation 2052/88 stipulates that Structural Fund measures shall be in keeping with the EC Treaty, legislation under it and Community policy including, inter alia, Community policy on the environment. Article 130r(1) of the Treaty of Rome provides that action by the Community relating to the environment shall have as its objectives, inter alia, preserving, protecting and improving the quality of the environment.

Given the importance of Mullaghmore in relation to both the Bern Convention and the Habitats Directive, Mary Banotti MEP sought to clarify the way the Commission interpreted the Treaty and the Regulations with the following parliamentary question:

Question H-1051/92:

Article 7.1 of Regulation 2052/88 stipulates that Structural Fund measures shall be in keeping with the EEC Treaty, legislation under it and Community environmental policy. Did the Commission take Article 7.1 fully into account before its decision of 7 October 1992 on complaints about the Mullaghmore visitor centre project in Ireland. If so, is it correct to conclude from its press statement of the same date that the Commission did not consider the objectives of the Habitats Directive and the Berne Convention as forming part of Community environmental policy for the purposes of its decision and its role in relation to the project?

The answer given:

> The Commission considers that it took full account of Article 7.1 of Regulation 2052/88. As regards the second part of the question, it is correct to so conclude.

Thus, the Commission confirmed that when it assesses whether projects financed by Structural Funds are in accordance with Article 7(1) of Regulation 2052/88, it will only examine whether these measures are in accordance with Community law despite the fact that Article 7(1) of Regulation 2052/88 explicitly states that the measures shall be in accordance with the Treaties, the instruments adopted thereto and with Community policy. This response (and a later response to Parliamentary question H-1240/92 also of Mary Banotti MEP) answers the question as to whether or not Directives have to be taken into account by the Commission as soon as they are formally agreed by the Council of Ministers, or only at the stage that Member States pass the necessary enabling legislation - often some years later.

The European Parliament took the same view as we did in our case lodged on 4 December 1992 when, on 22 April 1993, it passed Resolution B3-0520 and 0618/93 which states that:

The European Parliament

(D)(2): Believes therefore that the Berne Convention (Council decision 82/72/EEC) on the Conservation of European wildlife and natural habitats and the Habitats Directive (92/43/EEC) do form part of the Community's environment policy...;

(D)(3): Believes that, despite the fact that the Habitats Directive has not yet been transposed into national legislation, the Member States and the Commission alike are required to abide by its objectives, and points out that the Court of Justice judgement in case 80/86 confirms that a directive can have legal consequences even before it is transposed;

(D)(11): Expects the Commission from now on, in its decisions on spending under the Structural Funds, to comply fully with the objectives of the Habitats Directive, the Berne Convention, and other resolutions approved by the Council...

As a result of the interpretation which the Commission places upon Article 7(1) of Regulation 2052/88, WWF believes it fails to secure full compliance with this provision and Article 130r(1) of the Treaty of Rome. This constitutes the basis of the action brought by WWF UK and An Taisce against the Commission. As matters stand at present, WWF is gravely concerned that Community funding in the order of 141 billion ECU between 1994 and 1999 may finance major infrastructure projects which destroy and damage sites protected by Community environmental legislation and International Conventions.

2. The Question of Standing before the Court

WWF UK and An Taisce's action was brought on the basis of Article 173(4) of the EC Treaty (the former Article 173(2) of the EEC Treaty). This provision allows individual parties to challenge decisions of the Community Institutions which are addressed to third parties provided that these decisions are of direct and individual concern to the individual. We argued that the Commission took two decisions on 7 October 1992 - firstly, not to initiate an Article 169 proceeding against the Irish Government for a contravention of Community law and secondly, not to suspend or withhold funding for the project. We further stated that both WWF UK and An Taisce have *locus* with regard to this decision.

There have been no previous cases where *locus* of NGOs has either been granted or denied before the European Court or the Court of First Instance. As such, case law in this area is not yet established. On the question of individual concern, we relied on the case law of the Court on the admissibility of actions brought by consumer or industry organisations. In particular, we referred to the recent judgement of the Court in the *CIRFS* (case C-313/20 judgement of 24 March 1993, *CIFRS vs. Commission* [1993] ECR I-1125). In this respect, we invoked the important and active role WWF UK performed in the discussion on the reform of the Structural Funds in general and our extensive involvement in this particular project. We also drew the Court's attention to the fact that WWF UK is a formal observer on the Standing Committee on the Bern Convention (which WWF UK believes the Mullaghmore project contravenes), and that both the Commission and WWF UK are signatories to the final declaration of the joint meeting on conservation in Europe (Europe 2000). All of the above, therefore, contribute to our argument that our position as a negotiator was affected.

Concerning An Taisce, we pointed out that their principal aim is to conserve the physical heritage of Ireland for the benefit of the Irish Nation. An Taisce has rights under the Planning Acts and owns and manages property for its permanent preservation. At Mullaghmore, its land abuts the site of the proposed centre and, if the project were to proceed, its property would be adversely affected by the construction and operation of the centre.

Referring briefly to case law in Germany, one can also apply certain principles to our case. In general, an NGO can only challenge the Government before the Courts if they can demonstrate that the Government has violated a so-called subjective right of the NGO itself (a criteria comparable to the criteria of individual concern under Article 173 of the EC Treaty). It is not sufficient that the Government has violated the rights of its members or the rights of the general public. However, laws on nature protection of some of the German Lander (Berlin, Hamburg and Bremen for example) provide a right for NGOs to challenge the Government on environmental grounds for the violation of laws on nature protection - but not for the violation of any environmental law. The NGO must be registered. It may be registered provided that it fulfils a number of conditions:

- according to its statute it must support the objectives of nature protection and protection of the landscape;

- according to its statute its area of activity must at least comprise the area of one of the Lander;

- it must show that it is able to fulfil its objectives accordingly; in this regard the scope and kind of its former activities, its membership as well as its performance capability are taken into consideration;

- it must fulfil certain tax conditions;

- everybody who supports the objectives of the NGO must be allowed to join the NGO.

A registered NGO may challenge the Government with regard to a violation of law in the general public interest, or where a violation of the laws on nature protection influences the NGO in the pursuit of its constitutional objectives. One further condition is that the NGO must have made use of its right to participate in the administrative process leading up to the Government action which it wishes to challenge. We have argued in our case very much on the line of these provisions of German law, although we did not mention them.

Concerning the question of direct concern, we reject the Commission's argument that WWF UK and An Taisce could only be affected by the decision of the Irish authorities to build the centre, and not by the Commission's decision to finance the project. We referred to previous case law of the Court (Case 11/82 judgement of 17 January 1985 *Piraiki-Patraiki* [1985] ECR 207, 242; and the opinion of the Advocate General Verloren Van Themaat in case 11/82 [1985] ECR 208, 212) where the Court held that a measure is of direct concern to an individual party despite the fact that it requires the adoption of a further national implementing measure if it is possible to foresee with certainty (or with a high degree of probability) that the implementing measure will be taken. In this respect, we provided evidence which clearly indicated that the Irish authorities were only able to commence with plans for a centre once they were in a position to receive a 75% grant from the Structural Funds.

The Commission argues that neither group is directly and individually affected by its decision. We do not believe this to be the case.

However, it is also important to note that the Commission also contested that there was no "decision" as such to challenge as the decision not to initiate Article 169 proceedings against the Irish Government was distinct from any decision with regard to the funding of the centre. In any event, the

Commission argued that their involvement in the process does not extend beyond an examination of the Operational Programme. This is a requirement of Member States who apply for funding and gives a broad overview of the nature of projects to be funded, rather than the details of the individual projects themselves. Only during the oral hearing, and after having been confronted with evidence gathered by us, the Commission acknowledged that it may sometimes evaluate projects even after the adoption of an Operational Programme, although it denied having done so in this case.

3. The Judgement and its Implications

The Court of First Instance delivered its judgement on 23 September 1994. The Court ruled that the Commission only decided not to initiate an Article 169 proceeding, but did not decide to suspend or reduce funds for the project. The Commission's main argument was that such a possibility is open to the Commission at all times if it transpires that there are irregularities. In these circumstances, the Court rightly ruled that it was not necessary to determine "whether individuals have *locus* to contest a Commission decision".

Assuming that WWF UK and An Taisce decide to appeal, the issue of what constitutes a decision and the question of *locus standi* still remain to be resolved. If we appeal, and lose on the issue of whether or not a "decision" was taken, the question of *locus* will remain unresolved.

Whatever the outcome of this case, WWF UK believes that, in case such as the Cardiff Bay Barrage in Wales and the Acheloos river diversion scheme in Greece, individuals concerned (such as neighbouring landowners, expropriated farmers etc.) and NGOs with relevant rights or interests must be allowed to challenge funding decisions taken by the Commission where there is a question of non-compliance with Community law. Without such a right, we believe that EC funding will continue to be given to projects which may not only have been authorised contrary to European law but are also environmentally damaging. There will also be no judicial control although other Member States as well as the Institutions of the Community (especially the European Parliament) could, in theory, challenge the Commission's decision. Such a possibility appears, however, remote.

4. The Role of the Commission in Enforcing Community Law

If third parties are restricted in their access to the Courts, the role of the Commission in ensuring Member State compliance becomes even more significant. DG XI receives an enormous number of complaints every year. Some of these are pursued by the Commission and, following an exchange of correspondence, it commences Article 169 proceedings against the Member State. However, the number of cases that reach this stage is very small in relation to the number of complaints lodged.

This suggests one of two things. Either compliance is subsequently obtained, or (we can only assume) an "agreement" is reached which satisfies the Commission that there is no "net" environmental loss. In negotiating an "agreement" with a Member State the Commission may be under pressure to resolve the issue without recourse to litigation. This may be in the long term interests of retaining a good working relationship and the need to be seen to be treating all Member States in an even handed manner, even when there may be differing levels of implementation and enforcement of environmental protection at a national level.

The point is that the Commission appears to initiate very few cases against Member States. On occasion, it even fails to do so when the evidence for proceeding (as viewed by NGOs) is overwhelming. I would cite the Cardiff Bay Barrage in Wales as an example of this. This causes WWF UK concern as it would appear that, on occasion, important cases, where WWF UK believe serious breaches of Community environmental law have occurred have "fallen through the net".

5. Concluding Remarks

WWF UK believes that one of the answers must lie with a strengthened environmental directorate and legal service for the Commission to address the volume of complaints received by DG XI. This should be combined with transparent decision making an enhanced ability for third parties such as WWF UK to take action themselves where there has been a violation of the law which is detrimental to the public interest. This provision could complement actions taken by the Commission, and would also ensure that there was a mechanism by which the Commission is accountable for the legal consequences of its actions.

So, to conclude, I have outlined the events surrounding our action and provided a few brief thoughts on the issue of access to the Court. Hopefully, the case being pursued by Greenpeace in respect of Thorp (which we will hear more of tomorrow) will develop this issue further. Similarly, our own Appeal, should we decide to pursue one, may help to establish a precedent for the future.

Ladies and Gentlemen, that concludes my presentation on this issue. If you have any questions, I will be pleased to answer them - either now or at other times during the conference. For those questions of a more technical nature, our lawyer, Dr Georg Berrisch, is willing to answer questions on the telephone. Dr Berrisch practices at Schon Nolte Finkelnburg and Clemm, Rue Pere de Deken 33, B-1040 Brussels, Belgium. Telephone Brussels 732 2680 and fax Brussels 735 9604.

Chapter 8

Judicial Review of Government Decisions: The THORP Litigation in the U.K.

by James Cameron

We do not have a developed system of administrative law -perhaps because until fairly recently we did not need it. So it is not surprising that in dealing with new types of cases the courts have had to grope for solutions, and have found that old powers, rules and procedure are largely inapplicable to cases which they were never designed or intended to deal with." - Lord Reid, 1963[1]

Judicial review of government decisions has virtually transformed English law over the last three decades.[2] Ignited by Lord Reid, domestic courts have continued this flame of administrative review on a case by case basis. One case which outlines some complimentary developments in administrative law is *R. Secretary of State for the Environment, HMIP and MAFF Ex Parte Greenpeace and Lancashire County Council*, known as the *Thorp* case. In August 1993, Her Majesty's Inspectorate of Pollution (HMIP) and the Minister of Agriculture Fisheries and Food (MAFF) decided to grant applications by British Nuclear Fuels Limited (BNFL) for variations of authorizations to discharge radioactive waste. Pursuant to the Radioactive Substances Act 1960 (RSA), BFNL requested the applications to test its new thermal oxide processing plant (THORP) in Sellafield, Cumbria. Greenpeace challenged that decision; it sought an order of certiorari to quash the decision, and an injunction to stop testing pending a decision in favour of the main operation of THORP. Though the application failed, Otton J emphatically rejected BFNL's argument that Greenpeace lacked standing to bring such a challenge.

In a separate action, Greenpeace challenged the government's decision to commission THORP without holding a public inquiry and without proper application of the EC principle of "justification".[3] Though this application failed as well, the Court noted that it was responsibly brought and properly pursued.[4] The government and BFNL argued that their legal costs should be paid by the unsuccessful applicant. Despite their requests, Potts J exercised his discretion that there should be no order as to costs.

In *Thorp* we find first instance judges quietly exercising their "discretion" to override two of the principle obstacles traditionally placed in the path of the responsible public interest group: the standing objection and the cost burden.[5] Unfortunately, it is too early to predict whether these steps are progressive strides in judicial activism, or an unwelcome trip to the "Black Hole" of civil litigation, where future cases cannot surface. *Thorp* leaves us in the "twilight zone" of judicial discretion, for its subjective standard will inevitably produce disparate results. This paper will briefly outline *Thorp* while concentrating on the issues of standing and costs.

Standing

"The fact that some thousands of people joined together and assert that they have an interest does not create an interest if the individuals do not have an interest." - Schiemann J[6]

"... I reject the argument that Greenpeace is a ... 'meddlesome busybody'. I regard the applicants as eminently respectable and responsible and their genuine interest in the issues raised is sufficient for them to be granted *locus standi*." - Otton J[7]

BNFL submitted that Greenpeace did not have a sufficient interest in the matter to give them standing in the judicial review application. It was argued on behalf of BNFL that: "This is the classic case of the busy body. The nub of Greenpeace's complaint is that, although it has itself the opportunity to make comments, the decision is flawed because some person or persons should have been consulted. Allegations that procedural rights have not been respected are properly vindicated by those entitled to those rights and not by a pressure group which itself has no practical complaint."

The Judge held that once it was established that the Applicant was not a "meddlesome busybody", the matter of "sufficient interest" was primarily one of discretion. He considered it "appropriate to take into account the nature of the Applicant and the extent of the Applicant's interest in the issues raised, the remedy Greenpeace seeks to achieve and the nature of the relief sought." The Court found that Greenpeace's genuine interest was sufficient to grant standing.

His Lordship recognised certain factors which previous courts have not acknowledged as establishing locus standi. Greenpeace is a responsible and respected organisation commanding wide membership both internationally and domestically. It has a genuine concern for the environment. Furthermore, 2,500 members live in the Cumbria region. The Judge considered that the issues raised by the application merited determination and that the denial of standing to Greenpeace might well have resulted in variations of the authorizations going unchallenged. Furthermore, Greenpeace's expertise in the environmental field and their financial backing of the application ensured scarce court services were spared and that the Respondents could recover their costs.

Otton J's conclusion that Greenpeace had locus standi is consistent with "the desirability of the courts recognising...the right of responsible citizens to enter the lists for the benefit of the public, or a section of the public, of which they themselves are members, and thus the respectability of affording to individuals...liberal access under a generous conception of locus standi."[8] Though the courts' recognition is ideal, it has not been widely adopted.

Unfortunately, the majority of the courts still interpret locus standi in line with Schiemann J's analysis, where public interest groups are usually denied standing. According to the editors of the White Book, "...the formula 'sufficient interest' is not intended to create a class of person, popularly referred to as a 'private attorney-general', who seeks to champion public interests, in which he is not himself directly or personally concerned, under the guise of applying for judicial review."[9] However, Otton J's finding challenges this restricted notion, and establishes the framework for future public interest group participation. His Lordship's insight goes beyond the mere notion of the "citizen action", to the fact that a mature public law system should afford to a public interest group a position more favourable even than that of the "public-spirited citizen." Otton J expressed a preference for action by the responsible public interest group, over that of an individual citizen.

The heresy which the Otton judgment can be seen to have exploded is the notion that a public interest group (seeking judicial review) is to be treated as being akin to a group action (in "ordinary" civil proceedings). Previous group-applicant cases were viewed as an amalgam of individuals and could be in no stronger position than would any one of them. However, the *Thorp*-litigation has seriously weakened this limited view towards citizen actions.

Operation of the Plant

BNFL had sought planning permission for THORP between 1971 and 1977. In 1977, a public inquiry into the planning application was held and full planning permission was eventually granted in 1983. Construction of THORP was subsequently completed in 1992. In order to operate THORP, BNFL then applied to HMIP and MAFF for new authorizations for the discharge of radioactive wastes to sea and air from the Sellafield site. In December 1993, the Government decided not to hold a public inquiry and to grant BNFL the authorizations under Section 13 Radioactive Substances Act 1993. Greenpeace challenged the decision on the grounds that, inter alia, the Secretary of State had erred in law in believing that there was no obligation to justify the radioactive emissions in terms of the net benefit to the public, that any decision that the discharges were justified was irrational, that the decision not to hold a public inquiry was irrational, and that the authorization could not lawfully be granted without an environmental impact assessment first being provided in accordance with EC Directive 85/337.

Justification

The Judge found that the Secretary of State was legally obliged to justify the need for THORP under Articles 6(a) and 13 of the Euratom Treaty (Directive 80/836 Euratom).[10]11 BFNL unsuccessfully argued that Section 13 of the Radioactive

Substances Act 1993 is not concerned with proving or reviewing the justification of practices; it only deals with the authorization of discharges.[11] Although the 1993 Act, under which the authorizations were granted, did not in terms require justification, the Act had to be construed consistently with a directive made pursuant to the Euratom Directive, which lays down basic safety standards for the protection of workers and the general public against the dangers of ionizing radiation. It is a principle of Community law that national legislation is interpreted as far as possible consistently with the requirements of any relevant Community directive (See *Marleasing SA v. La Commercial Internacional de Alimentacion SA* (1990) ECR 1-4135)). This principle does not allow the plain meaning of the Statute to be distorted. The Euratom Directive provides that the various types of activity resulting in an exposure to ionizing radiation shall have been justified in advance by the advantages which they produce. Potts J found that although the 1993 Act is silent as to justification, the plain meaning of its relevant provisions was not distorted by being read in accordance with the Directive. In his Lordship's judgment, the Ministers erred in determining that the legislation did not require them to justify the authorizations.[12]

Despite this error in interpreting their administrative functions, it did not alter the Judge's findings. Potts J concluded that in fact the Ministers had considered justification, albeit they had not considered themselves legally obligated to do so. The Ministers had carried out a careful process of weighing the benefits against the detriments of granting the authorizations. Although the final *Thorp* decision is not the desired result, the Court's attention to administrative functions establishes a positive framework for future judicial review.

Environmental Impact Assessment

Annex II to the EIA Directive sets out projects for which an EIA will be required where Member States consider that "their characteristics so require". Among the projects listed in Annex II are "installations for the reprocessing of irradiated nuclear fuels". Greenpeace argued that the construction of THORP and the operation of the processes causing the emissions were two separate projects. Greenpeace maintained that the discharge of ionising radiation constitutes an "intervention in the natural surroundings", and thus a separate project within the definition in the Directive. If there were only one project then Greenpeace's application on this point would fail since the 1985 Directive does not apply to projects which either predate or were in the pipeline before its entry into force. However, it was held that the construction and operation of THORP were one project which had received its development consent before the entry into force of the Directive, so that the Directive did not apply.

Public Inquiry

Under the Radioactive Substances Act 1993, the Secretary of State has discretion to cause a local public inquiry to be held. Greenpeace submitted that the following matters, inter alia, were relevant in considering whether there should be a public inquiry:-

- the importance of the decision;

- the great public concern demonstrated by the number of responses received to consultations;

- the quality of the responses to the consultations;

- the need to properly test and consider economic and scientific issues; and

- the need to inform the public about radiation and to allay their fears.

The Judge considered the way in which the Secretary of State had exercised his discretion, and found that he had taken into account all relevant considerations and had weighed the arguments of those who sought a public inquiry. In order to impugn the Secretary of State's decision not to call an inquiry, it would have to be shown that his decision was so unreasonable that no reasonable minister could have reached the same conclusion. Here, there was no evidence that the Secretary of State had failed to apply his mind genuinely and rationally to the issue of whether or not to hold a public inquiry. It was not the place of the Court in judicial review to act as a "court of appeal" from the Minister's decision, but merely to consider whether the Minister had acted lawfully within the powers conferred on him by Parliament. While the Judge noted, significantly, that it might be thought that a Minister sensible to the scale of representations made and the desirability of allaying public anxiety would have directed an inquiry, nevertheless, he found that the decision not to do so was not irrational in English law.

Costs

Although the challenge was dismissed, the Judge did not order Greenpeace to pay costs, an indication of the public interest of the application. One irony which emerges is that one of the factors mentioned by Otton J in expressing a preference for Greenpeace as an applicant (rather than as an individual citizen), was its ability to meet an order for costs should it fail.

Utilizing his discretion, Potts J concluded that there should be no costs, which saved Greenpeace millions of pounds. His Lordship relied on three matters: (1) that this was a case of substantial public interest; (2) that leave had been granted; and (3) that Greenpeace had succeeded on one important point (justification under EC law), thus clarifying the law for the future.

The question is to what extent points (1) and (2) explode the heresy that in relation to costs judicial review proceedings to which the "ordinary" rule should apply. This is, after all, the premise which underlies the Crown Office's Notes for Guidance, which refers to the "general rule that the party which loses is ordered to pay the costs of the other side."[13]

The simple point is that judicial review is a special jurisdiction. It is certainly not always characterised as "civil proceedings".[14] There is a long line of reported cases which show that it is perfectly respectable for a court to refuse to impose costs burden on an unsuccessful applicant who has brought to light a matter of public interest.[15]

The Law Commission has seen the point. Its 1993 Consultation Paper considers the argument that "where an application brought in good faith in the public interest is unsuccessful, the applicant should not be obliged to pay the other side's costs", since "it could be said that the usual principle of costs being awarded to the successful party is really designed for civil litigation concerning the vindication of private rights."[16]

The Commission's (provisional) recommendation is that: "Where leave has been granted on the footing that the application discloses arguable grounds that the court ought to exercise its prerogative jurisdiction, we consider that it may be appropriate to disapply the usual costs rules, on the footing that they are inappropriate to the nature of the jurisdiction."[17]

Conclusion

Thorp indicates that English courts may no longer be willing to allow procedural rules to discourage public interest groups from bringing legitimate concerns to the judicial forum. The Greenpeace cases are steps in the right direction, but questions regarding standing and costs still remain. The Court's finding is a mixed signal, for it implies that the group-applicant must satisfy orthodox requirements of legal capacity in addition to the elements of standing. Moreover, citizen actions may still be forced to pay costs if their application is unsuccessful, which will hinder future litigation. If citizen action is to be properly recognised, our judicial system must blaze the trail of judicial review which Otton and Potts JJ have identified.

Notes

[1] See Fordham, M. and Cameron, J., Judicial Review and Public Interest Groups, 1 Environmental Judicial Review Bulletin page 5 (September 1994). Many thanks to Phyllisina Vinson, FIELD Legal Intern and J.D. Candidate, Duke University School of Law, 1995, for her assistance in preparing this article.

[2] Id.

[3] Fordham and Cameron, page 6.

[4] I understand that government lawyers take the view that

Greenpeace really won the case because of the Court's ruling on justification.

[5] Id.

[6] See *Regina v. HM Inspectorate of Pollution Ministry of Agriculture, Fisheries and Food* (Ex Parte Greenpeace), page 38 (quoting Schiemann J in Ex Parte Rose Theatre Company, page 520).

[7] See *Regina v. HM Inspectorate of Pollution* at page 45.

[8] Fordham & Cameron, page 5.

[9] Id.

[10] *Regina v. The Secretary of State for the Environment Her Majesty's Inspectorate of Pollution The Minister of Agriculture, Fisheries and Food* (Ex Parte Greenpeace and Lancashire County Council), page 30.

[11] Id. at 27.

[12] Id. at 30.

[13] Fordham & Cameron, page 6.

[14] Id.

[15] Id.

[16] Id.

[17] Id.

Chapter 9

Litigation to Protect the Northern Spotted Owl and the Ancient Forest Ecosystem

by Todd D. True

Since environmentalists filed the first lawsuit to protect the northern spotted owl and its ancient forest ecosystem over seven years ago,[1] the federal trial and appellate courts have issued more than fifteen published opinions addressing the wildlife and forest management responsibilities of three separate federal agencies under a half dozen environmental laws. In almost everyone of these cases, the environmental plaintiffs have prevailed. The political response to these cases and the ensuing legislative reaction[2] also has raised constitutional issues recently addressed by the U.S. Supreme Court.[3] One observer has described the litigation to enforce the environmental laws and protect the owl and the ancient forests as "the most stunning series of victories ever put together by an environmental litigation team."[4] This report will briefly identify the major cases and their current dispositions.

1. Background

The northern spotted owl is a medium-sized owl with dark eyes, dark to chestnut brown coloring, whitish spots on the head and neck, and white mottling on the abdomen and breast. The owl is monogamous, long-lived and highly territorial. It inhabits the forests of southwestern British Columbia (Canada) and western Washington, Oregon, and northwestern California in the United States.[5]

As one report by a team of U.S. scientists put it: "Why all the fuss about the status and welfare of this particular bird?" Their answer:

> The numbers, distribution, and welfare of spotted owls are widely believed to be inextricably tied to mature and old-growth forests. Such forests have been significantly reduced

since 1850 (mostly since 1950) ... most significantly, by logging in recent decades... As its habitat has declined, the owl has virtually disappeared from some areas and its numbers are decreasing in others.[6]

The courts have made the same point:

"The fate of the spotted owl has become a battleground largely because the species is a symbol of the remaining old growth forests."[7]

2. Litigation under the Endangered Species Act (ESA) against the U.S. Fish and Wildlife Service (FWS)

Litigation on the owl's behalf by U.S. environmental organizations promises to address virtually every provision affecting the government's duties under the Endangered Species Act.[8]

Thus far, the courts have ruled that the FWS[9] improperly refused to list the owl under the ESA,[10] leading to its listing as threatened; and that the agency improperly refused to designate critical habitat for the owl,[11] leading to the designation of critical habitat.[12] The courts also have addressed the scope of consultation between federal agencies required under the ESA to protect the owl,[13] and, in a case filed by the timber industry, the validity of ESA regulations that protect listed species.[14]

In addition, in May of 1992, the Endangered Species Committee (the ESC), a cabinet level committee established under section 7 of the ESA,[15] granted an exemption from certain provisions of the Act for 13 of 44 government timber sales in Oregon that FWS had concluded would jeopardize the continued existence of the owl. This decision followed an extraordinary 23 day formal administrative hearing on the exemption application in January of 1992.[16] The Committee's timber sale exemption was the first ever granted under the ESA following a full hearing[17].

A coalition of environmental groups that participated in the ESC administrative proceedings subsequently sought review of the exemption decision in the Ninth Circuit Court of Appeals under ESA section 7(n).[18] The court, in late 1992, ruled that the environmental plaintiffs could take discovery to determine whether then-President Bush had improperly attempted to influence the ESC decision.[19] Following this ruling, the new Clinton administration withdrew the government's application for an exemption from the ESA for the 13 timber sales.

3. Litigation under the Environmental Policy Act (NEPA) against the Bureau of Land Management (BLM)

In 1987, environmental groups filed suit in Oregon under NEPA[20] and other laws challenging on-going timber sales in spotted owl habitat by the Bureau of Land Management. Within two months after the plaintiffs filed their suit, at the urging of the Oregon congressional delegation, the U.S. Congress enacted a "rider" to the Department of Interior and Related Agencies Appropriations Act for Fiscal Year 1988[21] restricting access to the courts for review of BLM timber sale activities. In a series of opinions, the Ninth Circuit interpreted the rider, which Congress subsequently re-enacted twice, to bar the plaintiffs' NEPA claims.[22]

The district court, in the meantime, concluded that although the rider prevented it from enforcing NEPA against the BLM, the agency had violated the requirements of that statute in pursuing its timber sale program.[23]

When the final version of the appropriations rider expired in September of 1990, plaintiffs renewed their NEPA claim against BLM. Although the district court again initially dismissed the claim on procedural grounds, following a reversal in the Ninth Circuit,[24] the district court first issued a preliminary injunction and then, in June of 1992, summary judgment and a permanent injunction against BLM timber sales in spotted owl habitat pending the agency's compliance with NEPA.[25] The federal appellate court subsequently affirmed this ruling.[26]

4. Litigation against the U.S. Forest Service under NEPA and the National Forest Management Act (NFMA)

The U.S. Forest Service[27] manages over 70% of the spotted owl's remaining suitable habitat (approximately 6 to 7 million acres of forests). This habitat is scattered across 17 national forests in Washington, Oregon, and northern California. In December 1988, the Forest Service, after preparing an environmental impact statement (EIS), adopted a plan for managing owl habitat. Biologists both inside and outside the government, however, sharply criticized the plan as scientifically insupportable.[28]

In February of 1989, environmental groups sought court review of the agency plan and EIS for violations of NEPA, the NFMA and the Migratory Bird Treaty Act.[29] In March, the federal district court issued a preliminary injunction against certain Forest Service timber sales in spotted owl habitat but before the case came to trial Congress, at the behest of Northwest legislators, intervened with another appropriations rider.[30] This new rider addressed the *Seattle Audubon* and *Portland Audubon* cases by caption and docket number and directed the dissolution of the existing injunctions in these cases.

The plaintiffs in each case challenged the constitutionality of the rider on the grounds that the law was an improper interference by Congress in the adjudication of cases by the federal courts — a violation of the constitutional "separation of powers" doctrine. Both district courts rejected the plaintiffs' constitutional arguments and dissolved the existing injunctions against timber sales.[31] In September of 1990, however, the Ninth Circuit struck down portions of section 318 for violating the constitutional separation of powers.[32] Within weeks of the Ninth Circuit's ruling, section 318 expired by its own terms and Congress did not re-enact it. Nonetheless, the United States successfully sought review of the Ninth Circuit's ruling in the Supreme Court and in March of 1992, the Court reversed the Ninth Circuit's decision without reaching "any broad question of Article III jurisprudence."[33]

Following the expiration of Section 318, the *Seattle Audubon* plaintiffs renewed their challenge to the Forest Service owl management plan, which the agency had changed in light of recommendations by an Interagency Scientific Committee chartered[34] to develop a conservation plan for the spotted owl. In March of 1991, the federal district court in Seattle found that the new Forest Service plan violated the requirements of the NFMA.[35]

Subsequently, in May, following a one-week hearing, the court permanently enjoined the Forest Service from selling additional timber sales in spotted owl habitat pending compliance with NFMA.[36] In issuing the injunction, the court observed:

> More is involved here than a simple failure by an agency to comply with its governing statute. The most recent violation of the NFMA exemplifies a deliberate and systematic refusal by the Forest Service ... to comply with the laws protecting wildlife. This is not the doing of scientists, foresters, rangers, and others at the working levels of these agencies. It reflects decisions made by higher authorities in the executive branch of government.[37]

The court concluded:

> To by pass the environmental laws, either briefly or permanently, would not fend off the changes transforming the timber industry. The argument that the mightiest economy on earth cannot afford to preserve old growth forests for a short time, while it reaches an overdue decision on how to manage them, is not convincing today. It would be even less so a year or a century from now.[38]

Accordingly, the court directed the agency to develop and adopt by March of 1992 an owl plan and supporting EIS that would meet the requirements of the law.[39]

In response to the court's orders, the Forest Service prepared and issued a draft EIS on a new owl plan in September of 1991 and a final EIS in January of 1992. In March the agency announced its new owl plan - which looked surprisingly like its old owl plan. Not surprisingly under these circumstances, environmentalists again challenged the plan and in May of 1992, the district court ruled that the EIS for the new plan failed to address a number of critical environmental issues affecting the owl and other wildlife species that inhabit the old growth forests.[40] On July 2, 1992, following issuance in May of a preliminary injunction against Forest Service timber sales in spotted owl habitat, the court permanently enjoined the agency from selling such sales until it complied with NEPA and adopted an owl plan that meets the wildlife protection standards of the NFMA.[41] In a companion opinion to the decision affirming the ruling in the *Portland Audubon* case, the court of appeals affirmed this ruling too.[42]

Since July of 1992, the government agencies involved in management of spotted owl habitat (the Forest Service, the BLM and the Fish and Wildlife Service), under the direction of the Clinton Administration, have attempted to formulate a coordinated plan for protecting the ancient forest ecosystem in the Pacific Northwest. The government formally announced and adopted this plan in April of 1994, following an April 1993 "Forest Conference" in Portland, Oregon, led by President Clinton, Vice-President Gore and several members of the Clinton cabinet. The new plan is a significant improvement over past government planning efforts and may protect as much as 80% of the remaining ancient forest ecosystem on federal lands in the Northwest.

Nonetheless, independent scientists and environmental groups have concluded that the plan is far from adequate to assure the survival of this ecosystem. It fails to protect all of the spotted owl's remaining habitat and proposes continued logging across hundreds of thousands of acres of land that provide important habitat for many wildlife species, including many species of fish, that have now been recognized as threatened with extinction, primarily because of past logging activities. Accordingly, in May of this year, environmental groups once again returned to court to challenge the new Clinton plan. The timber industry too has challenged the Clinton plan because, in their view, it allows too little logging on national forest and BLM lands in the Northwest.

The environmental and industry cases have been consolidated before a single judge and the case is working its way through the court system. A court hearing on the environmental and industry claims against the new forest plan is scheduled for early November of this year in Seattle, Washington.

5. Conclusion

The still unfolding story of environmental litigation to protect the spotted owl and the old growth forests has focused attention on "a remarkable series of violations of the environmental laws."[43] It has also stirred an often heated debate over management of public forests and wildlife protection. Ultimately, this debate may lead to congressional action that will establish new standards for protecting these forest resources. In the meantime, environmental litigation has proved quite effective in compelling the government to take major steps to better protect these unique forests and the species that inhabit them.

Notes

1 *Portland Audubon Society ("PAS") v. Hodel*, 18 ELR 21,213 (D. Ore. 1988), rev'd, 866 F.2d 302 (9th Cir.), cert. denied, 492 U.S. 911 (1989).

2 For a discussion of this history see V. Sher & C. Hunting, "Eroding the Landscape, Eroding the Laws: Congressional Exemptions from Judicial Review of Environmental Laws," 15 Harv. Envt'l L. Rev. 435 (1991).

3 *Robertson v. Seattle Audubon Society* ("SAS"), 112 S.Ct. 1407 (1992).

4 See J. Jefferson, "Timmberrr!!" Journal of the American Bar Association (Oct. 1993)(quoting Professor Patrick Parenteau, University of Vermont Law School).

5 See generally U.S. Fish & Wildlife Service, "Endangered and Threatened Wildlife and Plants; Determination of Threatened Status for the Northern Spotted Owl; Final Rule," 55 Fed. Reg. 26114 (June 26, 1990).

6 Report of the Interagency Scientific Committee for the Conservation of the Northern Spotted Owl at 7 (1990).

7 *SAS v. Evans*, 771 F.Supp. 1081, 1088 (W.D. Wash. 1991).

[8] The Endangered Species Act is the basic U.S. law that protects species threatened with extinction. See 16 U.S.C. §§ 1531 et seq. Under the Act, the government promulgates and up-dates a list of species recognized as threatened or endangered by extinction. Other government agencies must then ensure that their actions do not jeopardize listed species. Both the government and private parties also must refrain from taking a listed species in the absence of obtaining special incidental take permits which the government may issue only under carefully prescribed circumstances.

[9] The U.S. Fish and Wildlife Service is the federal agency charged with implementing most of the requirements of the ESA for terrestrial species.

[10] *Northern Spotted Owl v. Hodel*, 716 F.Supp. 479 (W.D. Wash. 1988).

[11] *Northern Spotted Owl v. Lujan*, 758 F.Supp. 621 (W.D. Wash. 1991).

[12] The agency's designation of critical habitat under court order has been challenged by a number of Oregon counties in a separate and still pending case, *Douglas County v. Lujan*, No. 91-6423-HO (D. Ore.).

[13] *Lane County Audubon Society v. Jamison*, 958 F.2d 290 (9th Cir 1992)(finding BLM consultation inadequate and enjoining BLM timber sales in spotted owl habitat pending proper consultation).

[14] *Sweet Home Chapter of Communities for a Greater Oregon v. Lujan*, 17 F.3d 1463 (D.C. Cir. 1994)(striking down regulation protecting listed species from certain forms of habitat destruction). This case is likely to be heard by the U.S. Supreme Court, at the government's request, in 1995.

[15] 16 U.S.C. § 1536(e).

[16] See *Bureau of Land Management v. U.S. Fish and Wildlife Service*, ESC No. 91-1.

[17] Of the two prior exemption applications that reached the

Committee, one was denied (for the snail darter in Tennessee) and the other was granted (for the Gray Rocks Dam in Wyoming) following modification of the project to meet the concerns of the all parties.

[18] 16 U.S.C. § 1536(n).

[19] *Portland Audubon Society v. Endangered Species Committee*, 984 F.2d 1534 (9th Cir. 1992).

[20] The National Environmental Policy Act requires federal agencies to prepare an environmental impact statement (EIS) on all federal actions that may significantly affect the environment. This statement must describe and disclose the environmental consequences of the proposed federal action and alternatives to that action. See 42 U.S.C. §§ 4331 et seq.

[21] Pub.L. No. 100-202, § 314, 101 Stat. 1329-254 (1987). This particular statute is the annual funding bill for the Department of Interior. Ordinarily it is not a proper vehicle for substantive legislation but Congress does occasionally include substantive legislation in the funding laws. See Sher & Hunting, supra note 3.

[22] *PAS v. Hodel*, 866 F.2d 302 (9th Cir.), cert. denied, 492 U.S. 911 (1989); *PAS v. Lujan*, 884 F.2d 1233 (9th Cir. 1989), cert. denied, 110 S.Ct. 1470 (1990); *Oregon Natural Resources Council v. Mohla*, 895 F.2d 627 (9th Cir.), cert. denied, 110 S.Ct. 2621 (1990).

[23] *PAS v. Lujan*, 712 F.Supp. 1456, 1485 (D. Ore. 1989).

[24] *PAS v. Lujan*, 952 F.2d 297, 303-04 (9th Cir. 1991).

[25] See *PAS v. Lujan*, 795 F.Supp. 1489 (D. Ore. 1992).

[26] *PAS v. Babbitt*, 998 F.2d 705 (9th Cir. 1993).

[27] The Forest Service is an agency within the U.S. Department of Agriculture. It manages hundreds of millions of acres of national forests across the United States. These forests generally include some of the last undeveloped, natural ecosystems in the United States. Because the Forest Service manages these

lands under a "multiple-use" mandate, see 16 U.S.C. §§ 1600 et seq., and has traditionally worked closely with the timber industry to provide a source of raw material for the industry, resource use conflicts have dogged the agency over the years. The controversy over the spotted owl is but the most recent and most high-profile of these disputes.

[28] Some of the reasons behind the agency's actions became apparent only much later. In 1991, Dr. Eric Forsman, one of the Forest Service owl scientists explained the agency's 1988 plan by testifying that the plan had been subject to "a considerable - and I would emphasize a considerable - amount of political pressure to create a plan ... which had a very low probability of success and which had a minimum impact on timber harvest." *SAS v. Evans*, 771 F. Supp. at 1089 (quoting Dr. Forsman).

[29] *SAS v. Robertson*, No. C89-160WD (W.D. Wash.). The courts eventually rejected the plaintiffs' claims under the Migratory Bird Treaty Act. See *SAS v. Evans*, 952 F.2d 297, 302-03 (9th Cir. 1991).

[30] Section 318 of the Department of Interior and Related Agencies Appropriations Act for Fiscal year 1990, Pub. L. No. 101-121, § 318, 103 Stat. 701, 745-50 (1989).

[31] In two separate cases during 1990, the timber industry unsuccessfully sought to compel the Forest Service to sell additional timber under section 318. See *Gifford Pinchot Alliance v. Butruille*, 742 F.Supp. 1077 (D.. Ore. 1990); *Gifford Pinchot Alliance v. Butruille*, 752 F. Supp. 967 (D. Ore. 1990).

[32] *SAS v. Robertson*, 914 F.2d 1311 (9th Cir. 1990), rev'd, 112 S.Ct. 1407 (1992). The Ninth Circuit, in a separate appeal, also subsequently ruled that certain of the procedural requirements of section 318 that limited access to the courts should be equitably tolled for the plaintiffs. *SAS v. Robertson*, 931 F.2d 590 (9th Cir. 1991).

[33] *Robertson v. SAS*, 112 S.Ct. at 1414.

[34] In addition to the three agencies that had been defendants in the owl litigation (the Fish & Wildlife Service, BLM and the

Forest Service), the National Park Service, which also manages some owl habitat, joined organizing the Interagency Committee.

[35] *SAS v. Evans*, No. C89-160WD, Order on Cross Motions for Summary Judgment and Dismissal (W.D. Wash. Mar. 7, 1991).

[36] *SAS v. Evans*, 771 F.Supp. 1081 (W.D. Wash. 1991).

[37] Id. at 1090.

[38] Id. at 1096.

[39] In December of 1991, following appeals by the government and timber industry, the Ninth Circuit affirmed the district court's rulings on summary judgment and injunctive relief. *SAS v. Evans*, 952 F.2d 297 (9th Cir. 1991).

[40] *SAS v. Moseley*, 798 F.Supp. 1473 (W.D. Wash. 1992).

[41] *SAS v. Moseley*, 798 F.Supp. 1484 (W.D. Wash. 1992).

[42] *SAS v. Espy*, 998 F.2d 699 (9th Cir. 1993).

[43] *SAS v. Espy*, 771 F. Supp. at 1089.

Chapter 10

Citizen Rights and Litigation in Environmental Law NGOs as Litigants: Past Experiences and Litigation in Canada

by Yves Corriveau

1. Introduction

The fathers of Confederation could hardly have suspected that environmental protection would ever become a major preoccupation for Canadians. This is why the Constitution of 1867, which established the division of powers between the Canadian Parliament and the provincial legislatures, does not establish a specific jurisdiction for environmental protection.

Over the years, however, both levels of government have adopted environmental protection measures by taking advantage of their powers in areas such as transportation, navigation, agriculture, atomic energy, wildlife conservation, and public health.

It was not until the 1970s that the Canadian Parliament and the provincial legislatures endowed themselves with the first legislation which specifically targets environmental protection. This legislation aims at three things: regulating the quantity of contaminant emissions through an authorization structure; making potentially environmentally damaging activities subject to the obtention of permits; and creating procedures for environmental impact assessment.[1]

However, the implementation of these laws encounters a number of pitfalls. First, Canada has a vast territory. Actually, Canada is the second largest country in the world: from east to west, 5514 kilometers separate Cape Spear in Newfoundland from the Yukon-Alaska border[2]. It is therefore difficult for the 86 people responsible for enforcing the laws of Environment Canada and the personnel of the provincial Environment Ministries to maintain an adequate surveillance of all of the areas within their jurisdictions. In addition, there is the factor that the low population is unequally distributed. Canada's population ranks just 31st in the world[3], and it is concentrated in the central part of Canada, particularly in southern Ontario and Quebec.

Second, the constitutional and political context in Canada certainly contributes to the pitfalls in the enforcement of the laws that fall within the mandate of Environment Canada. This, at least, is the conclusion of the Canadian Environmental Advisory Council, which was mandated by the Environment Minister to study Environment Canada's enforcement of the laws of its mandate. According to the Council,

> "The Council is of the opinion that some current trends, such as the delegation of administrative powers to provincial authorities and excessive fears of federal-provincial conflicts, are having negative effects on the implementation of Environment Canada's legislative mandate, and undermine the confidence of Canadians in the Department."[4]

While these comments applied mostly to Environment Canada's performance in enforcing the *Fisheries Act*, recent statistics allow them to be extended to enforcement of the *Environmental Protection Act* as well. In fact, the Act has given rise to an average of one criminal prosecution per year[5].

However, Canadian environmental groups consider that the constitutional situation is a pretext which does not excuse the poor performance of Environment Canada. It can be seen that there is another pitfall in environmental law enforcement: a lack of political will. According to the Canadian Environmental Caucus,

> "It is our view, shared by many other commentators, that the federal government's concern with its jurisdictional authority is more perceived than real. The political purpose served by these concerns is that they provided the federal government with an excuse not to effectively implement and enforce CEPA. ... Enforcement of CEPA has been infrequent and disproportionately focused on only three regulations. This situation does not suggest, as has been proposed by ... Environment Canada, that a serious problem with environmental regulation in Canada has

been "overlap and duplication of effort". On the contrary, the serious problem with CEPA has been the federal government's own reluctance to assert its clear constitutional authority to regulate the environment and enforce these regulations. The absence of political will and leadership has significantly contributed to all the failings noted above. The inefficacy, inefficiency, and lack of certainty that surround environmental regulation in Canada are not because of the law, but because of the failing of those people whose elected responsibility is to see that the law is effectively implemented and enforced."[6]

This lack of political courage also explains the lack of human resources allocated to law enforcement at Environment Canada.

In fact, Environment Canada has allocated 86 people for enquiries and for enforcement of CEPA and of the *Fisheries Act* in the whole of Canada. This fact is put into proportion when it is known that the Ontario Environment Ministry uses the same number of people to enforce the laws of its provincial mandate. It is also possible to conclude that this lack of political will with respect to efforts to enforce laws also exists at the provincial level. In Quebec, for example, the number of inspectors will considerably be decreased as the Minister of the Environment announced this summer his intention to lay off 136 law enforcing inspectors and civil servants.

In a context where the size of the country, the political climate and the lack of resources and political will mean that environmental laws seldom give rise to criminal prosecutions, it is right to ask what has been and what could be the contribution of groups dedicated to the respect and conservation of the environment.

According to the Canadian Environmental Network, there are 2000 environmental groups in Canada. These groups are usually very small and have limited financial resources. They are essentially involved in public education campaigns and in lobbying the government and industry. The involvement of citizens and environmental groups at the judicial level remains quite timid.

In this study, we will be looking at the statutes and

regulations which have given rise to court cases, as well as the progress NGOs have made, through such court cases, toward achieving environmental objectives and creating precedents[7].

We will also be presenting the statutes and regulations which enable NGOs to refer environmental litigation to the courts, or which can themselves become the object of litigation to determine their substance or scope.

2. Environmental Assessment

Since the beginning of the 80s, an important part of the energies of NGOs has been consecrated to the compliance of developers and government with the environmental impact assessment procedures. Our analysis, however, will be limited to those cases which concern the Quebec and Canadian environmental impact assessment procedures.

2.1 In Quebec

Section IV.1 of the *Environment Quality Act*[8] describes the procedure of environmental assessment. In the first place, Section 31.1 establishes the following prohibition.

"31.1 No person may undertake any construction, work, activity or operation, or carry out work according to a plan or programme, in the cases provided by regulation of the Government without following the environmental impact assessment and review procedure and obtaining an authorization certificate from the Government."

This prohibition applies essentially to those projects which are likely to have important environmental impacts and essentially aims to permit the expression of popular opinion about such projects. In fact, this is the only process in Quebec where the population is consulted on development projects.

The L.Q.E. confers important powers on the Minister of the Environment. Among these is the power to grant a mandate to the "Bureau des audiences publiques sur l'environnement"[9] to hold inquiries and public hearings. BAPE acts exclusively on the mandate of the Minister of the environment. Under the terms of Section 6.3, BAPE's function is to inquire into all questions relating to environmental quality which are submitted to it by the Minister, and to report to the Minister its conclusions and the analyses. The Minister, therefore, has a certain discretionary power, and his decision about whether or not to submit particular enquiries to BAPE is by its nature purely political. It is by virtue of this power that, in 1990, the Minister of the Environment granted a mandate to BAPE to proceed with an inquiry on the problems of hazardous waste disposal in Quebec. It seems, however, that the Minister cannot, under this statute, give mandates systematically or globally for a given sector of activity, since to do so would be to imply a renunciation of his discretionary power[10].

On the other hand, Section IV.1 of the L.Q.E. establishes the environmental impact examination and evaluation procedure (PEEIE). Section 2 of the Reglement sur l'evaluation et l'examen des impacts sur l'environnement[11] enumerates the projects that must be submitted to this southern regime of environmental impact examination and evaluation.

Certain projects are automatically submitted to this process, while others are not submitted unless they exceed certain specifications[12].

This process of pre-authorization depends on the impact assessment study[13] conducted by the developer of the project affected by the regulation. The environmental impact assessment is prepared by the developer or its representative, and focuses on questions enumerated in a directive issued by the Quebec Ministry of Environment and Wildlife[14].

Upon receiving notice of a project from the developer, the Direction des evaluations environnementales (DEE) of the MEF determines the aspects which must be addressed by the environmental impact assessment.

The developer then prepares its impact assessment study according to the MEF directive. The developer has to anticipate and take into account the impact of proposed activities on the environment in general, as well as upon the health and quality of life of the neighboring areas. The impact assessment study must propose different variants of the project as well as giving the reasons which militate in favor of the chosen scenario. In addition, the impact assessment study must indicate what measures have been planned to mitigate the negative impacts of the project. Finally, the developer must include in the impact assessment study a plan for follow-up environmental studies of the harmful effects of the project on the area.

If the impact assessment is judged acceptable by the DEE, it is made public by the Minister. From that moment, the public has 45 days to consult the impact assessment study. During this period, any group or individual can call for a public hearing. The request for a hearing must be made in writing to the Quebec Minister of the Environment and Wildlife.

Section 31.3 of the L.Q.E. stipulates that the Minister of the Environment can refuse to mandate BAPE to make an enquiry if he judges the request for a public hearing to be frivolous. In order to evaluate whether a request is frivolous, the Minister can rely on two types of information which were "provided" to him in the request for a hearing itself. First, the Minister can judge a request frivolous if the request for hearing allows him to conclude that the applicant does not attach importance to the area which is being affected by the project. Second, the Minister can judge a request frivolous if the request for a hearing allows him to conclude that it has been made without motive in that "the applicant demonstrates ... a lack of seriousness which approaches impertinence," and that the step "is, at the least, taken lightly (and) entirely lacks seriousness." If the request for a hearing demonstrates that the applicant is concerned for the affected area and that his concerns are *a priori* serious, the Minister has to mandate BAPE to proceed to a public hearing on the project.

In the last few years, the Minister of the Environment and Wildlife has in fact judged certain requests for hearing to be frivolous and as a result refused to order public hearings. Upon analysis of certain of these cases, it appears that the Minister based his decision on criteria that are extraneous to the law. For example, the Minister concluded that requests for a hearing were frivolous when the applicants did not live close to the project site or when they themselves would not suffer any direct harm from the project. If the Minister persists in judging requests as frivolous, though they are otherwise well based, it is to be anticipated that the authorizations issued will be contested before the courts for undue process. Thus, an action in nullity and in injunction could be envisaged by the applicants.

When he does not conclude that a request for a hearing is frivolous, the Minister of the Environment must mandate BAPE to make an enquiry and to hold public hearings. The president of BAPE appoints an Environmental Assessment Panel and nominates its president. Generally three in number, members of the commission are chosen for their particular expertise and for their impartiality. The primary function of BAPE commissioners is to determine the truth in all cases where they have been mandated by the Minister and they are invested with the authority of a commissioner appointed by virtue of the *Loi sur les commissions d'enquête*[15].

The BAPE public hearing process is divided into two parts. In the first part, citizens can familiarize themselves with the ins and outs of a project and address specific questions to the experts associated with the developer. This stage of the hearing, then, provides for a collective questioning of the rationales of the project and allows the true stakes to become evident. It illuminates the value judgments and the interests which have guided the experts in their conclusions - a perspective that is otherwise hidden by "the universal objectivity of science."

It is, then, in the first part of the hearing that intervenors and commissioners can learn and focus on the ins and outs of a project. It is a unique opportunity for the public and environmental groups to obtain from the developers and ministries involved the information which they need in order to diagnose a situation and to form an informed opinion on the issue under examination.

This opinion, whether favorable or not, can be freely expressed during the second part of the hearing, and is transmitted to the decision-making political power via the BAPE's report of the enquiry and hearing.

In the four months following the beginning of its mandate, BAPE must report its findings to the Minister of the Environment. The role of BAPE is purely consultative. The decision on permission or refusal of the project returns to the political power, the Cabinet of ministers having the ability to authorize, by EARP Order, the issuance of certificates of authorization[16].

This process of environmental impact examination and evaluation is the only public tool which can be used to prevent the establishment of activities which could have harmful effects on environmental quality and public health. Nevertheless, we are obliged to observe that cases where the population has been consulted on some aspect of activities which could have damaging effects were rare indeed. This situation is not foreign to the "Not in my back yard" (NIMBY) syndrome: in effect, recent history teaches us that when the individuals concerned are systematically excluded from the decision-making process, they become fiercely opposed to any decision which is likely to alter the status quo.

For example, in the affair *Béchard v. Selenco*[17], residents of Senneterre in Abitibi opposed the development of a hazardous waste management plant. In the Bellefleur case, aboriginal communities opposed construction of a dam by Hydro-Quebec.

2.1.1 The PCB Saga

After the fire in the PCB storage warehouse at St. Basile-le-Grand, an important part of the Abitibi population (in the far west of Quebec), committed itself to a battle to the end against a project to dispose of hazardous waste in their region. Without relating the entire sequence of events and the important social conflict which arose from this project, suffice it to say that local environmental groups, supported by certain municipalities, tried to prevent shipments of PCBs from entering their area by peaceful demonstrations. The local population opposed the disposal of hazardous waste from the prosperous central Quebec region in their area.

In 1986, the developer filed notice of a project to create an integrated management facility for hazardous waste. In accordance with the L.Q.E., the DEE issued a directive for the environmental impact assessment study which was to be conducted on the project. This directive went unheeded. A new developer, Selenco, took over the project and obtained an authorization certificate under Section 22 to build a hazardous waste storage site. The developer had obviously divided its project in two so as to avoid a public hearing on the construction of the storage warehouse and the importing of hazardous waste into Abitibi. In this way, by the time that the justification of the project would have been questioned in public hearings on the construction of the PCB incinerator, the developer would have presented the local population with a *fait accompli*. One can easily understand that the opponents of the project would have difficulty contesting the building of an incinerator when a warehouse storing the bulk of the PCBs from the whole province had already been built on the site.

The citizens requesting public hearings presented an interlocutory injunction as well as an action for a permanent injunction to stop all work in progress on the depot and return to their senders all the wastes that were already stored. The applicants claimed that the larger project of an integrated system had been divided into two components in order to evade the application of the environmental assessment process. The Superior Court agreed and held that the authorization certificate issued by virtue of Section 22 contravened the process already put under way by the issuance of the environmental impact assessment directive.

This judgment was appealed by the Ministry of the Environment and the developer, Selenco. The Quebec Court of Appeal reversed the first judgment and declared the authorization certificate delivered in virtue of Section 22 to be valid. According to the Court, one cannot penalize the developer for realizing a project for which an environmental impact assessment is not required under Section 22 of the regulation on the evaluation and examination of environmental impact. The last paragraph of this regulation stipulates that, when a project is planned in several elements, all of which are subject to the evaluation process, the project must be evaluated as a whole. However, in this particular case, the Court of Appeal found that the warehouse project was separate from the incinerator since it was economically viable regardless of the development of the latter.

2.1.2 *The Lake Robertson Project*

In 1981, Hydro-Quebec planned to construct a dam on the Ha! Ha! River near Lake Robertson. this project was subject to the environmental impact examination and evaluation process. An impact assessment study was conducted by the developer in 1984 and public hearings were held in 1985 under the aegis of BAPE. BAPE returned a rather critical report to the Environment Minister. At the request of Hydro-Quebec, the Environment Minister suspended the process and the project was put on hold.

It was necessary to wait five years and five months before Hydro-Quebec reactivated its file with the Minister of the Environment. Hydro-Quebec updated its 1991 environmental impact assessment, and the government of Quebec authorized the realization of the project by decree. The Naskapi and Montagnais aboriginal communities which were to be directly affected by the project requested the Environment Minister to order new public hearings by BAPE. The hearings were denied. As a consequence, they turned to the Superior Court seeking an annulment of the decree authorizing the project, as well as an interlocutory injunction against the construction of the dam. The Superior Court decided in favour of Hydro-Quebec. In their appeal of this decision, the Naskapi and Montagnais emphasized that the five year delay between consulting BAPE and the issuance of the authorization decree was prejudicial. They claimed that the Minister should have ordered new public hearings because of the delay.

The Court of Appeal agreed that the original impact assessment studies (1984) and their updates (1990) were very superficial in their treatment of the repercussions that the dam would have on the Naskapi and Montagnais communities[18]. The Court deplored the ethical situation which had been created in these terms:

"We must, however, with all respect, question the legal and ethical character of a process which consists, as in the present case, of consultation, then of interrupting the realization of the project for a long period of time only to take it up again as if, on the one hand, it had in effect been well and duly completed (which is not the fact in the present case, seeing the grave shortcomings of the impact assessment study), and, on the other hand, as if the circumstances six years later had nevertheless remained strictly identical. The process allowed by the law can give rise to obvious abuses and I would not have hesitated to rule in favour of the appellants on this point, had it not been for the fact that in strict law, the proof, such as it is in this case, does not reveal the existence of a visible and palpable change."

Then, the Court validated the decree because it preceded the new request for a public hearing by the Naskapi and Montagnais. In terms of the law, their request came too late. Moreover, the Court considered that, given the broad discretionary powers given to the Environment Minister and the Cabinet of ministers in the process of environmental assessment, judicial control was practically impossible. Justice Beaudoin wrote for the majority:

"I will finish however by saying that in my opinion, the present procedure is more the process of the law itself, which (and my intention is not to criticize the legislative work) gives such discretion to the decision-making process that it has the virtual effect of forbidding any judicial control except in extreme cases where there is proof of bad faith, of the pursuit of illegal goals or of complete arbitrariness, which is not the case here."[19]

Justice Proulx (dissenting) replies to this fatalistic reasoning:

"With due respect, I do not believe that we can thus sacrifice the spirit of the law to the letter of the law. My reading of the cases which consecrate the principle of judicial intervention within the framework of judicial control of the legality of the administration does not permit the removal from judicial control of those acts of the administration which do not respect the "spirit of the law."[20]

2.2 The Federal Law

At the federal level, environmental groups and aboriginal communities have both given battle to the federal government and to developers in the name of the larger principles of environmental assessment and sustainable development.

2.2.1 Cases Relating to the EARP Order

The federal Environmental Assessment Review Process (EARP) is stated in the *Environmental Assessment Review Process Guidelines Order*[21]. The EARP Order was the object of a series of court actions initiated by NGOs in the late 1980s. Before we discuss some of these cases, it would be useful to summarize the content of the EARP Order.

Section 3 of the EARP Order summarizes the *raison d'être* of the federal environmental assessment process:

"The Process shall be a self assessment process under which the initiating department shall, as early in the planning process as possible and before irrevocable decisions are taken, ensure that the Environmental implication of all proposals for which it is the decision making authority are fully considered and where the implications are significant, refer the proposal to the Minister for public review by a Panel."

All federal ministries must yield to the environmental assessment requirement of the EARP Order when:

- The developer of a project is a federal ministry:

- A federal minister has the power to authorize a developer's project;

- The planned project may have environmental repercussions that fall within the federal jurisdiction;

- Federal funds are committed to the development of the project;

- The project will be realized on federal lands.

The first step of the process is an initial assessment of the project to determine *a priori* the environmental and social impacts to be expected. If it is obvious that these impacts are not significant, the minister responsible can give an immediate go-ahead for the project. However, when the expected impacts are unknown or important, or when public concerns require it, the minister reponsible must submit the project to the Minister of the Environment, who will mandate the Federal Environmental Assessment Review Office[22] to hold public hearings. Upon reception of such a mandate, FEARO creates an Environmental Assessment Panel.

The Environmental Assessment Panel works out a set of guidelines, based on the anticipated impacts, which outline the elements which must be addressed in the developer's environmental assessment. These guidelines are made public, and, within the framework of a meeting, anyone can comment on the environmental repercussions which ought to be studied. After this, the Panel makes public the final version of the guidelines so that the developer can complete the environmental impact assessment. Once the developer has completed the impact assessment study, it is submitted to the Panel, where it is made accessible to the public.

From there, the Panel holds a series of public hearings where those concerned can question the developer about the project and its environmental consequences. Then, the Panel holds a final hearing at which briefs may be submitted and opinions given as to the project's acceptability, given its environmental and social consequences. The Panel writes its report based on this information and transmits it to the Minister of the Environment. The Minister can recommend that the project should not go ahead, or he can authorize the project while stipulating mitigation measures. The decision to authorize the project belongs thus to the Environment Minister and the Minister responsible for the project. If there is disagreement between the two Ministers, it is settled by the Cabinet.

2.2.1.1 The Saga of the Rafferty-Alameda Project

Federal departments had always considered the EARP Order to be an internal policy without real legal force. This perception lasted until the judgment of the Federal Court in the case of the Canadian Wildlife Federation[23].

This case was the beginning of a veritable saga in which

environmental groups opposed the Rafferty-Alameda project to dam the Souris River in Saskatchewan. The project was to build a dam which would control flooding and facilitate irrigation. The Souris River crossed three different jurisdictions: the Provinces of Saskatchewan and Manitoba, and the State of North Dakota (USA).

After a controversial provincial environmental assessment, and despite the protests of environmental groups, the Canadian Environment Minister, in accordance with the *International River Improvement Act*[24], issued a permit to the Saskatchewan Water Corporation for the project. The Canadian Wildlife Federation contested the validity of the permits by *certiorari* because the Environment Minister had not proceeded to an environmental assessment as prescribed by the EARP Order. The Canadian Wildlife Federation requested an injunction from the court to oblige the Minister to proceed according to the Order.

The Court agreed with the plaintiff and revoked the permit, noting that "the EARP Guidelines Order is not a mere description of a policy or program, it may create rights which may be enforceable by way of *mandamus*"[25]. This decision had an explosive effect and the Environment Minister proceeded to an initial assessment of the project. Following the presentation of a preliminary report of initial assessment and a public consultation on the basis of this document, the Minister of the Environment issued a new permit to the Saskatchewan Water Corporation. This permit was again contested by the Canadian Wildlife Federation. The Court seemed exasperated by the laxity of the Environment Minister and suggested that an Environmental Assessment Panel be mandated in order to "unscramble the omelette which has been made of the EARP Guidelines in this case."[26] Subsequently, in another decision, the Federal Court ordered that the second permit be revoked unless an environmental panel was appointed to study the project within a predetermined period of time. Such a panel was therefore appointed and the construction work was halted -only to be resumed on the sly some months later.

Faced with the resumption of construction, the Panel halted its public hearings. Members of the Panel ended up resigning in protest, but the construction work made good progress. The federal Environment Minister tried without success to force the Saskatchewan Water Corporation to suspend its operations in order for the Panel to review the project.

2.2.1.2 The Oldman River Dam

The environmental group Friends of the Oldman River Society attempted to get the Federal Court, by means of *certiorari* and *mandamus*, to force the Minister of Transport and the Minister of Fisheries and Oceans to proceed to the environmental assessment of the Alberta government's project to build a dam on the Oldman River. The Alberta government had obtained the required permit under the *Navigable Waters Act*[27] without having had an initial environmental assessment. The plaintiffs argued that the federal ministries were all bound by the Order and that the dam project would have important impacts on several areas involving federal jurisdiction, such as fisheries, maritime navigation and aboriginal lands.

The case came all the way to the Supreme Court, where the plaintiffs won the decision with eight judges against one dissenting[28]. Confirming the Federal Court of Appeal decision in Canadian Wildlife Federation, the Supreme Court concluded that the Order is constitutionally valid and that, given the facts of the case, its application is mandatory. The Court explained:

"Here, though, we are dealing with a directive that is not merely authorized by statute but one that is required to be formally enacted by "order" and promulgated under s.5 of the Department of the Environment Act, with the approval of the Governor in Council. That is in striking contrast with the usual internal ministerial policy guidelines intended for the control of public servants under the minister's authority."[29]

Moreover, the Court rejected arguments to the effect that the provinces are immune to the application of the Order. The Court also rejected the claim that the environmental assessment is limited to the biophysical domain:

"Surely the potential consequences for a community's livelihood, health and other social matters from environmental changes are integral to decision-making on matters affecting environmental quality, subject, of course, to the constitutional imperative ..."

2.2.2 The Real Impact of these Lawsuits

All during the eighties and until just recently, environmental protection groups and aboriginal groups have initiated litigation to force the Canadian federal and provincial governments to comply with their own legislation on environmental assessment[30]. With HUNT[31], we believe that the Rafferty-Alameda and Oldman River cases have created a revolution in Canadian environmental law. First, they have engendered other cases across Canada. Second, these cases have put the federal ministers on the alert and forced them to take the EARP Order seriously. Third, these cases have pushed the Canadian government to elaborate and to adopt the new *Canadian Environmental Assessment Act*[32].

However, though we may rejoice in certain of the judicial precedents that have been made by these lawsuits, it is nevertheless true that, in many cases, the construction projects were already well under way, so that environmental assessment, meant to be a preventative tool, became relegated by the courts to a tool of mitigation of negative effects. On this point, Professor Bowden, in a commentary on Rafferty-Alameda, concluded: "It would appear proponents need only advance their proposals irrevocably beyond the planning stage to ensure that the environmental assessment process will be an academic exercise."[33]

2.2.3 Potential Cases under the C.E.A.A

In 1992, the Parliament of Canada adopted the *Canadian Environmental Assessment Act*[34]. This law is very recent and very complex. The two regulations which will allow its implementation have not yet been adopted, so that this law is not yet in force. It seems, however, that the Minster of the Environment has committed herself to bring the C.E.A.A into force at mid October 1994.

The judgments of the Federal Court of Appeal in *Canadian*

Wildlife Federation v. Canada and Oldman caused consternation in the government and, to some extent, precipitated the creation of a federal law on environmental assessment[35]. In doing this, the new law on environmental assessment closed certain loopholes in the EARP Order, while nevertheless limiting the scope that the Federal Court had given to environmental assessment in these cases.

2.2.3.1 A New Procedure

The C.E.A.A applies to the federal and the provincial crowns[36] and applies to the environmental effects[37] of projects[38] in the federal jurisdiction. Projects are subject to the environmental assessment process when they are

1. Undertaken by a federal authority

2. Financed by means of federal funding

3. Realized on lands falling within the federal domain

4. Require the issuance of a permit under a federal law enumerated in the regulation on the legislative list.[39]

The responsibility for engaging the environmental assessment procedure rests on the responsible authority of the project.

When the project belongs to one of the categories on the Comprehensive Study List, the responsible authority must proceed to a comprehensive study of the environmental impacts[40]. Upon the completion of this study and on the basis of its conclusions, the Environment Minister decides whether the project is subject to a public hearing. If the Minister judges that the environmental impacts of the project are important or unknown, or else that the concerns expressed by the public require it, he mandates the Canadian Environmental Assessment Agency to engage in a public examination of the project or in a mediation[41]. If, however, the minister comes to the conclusion that the impacts are not significant, he returns the project to the responsible authority to exercise its decision-making power on the project[42].

When the project does not appear on the Comprehensive Study List, the authority responsible for the project itself evaluates whether the repercussions of the project are significant[43]. If the responsible authority determines that the repercussions of the project are not significant, it authorizes the realization of the project[44]. If, on the contrary, the responsible authority considers that the project will have significant or uncertain effects, it refers the project to the Minister of the Environment in order that a public examination commission or a mediation commission may be named[45]. Upon completion of the exercise, the responsible authority decides whether or not to authorize the project according to the severity of the anticipated impacts and the circumstances in the case[46].

2.2.3.2 Foreseeable Points of Litigation

Section 7 of the C.E.A.A determines the projects which can be excluded from the environmental assessment procedure. Paragraph c) allows those projects which are undertaken in reaction to an emergency which threatens persons, good or the environment to be excluded from the assessment process. This paragraph is worrisome, however, because, as has already happened in Quebec, it is possible to create emergency situations by letting natural phenomena which are repetitive (and therefore foreseeable) develop without intervention until the critical moment when intervention becomes urgent.[47].

Section 16 (1) a) of the C.E.A.A requires that the cumulative effects of a project be evaluated at the initial assessment stage as well as at the stage of the comprehensive study, the mediation or the public examination by a commission. Since the evaluation of the cumulative impacts of a project, taking into account other projects being realized in the same area is a little-used practice and resisted by the developers and consultants, it is to be anticipated that the methodology and the scope of cumulative impact assessments will give rise to litigation.

Section 11 of the C.E.A.A establishes a true obligation of diligence on the part of the responsible authority. According to this disposition, environmental assessment must be performed as early as possible, at the planning stage of a project and even before any irreversible decisions have been made. In situations such as Oldman and Rafferty-Alameda, a *mandamus* could have been taken against the responsible authority in order to enforce procedures according to the law as early as the planning stages. Recourse to the courts in such a situation is far from being purely hypothetical, since we have seen that the different federal ministries resisted environmental assessment or barely included it in their decision-making process.

Finally, the responsible authority or the Minister of the Environment (when the project is subject to mediation or to public examination by a commission) determines the scope of the project with regard to which the environmental assessment shall be done[48]. Nevertheless, the responsible authority, or the Minister of the Environment when the project is subject to mediation or public examination by a commission, decides whether two projects are sufficiently related to be considered as one project[49]. In both of these cases, we may ask ourselves what is the extent of the discretion of the responsible authority and of the Minister as to the scope of the environmental assessment which they establish.

The answer to this question is obscure, and some writers literally deplore the existence of such a discretionary power:

> "Given the principles of comprehensive assessment and unfortunate experience elsewhere, it would have been preferable to include a clear and entirely non-discretionary prohibition against project segmentation for the purposes of assessment."[50]

The coming into force of the C.E.A.A in a few weeks will render purely theoretical the numerous decisions given by Canadian courts on the EARP Order in cases brought by NGOs. However, it is to be expected that the new C.E.A.A will also be the object of court cases. According to one author,

> "As a result, we can predict with some confidence that the new Canadian Environmental Assessment Act will engender even more litigation than we have seen under the EARP Order in recent years. Such litigation will no doubt involve division of powers and charter challenges, questions relating to confidentiality of business information, disputes relating to the

procedure used in conducting impact assessment and attempts to define the rights of interested parties to participate in impact assessment."[51]

This prediction is made that much more likely because the NGOs will now have certain resources at their disposal in order to participate in environmental assessment. In effect, the Environment Minister will shortly announce amendments to the C.E.A.A which would fund the participation of the public and NGOs in the process. Such financing already exists in Ontario and has been announced in Quebec in the latest legislative modification of the L.Q.E., although no serious budgetary commitment has been made in this matter.

3. Intervention by NGOs

Unless otherwise specified in provincial legislation[52], anyone can initiate the penal prosecution of a polluter[53]. In Ontario, an individual or group dedicated to the protection of the environment can, with the permission of the Court, act as the prosecutor in order to initiate a penal prosecution against a polluter[54].

Very few private penal prosecutions exist in environmental law. Over a twenty-year period, we have found barely more than ten[55]. Before trying to explain why Canadians and their environmental groups participate so little in the application of the law, we believe it is useful to look at some of the lessons we can draw from certain cases.

3.1 When the Citizen is Wrong Even If He's Right

In the case of *Cyanamid*[56], the accused was dumping ammonia-laden effluents into the Welland River (Niagara, Ontario) in contravention of Section 33 (2) of the *Fisheries Act*[57]. Since the proofs given by the private prosecutor were unequivocal, the Court had no choice but to render a guilty verdict. However, taking into account the responsible behavior of the corporation and of the clean-up programs which it had contracted for with the Ontario Ministry of the Environment, the Court assessed a fine of $1 and added that the corporation had a month in which to pay. The Court explained:

"The penalty section of the Fisheries Act which applies to the charge before this Court provides that a fine is the penalty to be imposed by this Court. The maximum penalty permitted is a fine of $50,000 for a first offense. There is no minimum penalty prescribed. The Court, therefore, is left with a wide discretion as to the penalty to be imposed. It is the function of the Court to weigh the severity of the offence before the Court and by the fine imposed to indicate how severe an offense the Court deems the particular offense before it to be. I trust that the penalty that I am about to impose will reflect where I consider this case rests on any scale of severity. In imposing the penalty, I am mindful of the many mitigating factors ...

... On this offense before the Court said to have occurred on March 23rd, 1981, contrary to Section 33 (2) of the Fisheries Act, Cyanamid Canada Inc. is hereby fined the sum of $1.00 in default of payment distress to issue.

The Corporation may have one month to pay the fine."[58]

This decision does indeed show where, in the scale of values of some judges, environmental protection falls.

In the case of *Adventure Charcoal Enterprises*[59], the informant, a private individual, declared he had reason to believe that the defendant had undertaken the construction of charcoal kiln without having first obtained the necessary permits, in violation of Section 8 (1) of the *Environmental Protection Act*[60]. The Court scolded the informant sharply, saying,

"In addition to the assurances set out in the above letter, there is the fact that on February 10, 1972, the plant was not in operation, and that, in light of the above paragraph, would not be until approval was given. The informant insisted on proceeding.

"*It is interesting to note that the informant did not give evidence nor was it established that he lived in the community, and his conduct was such in Court that I was obliged to reprimand him.* I hold that the prosecution served no useful purpose that was not already under the firm control of the Air Management Branch. There is no evidence that the Department refused to prosecute, therefore, the private prosecution was costly in time and effort, irresponsible and frivolous.

"I therefore award costs against the informant, a peril that private informant must suffer.

Accused convicted."[61]

(Our emphasis added.)

3.2 Local, Well-Organized, Well-Regarded Prosecutions

In the case of *INCO*[62], the Ontario Provincial Court found the accused guilty of having contaminated the air in contravention of the *Ontario Environmental Protection Act.* In this case, the plaintiff was the Sudbury Environmental Law Association. Its proof rested essentially on the observations of a citizen acting as an informant and on the expertise of a former inspector of the Air Quality Division of the Ontario Ministry of the Environment. Thanks to the combined efforts of these legally well-informed citizens, INCO was fined $1,500.

In the case of *Cherokee Disposals and Construction Ltd.*, waterways crossing the property of the informant were contaminated by the accused in contravention of Section 32 (1) of the *Ontario Water Resource Act*[63]. The Court recognized the capacity of citizens to give their opinion on the contamination of water by waste material:

"I realize that these witnesses do not fall into the category known to the Court as expert witness. I explain my willingness to allow them to express opinions in the following manner:

- the opinions expressed were expressed by people who struck me as having at least ordinary intelligence - if not more than ordinary intelligence;

- any opinion that was expressed by any witness was an opinion arrived at from facts known to the witness from his own personal knowledge gained by his attendance at the location where the infraction of the law is said to have occurred, and,

- The subject upon which the opinion was expressed is one of the manifestations which are now as familiar to almost every man because of our experiences with the subject within our present-day social environment.

What I have said really is that today most people of ordinary intelligence can look at a stream or other body of water and upon seeing garbage in it and upon seeing a brown slimy-looking substance flowing into it, form an opinion as to whether or not the quality of the water might be adversely affected. I personally do not think that it takes an expert to tell one that."[64]

While the facts in this case were particularly simple for an environmental lawsuit, it is nevertheless remarkable that the Court recognized that the average person could have the expertise required to give his opinion on contamination by visible and smelly garbage and wastes.

3.3 A Matter of Financial Resources

There have been a small number of private prosecutions in Canada. This situation can be explained by the cost of following a suit to its end. On this topic, one author reports that a prosecution for a violation of the L.Q.E. costs the government approximately $20,000[65]. Few non-profit organization can afford the luxury of initiating a criminal prosecution. There is little comfort to be had from CEPA or the *Fisheries Act* which provides that the prosecutor may be awarded 50% of the fines imposed. In fact, the Court has complete discretion in the awarding of this amount. In order to claim this sum, the prosecution must convince the Court that the cost of the procedure are reasonable and that it served a useful purpose.

4. The Right to a Healthy Environment

Unless they are directly and materially injured, environmental protection groups do not have the *locus standi* to resort to the justice system. Nevertheless, historically, environmental protection groups have bypassed the roadblocks set up by the question of standing by actions such as the outright purchase of a plot of land[66]or by assignment of claim from pollution victims[67]. In the latter case, Section 1637 of the *Civil Code of Quebec* allows the claimant in a court action to cede part or all of his claim to a third party. Thus, by acquiring a partial right to prosecute against a polluter, environmental protection associations can take action to obtain damages and/or issuance of an injunction. There is, however, the risk that the courts will not be particularly sympathetic to groups which involve themselves in a lawsuit between private parties by obtaining legitimacy with the complicity of the complainants.

By this time, it seems to us that environmental groups would find it an advantage to find a basis of action and standing within the statutes which provide specifically for the public involvement in environmental protection. We call these statutes by the collective epithet “Environmental Bills of Rights.”

4.1 In Quebec

In 1972, Quebec adopted its first law which aimed specifically at the protection of the environment. The L.Q.E.[68] was distinct from other pieces of legislation, because, for the first time, it treated the environment as a subject for law in itself. Thus, independently of property rights, the environment became the object of protective measures.

These protective measures were essentially of two types. On the one hand, the law forbade anyone to release contaminants into the environment without having obtained a pollution permit from the government[69]. On the other hand, it is forbidden to engage in an activity or a business which is likely to have harmful effects on the environment without having obtained the prerequisite permits from the government[70].

As we can see, the L.Q.E. of 1972 established a regime for environmental protection which relied solely on the diligence and responsibility of the government when it came to environmental management and prevention of pollution. In 1978, fundamental modifications were made to the law in order to include the role of citizens in environmental protection.

With this reform, Quebec became the first Canadian province to have endowed its citizens with the right to a quality environment. Section 19.1 of the L.Q.E. states that:

"Every person has a right to a healthy environment and to its protection, and to the protection of the living species inhabiting it, to the extent provided for by this act and the regulations, orders, approvals and authorizations issued under any section of this act."

Although all of the legal doctrine speaks of "the" right to a healthy environment, the terminology of Section 19.1 suggests at least two distinct rights. First, there is the right to enjoy a certain quality of environment[71]. Second, there is the right to act to protect this environmental quality and to safeguard the species of life which inhabit it.

While the language of Section 19.1 seems to be very general, these rights to a healthy environment are not absolute, since they are demarcated by the law[72] and the regulations which follow from it[73]. Nevertheless, these rights are substantive rights and this characteristic confers upon them "...a status, if not distinctive, at least equal to the right of property with which it is often in conflict."[74]. The right to quality of the environment can be implemented by recourse to injunction as expressly provided for in Section 19.2. This section stipulates that

"A judge of the Superior Court may grant an injunction to prohibit any act or operation which interferes or might interfere with the exercise of a right conferred by Section 19.1."

The majority of the doctrine considers that an injunction issued by virtue of Section 19.2 is not mandatory[75]. Thus, the terms "to prohibit any act or operation" are interpreted to mean an injunction can only prevent the commission of an act. Upon reflection, this interpretation does not appear to us to be well-based, and appears uselessly restrictive given the objectives of the law. In effect, we do not believe that the term "pour empêcher" are synonymous with an obligation not to do, but rather that they establish the objective of the order to prevent any act or operation which undermines or is likely to undermine the exercise of a right conferred by Section 19.1. According to our interpretation of Section 19.2, the Superior Court could issue a mandatory injunction in order to put an end to a violation of the L.Q.E., whether it is a matter of obliging the defendant to install anti-pollution device or of obliging him to perform work to prevent the expansion of an illegal contamination source.

Section 19.2 of the L.Q.E. establishes the *locus standi* for a party to be able to have recourse to an injunction which accompanies the right to a healthy environment:

> 19.3 The application for an injunction contemplated in section 19.2 can be made by any natural person domiciled in Quebec frequenting a place or the immediate vicinity of a place in respect of which a contravention is alleged.

The first observation which springs to mind is that only a natural person can have access to this particular recourse. Companies, environmental and other incorporated groups are therefore excluded[76]. The burden of the establishment of the rights of every person to healthy environment rests therefore on the citizen, who finds himself alone when facing the justice system. Moreover, to have the *legal standing* such a person must reside in Quebec and frequent the area targeted by the injunction. This criterion of frequenting is, indeed, the characteristic which makes Section 19.2 a considerable widening of the *locus standi* in common law. Common law required a sufficient interest, that is to say a direct and personal interest[77]. Thus, the fact that someone participates in sports, recreational activities, tourism[78], or simply walks through a particular area on the way to work will satisfy the criterion of frequenting[79].

Although less restrictive than that in common law, the concept of legal standing established in Section 19.3 of the L.Q.E. seems to us too anthropocentric. It would have been preferable to have a broader notion of interest in order to recognize the right of every physical or corporate citizen to preserve the quality of the environment even if he or she does not have access to it or even if such an area is not frequented by people. In the present state of the law, the right to the environment and the recourse to injunction which accompanies it cannot be invoked for the sake of a harmful and illegal activity which is underway in a distant or unfrequented area. Let us not forget that this injunction aims to prevent the commission and the perpetuation of an infraction. We have the right to ask ourselves what logic justifies limiting to certain people the right to justice in such circumstances.

Be that as it may, a series of decisions by the Superior Court has considerably limited the concept of *locus standi* of Section 19.3. In the case of *Archambault*[80], a citizen turned to the Superior Court seeking a class action. In examining the citizen's right to legal action, the Court interpreted Section 19.3 in an excessively restrictive manner. According to the Court, the applicant for injunction must advance and prove a particular interest apart from a general interest, and he must also establish that he has suffered personal damages, in order to request the cessation of the damage to his environment. In turning its back on a broad and liberal interpretation, the Court seemed to consider that instead of broadening the notion of locus standi, Section 19.3 was only intended to add further conditions to the common law concept of the right to act.

In the case of *Maurice v. Corporation municipale de St-Claude*[81], a farmer sought an injunction under Sections 19.2 and 19.3 in order to stop the overflow from the sewage system into the stream from which his dairy cattle drank. The farmer had already been successful in a Superior Court suit asking for compensation for damages caused to his stock as a result of this contamination. Subsequently, he returned to the Superior Court, seeking an injunction to stop the overflow. He based his suit on the right to a healthy environment. The Court, following the decision rendered in Archambault, rejected the case on the grounds that the applicant had not showed that he had the legal interest or had suffered personal harm.

On appeal, the Court had to determine the scope of legal standing under the L.Q.E.. The Court authorized the Quebec Environmental Law Center (C.Q.D.E.) to intervene in order to represent the public interest and to clarify this issue for the Bench. The CQDE argument was based on the necessity for a broad and liberal interpretation of the rights conferred by the L.Q.E.. Moreover, the CQDE pleaded that the decision at first instance had the effect of rendering sections 19.1 and 19.2 meaningless, while limiting the injunction recourse to the Attorney General.

The Court of Appeal decided in favor of Maurice and the CQDE. However, the Court did not address the issue of a liberal interpretation of the right to a healthy environment advocated by the CQDE, preferring to rely solely on the text of the law. Thus, although the case was a success from the environmental point of view, the precedent expected by the environmentalists did not materialize.

Aside from a permanent injunction, the Superior Court can grant an interlocutory injunction in order to prevent damages until a fundamental judgment is rendered. The motion for an interlocutory injunction and the action on a permanent injunction must be served on the Attorney General[82]. Upon granting an interlocutory injunction, the Court can oblige the plaintiff to pay a security deposit not exceeding $500, in order to cover the eventual damages suffered by the defendant in the case of the request for a permanent injunction being denied.[83] Moreover, by virtue of Section 19.7 of the L.Q.E., an injunction cannot be granted if the activity in question has been authorized under the law and if it complies with a depollution attestation.

Because the right to environmental quality is conditional upon the existence of an activity contravening the L.Q.E., it has been argued in defense that recourse to an injunction was not possible unless the defendant had previously been prosecuted for and found guilty of the infraction. The Superior Court rejected this interpretation, which, had it been accepted, would have meant the injunction would have lost its essentially preventive nature[84].

The rights to a healthy environment in Section 19.1 of the L.Q.E. are associated with every person's right to obtain from the Minister of the Environment all the information concerning the presence of contaminants in the environment[85]. In the case of *Goodfellow*[86], the applicant, a member of an environmental protection group, addressed the Commission for Access to Information in order to review the MEW's decision to refuse access to Goodfellow's studies of the characterization of contaminated soil. In its decision, the Commission recognized the close links between the right to put a stop to activities which infringe the right to a healthy environment, and the right to be informed about the presence of contaminants in contravention to the L.Q.E.. Appealing this decision, Goodfellow claimed that the company's right to confidentiality prevailed over the right of access to information conferred by Section 118.4 of the L.Q.E..

The case has not yet been heard by the Court of Quebec sitting in appeal of the Commission's decision. The decision of this Court is eagerly awaited. In fact, the importance of this decision is so great that, should the Court of Quebec declare that the right of confidentiality prevails over the right of access to information, the right to a healthy environment would be ignored, since the information required to enforce it would be completely inaccessible.

4.1.1 Environmental Groups and the Right to a Healthy Environment

Thus armed with the "right to a healthy environment" and the "right to know," citizens who notice an act of pollution which contravenes the L.Q.E. in an area which they frequent, can ask a judge of the Superior Court to order a polluter to cease polluting immediately[87]. However, the legislature chose to limit the ability to do this to natural persons; recourse to injunction in cases of activities undermining the right to a healthy environment is impossible for corporate citizens. We have the right to ask ourselves why the Quebec legislature is not in favour of judicial interventions by corporations dedicated to the protection of the environment to ensure conformity to environmental laws. We discern in this choice the fear that allowing environmental groups this recourse would only give rise to abuses and to a flood of lawsuits by environmental groups against those, who, by their development projects, contribute greatly to the strength of our economy.

This unfortunately has been followed in the last few years by a complete lack of interest on the part of the government in the right it has conferred on its citizens. In fact, of all the cases where a court has had to decide on the role and the scope of the right to environmental quality, the Quebec Attorney General intervened only once to promote a broad and liberal interpretation of these dispositions.[88] As a consequence, certain decisions of the Quebec Superior Court, by a too-narrow interpretation of the law, have had the effect of restricting the conditions under which citizens can have recourse to injunctions. Moreover, numerous modifications to the L.Q.E. have had the effect of restricting the scope of the right to know, and, as a result, of the right to a quality environment[89]. Finally, since the right to a healthy environment is delimited by the L.Q.E., each new environmental law takes away some of the scope of the right to a healthy environment.

We consider that the right to a healthy environment is not allotted exclusively to natural persons, and that corporations such as environmental groups are equally entitled to it[90]. Although the recourse to injunction of Section 19.2 is not open to corporations, the recourse to injunction in common law remains. In effect, being entitled to a right to a healthy environment and to a right to safeguard living species, environmental protection groups can claim a sufficient interest[91] to introduce an injunction application associated with a request for an interlocutory injunction[92]

4.1.2 NGOs and Class Action

Class action suits have found an important application in environmental law in Quebec. First of all, however, let us recall that, despite its evocative name, class action is not the same as recourse. It is more of a procedural mechanism intended to promote access to justice. Using it, a person (the representative) can, with the authorization of the Superior Court, initiate a suit against a defendant in the name of all the people who have suffered damages. To qualify as a class action, cases must have a similarity of facts and raise identical points of law.

In the case of *Comité d'environnement de La Baie Inc. v. Société d'Electrolyse et de Chimie Alcan*, the citizens of La Baie requested permission to bring a class action for damages. The plaintiff claimed to represent 2400 residents who had suffered damages due to the harbour operation of the accused, SECAL[93]. Following the precedent of other decisions rendered in this instance, the request for permission to bring a class action suit was rejected, on the grounds that the existence of similar events and of "events causing the fault" had not been demonstrated. Moreover, the Court considered that the plaintiffs had not shown a real difficulty in the application of Section 59 of the Code of civil Procedure. This decision was reversed on appeal in what was seen as the "most important judicial development that Quebec has seen in environmental matters in ten years."[94]

In this decision, the Court of Appeal interprets the conditions of exercising recourse in a broad and liberal manner:

"In short, the class action provisions of the Code allow considerable flexibility in determining which questions will be decided collectively, which questions individually, and how the action will proceed. These provisions are, in my view, sufficiently broad to contemplate the bringing of a class action for damage involving a number of important questions that are common to all of the members of the group even though the damages suffered by members may vary."[95]

Following this decision, it is no longer necessary that the nature and the extent of damages be perfectly similar in order for the class action to be permitted.

This more liberal interpretation presents class actions in a new perspective:

"The class action recourse seems to me a particularly useful remedy in appropriate cases of environmental damage. Air or water pollution rarely affect just one individual or one piece of property. They often cause harm to many individuals over a large geographic area. The issues involved may be complex and expensive to litigate, while the amount involved in each case may be relatively modest. The class action, in these cases, seems an obvious means for dealing with claims for compensation for the harm done when compared to numerous individual law suits, each raising many of the same issues of facts and law."[96]

Another interesting decision relating to class action was rendered in the case of *Robitaille v. Les Constructions Desourdy Inc.*[97]. In this case, the Superior Court confirmed that it is possible to bring a class action suit to obtain an injunction against the defendant to cease operation of his quarry and concluding with the concession of damages.

The decision rendered by the Court of Appeal in Comité de l'environnement de la Baie Inc begins a new era in the area of compensation for victims of environmental damage. Its application to cases of damages resulting from the commission of a mismanagement of wastes or contaminants (circumstances analogous to the events at St-Basile le Grand) seems obvious. In addition, since the action for damages can be added to the injunction under the L.Q.E., the class action becomes an effective mechanism of access to justice. In this way, environmental groups can act as initiators of class action suits in order to compensate victims of pollution and stop the pollution itself. In effect, the Code of civil Procedure allows a non-profit corporation or a cooperative to request the status of representative of a group of natural persons to the extent that a natural person would intend to exercise a class action[98]. However, the corporation must include at least one of the persons whom it will represent for the purposes of the class action.

Numerous advantages must, in our opinion, encourage environmental groups to act as representatives in the framework of the class action. First, these organizations can benefit from support of the Fonds d'aide aux recours collectifs, which, depending on the importance of the case, can finance the class action in part or in whole. Second, a corporate citizen is better able to resist the pressures and the inconveniences of lawsuits which often involve sums of more than a million dollars.

4.2 In Ontario

After fifteen years of lobbying by environmentalists[99], the Legislative Assembly of Ontario adopted, in December of 1993, an environmental bill of rights[100]: An Act Respecting Environmental Rights in Ontario[101]. In many respects, the Ontario EBR reflects the most recent trends in the area of the public's right to the protection and management of the environment[102]. Among its innovations, the Ontario EBR:

- Guarantees the participation of the public in the development of environmental laws, regulations and policies;[103]

- Guarantees access to information through a computerized register containing the decisions that the ministers involved in environmental matters are about to make;[104]

- Guarantees the public's right to be informed of environmental permits which are about to be issued as well as the right to make representations before a decision is made;

- Guarantees to injured persons the right to appeal of a decision to issue a permit to pollute and allows the intervention of the public in such an appeal;

- Obliges ministers involved in environmental matters to ensure that all reasonable efforts have been made to consult the public and to consider its comments before a decision is taken;[105]

- Guarantees the protection of employees who denounce the infractions committed by their employers. The charter gives recourse to employees who suffer from reprisals because of their participation in ensuring that environmental laws are respected[106].

But the major innovation of this charter is in the creation of the post of Environmental Commissioner[107]. A true guardian of the rights conferred by the Charter, the Commissioner is directly responsible to the Legislative Assembly[108], to which he presents a report at least once a year[109].

The Commissioner's main function is to oversee the application of the EBR by all of the ministers involved in the environment[110]. In order to do this, the Commissioner possesses important powers which allow him to hear secret testimony and to constrain a person to divulge documents[111].

Guarantor of both transparency and the effectiveness of the Charter, the Commissioner can receive applications for review from the public about the effectiveness and the application of laws, regulations and permits. On the basis of this application, the Commissioner must ask the ministry concerned to proceed to a reevaluation and a public review of the laws in its jurisdiction[112].

Moreover, when requested to do so by citizens, the Commissioner can demand that a ministry performs an enquiry on an infraction of an environmental law[113].

4.2.1 A New Type of Recourse

If the enquiry falters or arrives at an unreasonable conclusion, a citizen has the right to prosecute the implicated polluter, when the infraction has caused or is on the verge of causing "considerable injury to an Ontario public resource"[114]. However, this prosecution cannot be used in the case of odors, noises or dust produced by agriculture except when the citizen has already informed the Farm Practices Protection Board of the facts and when this request is still pending[115].

The burden of proof rests on the claimant, who has to show, on the balance of probabilities:

- That the defendant has committed or is about to commit an illegal act;

- That this violation has caused or will cause a significant harm to Ontario public resources[116].

In the case of an emergency, that is, when the delay involved in bringing a complaint is likely to cause significant damage to public resources, the request can be presented in court without foregoing measures[117]. The Ontario Attorney General must be informed of the legal action, except when the government is the defendant or co-defendant. The action must also be publicized in the register.

In defense against such an action, the defendant can show that he:

- has used due diligence;

- holds administrative authorization for the acts of which he is accused;

- has conformed to a reasonable interpretation of the authorizations which he holds[118].

This last defense is somehow surprising since it permits the defendant to claim an "honest" mistake about the law.

In this instance, anyone can participate in the debate according to the conditions determined by the Court about the nature and the scope of such an intervention[119]. The claimant who requests the issuance of an interlocutory injunction can be assessed a security deposit at the discretion of the Court. This deposit serves to cover the damages to the defendant if the action is rejected. However, the Court can dispense with the deposit if the action will created a legal precedent or raises new questions of law[120].

If the claimant's proofs satisfy the Court, the judge can order that the illegal activities cease and that the parties negotiate a restoration plan[121]. The Court cannot grant damages to the plaintiffs[122] but it can order that the polluter contribute a specific sum to a fund administered by the Minister of Finance to protect or conserve the environment[123].

4.2.2 The Environmental Bill of Rights and NGOs

It is with good reason that the Environmental Bill of Rights (EBR) has been described as representing an important "evolution" without however being the "awaited revolution"[124]. Although it is the fruit of long negotiation and of laborious compromises between environmentalists, developers and bureaucrats, this law remains an example for all of the Canadian provinces.

By virtue of the EBR, environmental groups will:

- have access to more information;

- be able to comment on proposed legislation and regulations;

- be able to appeal certain unreasonable decisions of the government relating to permits or authorizations likely to have significant environmental impacts.

Nevertheless, it seems that NGOs will not be able to bring complaints to the Commissioner and initiate a prosecution for the violation of an environmental law.

4.3 The Federal Law

The entrenchment of a right to a healthy environment in the Constitution is seen by many Canadian environmentalists as the ultimate solution to problems of legitimacy of access to justice for the defenders of the environment. Thus, the right to a healthy environment would be protected by the Constitution in the same way as other rights such as the right to vote, the right to life and security of the person.

However, making everyone's right to a healthy environment part of the Canadian Constitution poses certain conceptual problems. First, how can the right to a healthy environment be defined? Second, when this right comes into conflict with another right recognized by the Constitution (for example, the right to privacy), how will the courts establish the predominance of one over the other?

Aside from these questions, a pragmatic problem arises. The Canadian political and constitutional context makes the reopening of the Constitution for the entrenchment of a new right practically impossible. In effect, to "open" the Constitution, the amending formula calls for a majority of the members of Parliament, of the Senate and of the Legislative Assemblies of 2/3 of the provinces accounting for 50% of the Canadian population to agree with each other to pass resolutions to this effect. But the agenda of eventual constitutional negotiations includes recognition of self-determination for aboriginal peoples, the demands of Quebec regarding the division of powers and recognition of a distinct society, and Senate reform, and it is unlikely that the required unanimity can be achieved.

5. Conclusion

The intervention of citizens and of environmental protection groups in the domain of environmental enforcement is an obvious benefit which many legislators have been slow to recognize.

Quebec and Ontario have been the pioneers in this area, but in many Canadian provinces, citizens still do not have equivalent legal measures. This partly explains why prosecutions initiated by environmental groups are still a relatively rare phenomenon in Canada.

This inability of Canadian environmental groups to participate in the enforcement of environmental laws rests on other factors as well. Among these, let us mention the lack of financial resources allocated to environmental justice and the insurmountable obstacle presented by the concept of standing in both civil and Common Law.

While Quebec was endowing itself with a right to a healthy environment, Ontario equipped itself with a legal clinic specializing in the environment in order to facilitate access to justice for those who protect the environment. Aside from Ontario, then, legal aid for Environmental litigation is not available to Canadians in other provinces.

The case of Quebec is a good illustration of this situation. While the amount of legal aid consecrated to the environment in Ontario was more than $600,000 this year, Quebec spent $7,560 in 91-92.[125]. A person's eligibility for legal aid depends on his financial resources, taking into account the amounts necessary to provide for him and his dependents. The *Règlement sur l'admissibilité à l'aide juridique* sets the thresholds below which a person is eligible for legal aid. The last modification of this regulation dates back to 1985. In order to qualify, a person living alone without dependents would have to have a weekly gross income of less than $170 ($8,840/year). Aside from income, the value of the candidate's belongings is also counted, which automatically excludes owners of real estate from any legal aid.

Non-profit organizations are eligible for legal aid if their members are collectively eligible. On this matter, in 1985, the Commission des services juridiques noted that there was a lack of representation of public interest groups by a lawyer before regulatory organizations and commissions of enquiry among others. According to the Commission, this lack of representation could "create a distortion of facts leading to decisions on the part of the decision-making bodies, made in good faith but biased."[126] Despite this observation, legal aid is still not available except to non-profit organizations where "an important number of members are economically underprivileged."[127] And yet, for the very reason that they represent a diversity of interests[128], environmental protection groups do not qualify, and have not, to our knowledge, ever had access to justice in environmental protection matters by the route of legal aid.

The second obstacle to litigation by Canadian NGOs is the quasi-absence of provincial and federal legislation granting them the required standing in order to stop harm to the environment. In the absence of such measures, the NGOs do not have any choice but to finance their suits by their members as individuals.

The fact remains that the reluctance of legislators to recognize the contribution of environmental groups to the protection of the environment by giving them legal standing is difficult to justify. In fact, the obstacle of legal standing seems to us to be a pretext used by the Crown to paralyze legal action by NGOs than a measure intended to repress abuse of the judicial forum. In this sense, we subscribe to the proposal of ROMAN when he writes,

"Thus, the principal effect of the Law of standing is not to screen unmeritorious cases but to delay and increase the cost of proceedings brought by litigants who are not the principal or traditional users of the courts. Accordingly, public interest groups should anticipate rather than be surprised by standing challenges, and should prepare their pleadings and application so as to make the challenges more difficult. ...

Even a cursory examination of the case Law on standing reveals that the majority of the standing challenges are brought no by private corporation but by government department and the Crown agencies. Clearly, such standing challenges are part of the corporate culture of the Crown litigation bureaucracy.(...)"[129]

The coming years will be marked by a trivialization in the public eye of the environmental problems which face us. The intervention of NGOs is already suffering from backlash, at the level of fund-raising as much as at the level of public credibility. If this tendency continues, it will be difficult not only to finance environmental litigation, but also to support the existing lobbying at the provincial level to make the legislative tools available so that the NGOs can participate in the enforcement on environmental legislation. However, protection of our collective heritage an compensation for pollution victims are essential preoccupations of Canadians and the government has recognized their legitimacy on numerous occasions.

Notes

[1] At the federal level, see generally:

Canadian Environmental Protection Act, R.S.C. (1985) c. A-12; *Environmental Assessment and Review Process Guidelines Order*, SOR//84-467; *Canadian Environmental Assessment Act*, S.C. 1992, c. 37; *Fisheries Act*, R.S.C. (1985) c. F-14; *Canada Shipping Act*, R.S.C. (1985) c. S-9; *Navigable Waters Act*, R.S.C. (1985) c. N-22; *Hazardous Materials Information Review Act*, R.S.C. (1985) c. 24 (3 rd Supp.) Part III ; *Transportation of Dangerous Goods Act*,1992, S.C. 1992, c.34 ; *Pest Control Products Act*, R.S.C. (1985) c.P-9; *Canada Water Act*, R.S.C. (1985) c.C-11; *Canada Wildlife Act*, R.S.C. (1985) c. W-9 ; *Fisheries Act*, R.S.C. (1985) c. F-14.

For the Province of Quebec, see generally: *Environment Quality Act*, R.S.Q., c. Q-2; *Loi sur les espèces menacées ou vulnérables*, R.S.Q., c. E-12.01; *Pesticides Act*, R.S.Q., c. P-9.3; *Ecological Reserves Act*, LQ, 1993 c. 32.

For the Province of Ontario, see generally: *Conservation authorities Act*, RSO (1990) c. C-27; *Dangerous Goods Transportation Act*, RSO (1990) c. D-1; *Endangered Species Act*, RSO (1990) c. E-15; *Environmental Assesment Act*, RSO (1990) c. E-18; *Environmental Protection Act*, RSO (1990) c. E-19; *Ontario Water Resource Act*, RSO (1990) c. O-40; *Pesticides Act*, RSO (1990) c. P-11; *Waste Management Act*, SO 1992 c.1.

[2] Statistique Canada, Le portrait du Canada, 53 ed., Ottawa, Approvisonnement et Services Canada, 1992, p.1.

[3] Id., p.21.

[4] Canadian Environmental Advisory Council, A Statement by the Canadian Environmental Advisory Council on Enforcement practices of Environment Canada, Ottawa, Minister of Supply and Services Canada, 1987.

[5] Clark, K., Rutherford, B., "CEPA and Environmental Law Enforcement" in: Mausberg, B., Muldoon, P., Winfield, M., Reforming the Candaian Environmental Protection Act Ot-

tawa, Toxics Caucus of the Canadian Environmental Network, 1994, p.12.

[6] Id. p.12-13.

[7] Our report of foregoing jurisprudence will necessarily be highly summarized. British Columbia, Nova-Scotia and the Northwest Territories have had certain important cases dealing with major Hydro-electric projects and road construction, among others.

[8] R.S.Q., c. Q-2, hereinafter L.Q.E.

[9] Environmental Hearing Board, Hereinafter BAPE.

[10] *Construction Bérou v. Paradis* [1993] R.J.Q. 1497.

[11] R.R.Q. 1981, c. Q-2 r.9.

[12] However, certain paragraphs of Section 2 of the Environmental Assesment Review Regulation, which make important indutrial projects subject to the environmental impact evaluation and assessment procedure are not in force, because they have never been proclaimed. The result is that these projects, which have been and continue to be an important source of environmental litigation, are not subjected to a true environmental impact assessment nor to the public scrutiny.

[13] The impact assessment is an anticipatory exercise based on a knowledge of the human and natural environment, and its goal is to identify and evaluate the positive and negative impacts (socio-economic, biological and physiological) of a project.

[14] Hereinafter MEF.

[15] Section 6.5 of the L.Q.E reads: "6.3 The functions of the Office are to inquire into all questions relating to the quality of the environment submitted to it by the Minister, and to report to the Minister its conclusions as well as the analysis which it has made of these questions. (...) "6.5 In order to perform the enquiries with which they are entrusted, the members of the Office dispose of the powers and the immunity of Commissioners

named under the *Loi sur les commissions d'enquête* (chapitre C-37)."

Section 6 of the Loi sur les commissions d'enquêtes states: "In order to discover the truth, Commissioners may, by those legal means which they judge the best, inquire into the things whose investigation has been entrusted to them."

[16] L.Q.E, Section 31.5.

[17] *Béchard v. Selenco Inc.* [1988] R.J.Q. 2267 (S.C.) rev'd (1989) 3 C.E.L.R. (N.S.) 307 (C.A.).

[18] *Bellefleur v. Québec* (A.G.) and Hydro-Québec, [1993] R.J.Q. 2320 (C.A.), at page 2333.

[19] Id., p.2346.

[20] Idem.

[21] Supra note 1 [Hereinafter EARP Order].

[22] Hereinafter, FEARO.

[23] *Canadian Wildlife Federation v. Canada* (Min. of the Environment) [1989] 3 C.F. 309, confirmed on appeal [1990] 2 W.W.R, 69 (F.C.A.).

[24] R.S.C. 1985 c. I-20.

[25] Supra, note 23, p.322.

[26] (1989) 4. C.E.L.R. (N.S.), 201, p.226.

[27] R.S.C., 1985, c. N-22.

[28] *Friends of the Oldman River Society v. Canada* (Minister of Transport) [1992] 2 W.W.R., 193.

[29] Supra note 23.

[30] See generally: Rafferty-Alameda dam; *Association to Stop Construction of Rafferty-Alameda Projects Inc. v. Saskatch-*

ewan (Minister of Environment and Public Safety), (1988) 3 C.E.L.R. (N.S.) 236; *Canadian Wildlife Federation Inc. v. Canada* (Minister of the Environment) (1989) 3 C.E.L.R. (N.S.) 287, aff'd (1989) 4 C.E.L.R, (N.S.) 1; *Canadian Wildlife Federation Inc. v. Canada* (Minister of the Environment) (1990) 4 C.E.L.R. (N.S.) 201; *Canadian Wildlife Federation Inc. v. Canada* (Minister of the Environment) *and Saskatchewan Water Corporation* (1990) 121 N.R. 385; *Canadian Wildlife Federation Inc. et al. v. Canada* (Minister of the Environment) *and Saskatchewan Water Corporation* (1991) 40 FTR (C.F.) 114.; Oldman River Dam; (1987) 56, Alta L.R., 368; *Friends of the Oldman River Society v. Alberta* (Energy Ressources Conservation Board) (1988) 56, Alta.L.R.(2d), 286; *Friends of the Oldman River Society v. Canada* (Minister of Transport) [1992] 1 R.C.S., 3. *James Bay dam: Eastmain Band v. Robinson* (1991) 7 C.E.L.R. (N.S.) 230; *Eastmain Band v. Robinson* (1991) 9 C.E.L.R. (N.S.) 257; *Cree Regional Authority v. Canada* (Federal administrator) [1991] 3 C.F.R. 533; *Canada (A.G.) v. Mathew Coon Come and al.*[1991] R.J.Q., 922.; *Grand Conseil des Cris v. Canada (A.G.) et al.* [1994] RCS.

NATO's low level flights: *Naksapi-Montagnais Innu Assembly v. Canada* (Minister of National Defense [1990] 3 C.F.R 381. *Nova-Scotia-Prince-Edward-Island bridge: Friends of the Island Inc. v. Canada* (Minister of Public Works) (1993) 10 C.E.L.R. (N.S.), 204.

[31] Hunt, C.D., The changing face of environmental law and policy, 1992, 42 UNB L.J., 87.

[32] See infra Potential cases under the C.E.A.A, p.11.

[33] Bowden, Marie-Ann, Damming the opposition: EARP in the Federal Court.1990, 4 C.E.L.R. (N.S.) 227, p.235-236.

[34] S.C. 1992, c. 37, hereinafter C.E.A.A

[35] Gertler, F.S., The Federal Law of Environmental Assessment after Oldman: The EARP Order and the Canadian Environmental Assessment Act, unpublished manuscript, 1992, p.106.

[36] C.E.A.A, section 3.

[37] C.E.A.A, section 2 (1) where "environmental effect" is defined as meaning "the components of the Earth and includes

a) Land, water and air, including all layers of the atmosphere,

b) All organic and inorganic matter and living organisms, and

c) the interacting natural systems that include compo nents referred to in paragraphs (a) and (b).

[38] C.E.A.A, section 2 (1) where "project" are defined as: in relation to a physical work, any proposed construction, operation, modification, decommissioning, abandonment or other undertaking in relation to the physical work, or any proposed physical activity not relating to a physical work that is prescribed or is within a class of physical activities that is prescribed pursuant to regulation mate under paragraph 59 (b).

[39] C.E.A.A, section 5(1).

[40] C.E.A.A, section 21.

[41] C.E.A.A, section 21 (1) b).

[42] C.E.A.A, section 23 a).

[43] C.E.A.A, section 18 (1).

[44] C.E.A.A, section 20 (1) b).

[45] C.E.A.A, section 20 (1) a)

[46] C.E.A.A, section 27 a) and b).

[47] It is in this way that, in Quebec, a project to spread pesticides in forest areas was excluded from environmental assessment because intervention had become urgent.

[48] C.E.A.A, section 15.

[49] C.E.A.A, section 12 (2).

[50] Op. cit. note 35, p.115.

[51] Id., p.137.

[52] See Section 112.1 L.Q.E., by virtue of which criminal prosecutions are undertaken by the Solicitor General or by a person whom he gives written authorization for this purpose. The Quebec legislature clearly wished to provide for a strict control on private criminal prosecutions in the environmental domain, since without this disposition, anyone could have brought a criminal action, given permission from the Court.

[53] For criminal prosecutions, see the definition of the word «prosecutor» in Section 2 of the Criminal Code. In regard to infractions under the majority of federal environmental laws, see the Criminal Code relating to summary prosecutions, in particular the definition of "prosecutor" given in Section 785 of the Criminal Code.

[54] See *Provincial Offence Act.* RSO, c P-33, Sections 1, 23, 24.

[55] Among others, see the following cases: En outre, les affaires suivantes: *R. v. Adventure Charcoal Entreprises Ltd* (1972, 9 C.C.C. (2d); *R. v. Sheridan,* [1973] 2 O.R. 247, 3 C.E.L.N., 75 (Cour de district de l'Ontario); *R. v. Lake Ontario Cement Ltd* [1973] 2 O.R.24 (H.C.); *R. v. Young* (1973) 1 O.R. (2d) 564 (CA); *R. v. Cherokee Disposals & Construction Ltd.* [1973] 3 O.R., 599 (Cour provinciale de l'Ontario); *R. v. International Nicker Company of Canada* (1974) 3 C.E.L.N., 75 (Cour provinciale de l'Ontario); *R. v. Lieberman* (1974) 3 C.E.L.N.,47; *R. v. Hale* (1976) 6 CELA Newsletter, 77 (Cour provinciale de l'Ontario): *R. v. Snow* (1981) 11 C.E.L.R, 13 (Cour provinciale de l'Ontario); *R. v. Cyanamid Canada* 1981 3 FPR, p.151.

[56] *R. v. Cyanamid Canada Inc.* (1981) 11 C.E.L.R., 31.

[57] Supra, note 1.

[58] Supra, note 56, p.41.

[59] *R. v. Adventure Charcoal Entreprise* (1982) 9 C.C.C. (2d), 81.

[60] 1971, (Ont.) c. 86.

[61] Supra, note 59 p.85.

[62] R. v. International Nickel of Canada, (1974) 3 C.E.L.N., 75.

[63] RSO, 1990, C.332.

[64] Id. p.609.

[65] Hétu, J., Les sanctions pénales et la protection de l'environnement, (1989) 49 R. Du B., 494.

[66] *Environnement Laterrière Inc. v. M.R.C. du Fjord-du-Saguenay* [1988] R.J.Q, 747.

[67] *Fusano v. Ville de Pierrefonds* [1974] C.S. 460.

[68] R.S.Q, c. Q-2. (Hereinafter L.Q.E.).

[69] L.Q.E., Section 20.

[70] L.Q.E., Sections 22 and 31.1.

[71] In the French version of Section 19.1, the words "qualité de l'environnement" are used, which seems to us a different and narrower concept than a healthy environment.

[72] L.Q.E., Sections 20, 22, 31.5, 32, 48, 54 and 55.

[73] See regulations passed under Sections 31, 46, 53, 70, 87 and 95 of the L.Q.E.

[74] Daigneault, R., Paquet, M., L'environnement au Québec, Farnham, Éditions CCH/FM Ltée, 1994, p.1091, no.5200.

[75] See, amongst others; Yergeau, M., Loi sur la qualité de l'environnement, texte annoté, p.50; Daigneault, R., Paquet, M., M, loc. Cit, note 74, p.1193, no.5320.

[76] Infra, p.31.

[77] *Banque Canadienne Nationale v. Carette* [1931] R.C.S. 33.; *Cotroni v. Commission de police du Québec* [1978] 1 R.C.S., 1048; CÔTÉ, P.A. Interprétation des lois, (2d), Cowansville, Yvon Blais, 1990, 477-481.

[78] Duplessis, Y., Hétu, J. and Piette, J., La protection juridique de l'environnement au Québec, Montréal, Éditions Thémis, 1982, 707 p.62-63.

[79] *Bernier v. Immeuble Charlesbec Inc.*, C.S. Québec 200-05-001640-791.

[80] *Archambault v. Construction Bérou Inc.* [1992] R.J.Q., 2516.

[81] *Gaston Maurice v. St-Claude* (Mun. of..) C.S. St-François, no. 450-05-000558-938, July 15 th. 1993, j. L. Daigle.

[82] L.Q.E., Section 19.5.

[83] L.Q.E., Section 19.4.

[84] *A.G. of Québec v. Pro-Bri Transport* 1991 R.J.Q. 478.

[85] L.Q.E., Section 118.4.

[86] *Goodfellow Inc. v. Ministre de l'Environnement C.A.I.*, no.909993, June 13n 1990, Mr. J. O'Brady, Pres.

[87] L.Q.E, Sections 19.2 and 19.3.

[88] After criticism form the Appeal Court for his equivocal position on the CQDE intervention and for being absent from the first instance, the Attorney General decided to intervene in the Maurice Case. Acting as a representative of the public interest, the Quebec Environmental Law Centre pleaded for a broad and liberal interpretation of section 19.1 and 19.2. The Attorney General argument in the end limited endorsing the arguments of the appellants and the CQDE.

[89] See *Pesticides Act*, R.S.Q c.P-9.3, of the *Loi sur la protection du territoire agricole*, R.S.Q, c. P-41.1 and of the *Loi sur l'aménagement et l'urbanisme*, R.S.Q c. A-19.1.

[90] Contra, Daigneault, R., Paquet, M., loc. cit. note 74, p.1251, no.5360.

[91] Section 55, *Code of Civil Procedure of Quebec* (Hereinafter C.C.P.).

[92] C.C.P., Section 755.

[93] (1988) CS, # 150-06-000002-865, Feb. 17 1988, Jacques Philippon.

[94] Yergeau, Michel, "Contamination et responsabilité; Ne pas ériger la panique en système." op. cit, p.43.

[95] CA, # 200-09-000166-881, 6 février 1990, Chouinard, Rothman and Savoie.

[96] Id., pp.17-18.

[97] (1988) CS, # 460-06-000001-886, Dec. 5 1988, J. George Savoie.

[98] C.C.P, Section 1048.

[99] See, Estrin, David, Swaigen, John, Environment on Trial., 3ed, Toronto, Emond Montgomery Publications Ltd., 1993, pp.793-819.

[100] Hereinafter, EBR.

[101] S.O. 1993, c. 28.

[102] See Walker, Sandra, "The Ontario Environmental Bill of Rights"; See also Lindgren, Richard D., Environmental Bill of Rights: An Overview, Toronto, Canadian Environmental Association, 1993, 45 p.; 1992, Task Force on the Ontario Environmental Bill of Rights, Report of the Task Force on the Ontario Environmental Bill of Rights - July 1992, Toronto, Queen's Printer for Ontario, 1992, 225 p.

[103] EBR, Sections 3 to 48.

[104] EBR, Sections 5, 6, 8(2), 8(3), 9, 15, 16, 22, 27, 47 (1) and 87.

[105] EBR, Section 35.

[106] EBR, Section 105.

[107] EBR, Section 49 to 60.

[108] EBR, Section 49 (1) and (2).

[109] EBR, Section 58.

[110] EBR, Section 59 a.

[111] EBR, Section 60 (1).

[112] EBR, Section 62.

[113] EBR, Section 74.

[114] EBR, Section 84.

[115] EBR, Section 84 (4); see also Section 5 of the *Farm Practices Protection Act*, RSO 1990, c. F.6. which makes agricultural operations using normal methods immune to prosecution for noise, odours and dust.

[116] The term "public resources of Ontario" is understood to include:

- The air (except indoor air);

- Water (except for private and non-navigable watercourses);

- Public lands which have not been altered;

- Any lot or public land larger than five hectares which is used for recreation, conservation, quarrying, or resource management;

- All plant or animal life and the ecosystems associated with any of the categories enumerated above.

[117] EBR, Section 84 (6).

[118] EBR, Section 85 (1) to (3).

[119] EBR, Section 89.

[120] EBR, Section 92.

[121] EBR, Section 93 (1).

[122] EBR, Section 93 (2).

[123] EBR, Section 95 (8).

[124] Lindgren, R.D., loc. cit., note 102, at p.44.

[125] État des produits et charges du Fonds d'Administration de la Commission des Services Juridiques (1991-92), Ministère de la Justice, L'Aide juridique au Québec une question de choix, une question de revenu. Gouvernement du Québec, June 1993, p.6.

[126] Commission des services juridiques, 13e Rapport annuel.

[127] See Section 1 b) *Legal Aid Act* R.S.Q, c. A-14, Section 7(3) *Règlement sur l'admissibilité à l'aide juridique.*(Décret 941-83, 11 mai 1983, amended by, Décret 1307-85, 26 juin 1985): See also the Review Panel Decision Comité 19892, of June 26 1991, commissioners J. Frémont, M. Charbonneau and JM Hébert-Dufaux.

[128] Its members come from all levels of society.

[129] Roman, A.J., Pikkov, M., Public Interest Litigation in Canada, in: Into the future, Edmonton, Alberta Environmental Law Centre 1990, 165, p.180.

Chapter 11

The Oeresund Litigation in Denmark

by Ulf Kjellerup

Judicial review of parliamentary legislation is extremely rare in Denmark. Although the competence to exercise such review is confined to the ordinary court system according to the Danish Constitution, practice is virtually non-existent. Instead of challenging parliamentary action the judicial initiative in such cases is rather directed towards the legality of executing the administ rative discretion according to the legislation in question. One of the consequences of a successful litigation by such methods is of course an indirect criticism of the legislator - but the method has the advantage that the courts can restrict their action to exercise review of administrative action. In this way a major conflict between courts and Parliament might be avoided, which particularly in Denmark seems to be important because although there are undoubtedly confined powers to courts to exercise review of parliamentary action - these powers are implicatory and not expressly founded in the Constitution. These considerations have been emphasized since the initiation of the litigative thoughts behind the *Oeresund* case[1] and even more so because the case involves EC law being confronted with Danish constitutional practices. Putting it very brief it involves the question of whether an EC Directive in any way can derogate or modify constitutional procedures in the light of the contents of the EC Directive in question. My article will not go into details about this discussion, but the nature of these interests must be taken into consideration as an implication of the extremely ambiguous wording of article 1.5 of the EIA Directive[2]. This article says:

> "This Directive shall not apply to projects the details of which are adopted by a specific act of national legislation, since the objectives of this Directive, including that of supplying information, are achieved through the legislative process".

The interpretation of this article forms the central element of the litigation on the Oeresund bridge. My article will contain a brief outline of the project, procedures undertaken in Denmark and Sweden, environmental problems arising from the project, and a more detailed description of the litigation and its legal implications.

The Fixed Link across the Sound (Oeresund)

The project in question is a combined fixed link, containing a two-tracked railway and a four-lane motorway that links the city of Malmoe in the southern part of Sweden with the city of Copenhagen in Denmark. The link crosses the water between these two cities - called the Sound (in Danish "Oeresund"). The project is subject to obligatory assessment under the provisions of the EIA Directive, according to art. 2.1.

Historically speaking, the project has been discussed for nearly a century. Several joint-investigation committees have worked over the years to design this project. During the last thirty years 6 different reports have dealt with various ways of establishing a link between the two countries.

The present project is based upon an agreement signed by the relevant ministers in Denmark and Sweden in March, 1991. The main article, art. 2, subsections 1 and 2 of the agreement states that:

> "The Oeresund link is constructed as a combined rail- and motorway connection comprising a two-tracked railway and a four-lane motorway between Kastrup and Limhamn.
>
> The link begins from an artificial peninsula by Kastrup Airport and crosses Drogden in an immersed tunnel to an artificial island south-west of the island of Saltholm. The link continues from the artificial island as a bridge crossing Flinterenden and Trindelrenden and ends to the south of Limhamn".

It is also mentioned in the agreement that the technical details and the actual position of the link has been agreed upon by the parties of the agreement in Annex 1. The agreement establishes a consortium to implement the project. The consortium is owned by Denmark and Sweden respectively on a 50-50 basis. Furthermore it is agreed that the consent procedures established in national regulations in the two countries may lead to alteration of the project, as described in Annex 1.

Procedures Undertaken in Denmark

The Danish Government submitted a bill for adoption in Parliament in May 1991, where it is settled in art. 4 that:

"The definitive design of the link ... is to be constructed taking into consideration what is ecologically motivated, technically possible and economically feasible, hereby preventing possible damaging effects on the environment".

Furthermore it is mentioned in art. 15 of the Act that:

"The Minister of Transport defines the final positioning of the link in Danish waters".

The Bill was adopted by Parliament in August, 1991[3] and the agreement with Sweden was ratified one week later. In connection with the adoption of the Bill a majority in Parliament declared the project exempt from the EC Directive (85/337) on EIA, according to art. 1.5 of the Directive. The Act was supplemented with a 1500 pages long EIA study[4].

Procedures Undertaken in Sweden

Due to a different way of legislating in Sweden, the Swedish consent procedures started after the formal decision to carry out the project. The Swedish legislation prescribes a number of procedures under different acts, stating that such procedures might be undertaken after the adoption of decisions to act - these acts have later been amended in order to bring Swedish environmental regulations in compliance with EC regulations. The consent procedures in Sweden ended in June, 1994[5] with a formal adoption of the project - but, at this stage, in a much altered design. Amongst others the Swedish Board on Consent Procedures rejected the project in accordance with the procedures established in the *Environmental Protection Act*[6]. The Regional Water Court of Southern Sweden rejected the proposed project twice, stating that nature of the material presented to the Court did not satisfy the demand of evidence that the proposed projects would not have a severe impact on the sensitive balances of the Baltic Sea. After having presented 6 different design proposals the consortium succeeded in convincing the Water Court that the latest proposal would have zero effect on the Baltic Sea. Due to the Swedish *Act on Use of Natural Resources*[7], the final decision in the consent procedure is in cases of national interest adopted by the government. In June 1994, the Swedish Government granted the final consent to the proposed project.

The project granted in Sweden is not the equivalent project that was adopted by law in Denmark in 1991.

Environmental Problems Arising from the Project

The special sensitivity of the Baltic Sea has been the domineering subject in the Oeresund debate. The salinity of the waters in the Baltic Sea is dependent solely on the in- and outflow of water through the Danish Straits. As such the straits are the corridors which connect the Baltic Sea with the North Sea. The Baltic Sea is the world's largest brackish water area, and it is also designated by the IMO in the MARPOL Convention (73/78), Annex 1, as one of the few areas where oil pollution from ships must be strictly controlled.

The problems of building a bridge across Oeresund is not just a question of placing a row of pillars in the water to carry the bridge. The establishing of an artificial peninsula and an artificial island in Oeresund will decrease the cross section of Oeresund and as such block the in- and outflow of water through Oeresund. Of course it would be possible to deepen the waters of Oeresund in order to compensate for the decreasing cross-section of the corridor, but this will just represent a removal of the environmental damage from one biotope to another. Compensatory dredgings are foreseen in the adopted project in Denmark, and is estimated to be of a magnitude of 11.5 mio. tonnes, if total compensation is to be reached. Different techniques to reduce the spilling effect have been discussed, and a maximum level of 5% spilling of lime into the water is settled as a condition. (Even when the spilling is reduced to this level it equals 200 years emissions from the largest operating lime works in Denmark). If carried out it will leave Oeresund milky white in large areas for at least 4-5 years, having a significant impact on migrating fish (mainly herring).

The problems of the Baltic Sea's dependence of the in- and outflow of water through Oeresund have never been investigated thoroughly, consequently it is still uncertain which impacts may arise from the implementation of the project. It is still - in February 1995 - uncertain whether it is possible to establish the link without significant impacts on the salinity of the Baltic Sea.

The air pollution problems of the project have been partly examined, but are solely based on prescriptions of local traffic impacts. There is no overall assessment of the impacts of the easier traffical access to the European Continent and vice versa.

Finally, the project will penetrate a specially protected area, designated under the EC Directive 79/409 on bird protection. The island of Saltholm and the shallow waters surrounding it constitutes the area no. 110 designated to the directive in Denmark. The island is in principle uninhabited and there is a general restriction on any kind of access to the area. A little less than 5% of the designated area will be cut off from the rest of the area as a consequence of the implementation of the project.

Of course there are a vast number of impacts from such a project, but the above-mentioned are the most debated subjects of the project.

The Litigation

In March 1993, Greenpeace (DK) decided to challenge the decision in the Danish High Court. A number of problems were considered before entering litigation. First of all, no organization has been able to get legal standing in the field of environmental law to challenge discretionary powers of governmental or local administrations in court cases in Denmark before. Secondly, the utmost consequence of the litigation will be that the court will have to overrule a vast majority in

Parliament, if Greenpeace is successful in their doing - which eventually will be a sensational development in the national legal practice.

As mentioned ordinary courts have implied powers to exercise judicial review of parliamentary legislation in the Danish Constitution. According to the Danish Constitution art. 63 the ordinary courts have expressly stated powers to exercise judicial review of administrative decisions.

Legal Interest

The concept of legal interest is the central procedural requirement by which the question of standing is evaluated. As nature cannot defend itself in a human law court, someone must be given a right to appear before authorities or courts, if this representation is not given to the deciding authority alone. In Denmark, the concept of legal interest is in Denmark developed through court practices and comprises several dimensions.

In principle the question of legal interest is related to matter of the case, actual interest and personal interest. I will concentrate on the questions of actual and personal interest, as these questions are central for the understanding of the development of the *Oeresund* case. Actual interest relates specifically to whether there is an actual conflict that does not turn litigation into a general responsive activity. Personal interest relates specifically to who is entitled to sue.

First of all, legal interest is a mixed question of fact and law. The test of whether a plaintiff has sufficient legal interest will depend on the remedy sought and therefore it will always be necessary to look at the statute under which the duty in question arises. As the case is based upon the obligation for Member States to carry out EIA procedures for certain projects, according to EC Directive 85/337, it was a natural part of the case to examine whether Greenpeace was one of a number of organizations which under normal circumstances - administratively decided projects - would have the right to be consulted and to complain about breaches in duties to carry out EIA procedures.

The normal procedures on EIA is established in the *Planning Act* in Chapter 3 on regional planning. According to art. 58-59 of the *Planning Act* all citizens have the right to appeal if they have a legal interest herein. The interpretation of the term legal interest under this provision must be made in view of the purpose of the law, which, among others, stresses the importance of the participation of all citizens in the planning of the society. Of course the legal interest in complaint will vary from case to case dependent on the nature of decisions challenged in appeal.

In the case of court litigation these suggestions do not carry all the way. On the other hand it is beyond doubt that the practices evolved according to the *Planning Act* and other acts where the term legal interest is used as the decisive criteria as to whether a person or an organisation is given a right to appeal administrative decisions also influence the attitude of the ordinary courts of law. Though, it must be stressed that the courts in the very few cases they decide balances the procedural and personal requirements differently than administrative appeal boards. In some cases this difference is seen in the assessment of the structural requirements posed on organisations in administrative appeal compared to the assessment of the corresponding requirements in courts. Informal organisation's or citizen's initiatives are admitted in administrative appeal but often excluded from litigation in courts with a specific reference to the lack of formal structure.

Under normal circumstances Greenpeace would have the right to complain about breaches in EIA procedures according to the provisions in the *Planning Act*, articles 58-59. A central element in their argumentation for showing sufficient legal interest in litigation was that the adoption of the specific *Act on the Oeresund bridge* in fact cuts off the right Greenpeace already held to have a judicial review of procedures undertaken. Furthermore it was argued that the fact that the EC Directive in art. 1.5 does impose certain obligations on member states in order to qualify for the exemption the non-compliance with these obligations were judicially reviewable. The consequence of cutting off a judicial review on the grounds of not showing sufficient legal interest would in fact equivalate a final decision on the material questions of the case. Consequently it would lead to Greenpeace being deprived of the rights that citizens in the Member States are given in the EIA Directive.

Danish court practices suggest that surprisingly few environmental organisations have tried to protect the legally based positions under the relevant environmental regulations. One could point at the fact that the reluctance to do so is very much the reason for the very weak position of environmental organisations in the judiciary system, which is in strong contrast to the stronghold of these organisations in the relevant acts. In a vast majority of these acts the organisations are given extensive rights on hearing and complaint.

Nature of Remedy

The nature of the remedy sought in litigation must play an important role as well as the question of representation of the interests which Greenpeace purports to favour in general and by litigation.

Cases concerning the enforcement of public law can often be divided into two categories. The first category is concerned with the problem of compelling an authority to carry out a duty. The second category is concerned with the problem where an authority to the detriment of the complainant has exceeded its powers. In the latter example it will probably be much easier to meet the test of sufficient legal interest in courts.

The remedy sought is formulated in the following demand that:

"The Minister of Transport recognizes that he acts unlawfully if the construction works under the *Act on the Link* are carried out".

The arguments stated in favour of the claim are:

1. The *Act on the Link* does not constitute an exemption according to Art. 1(5) of the EC Directive 85/337 on EIA.

2. Therefore the Minister of Transport is obliged to subject the project to an EIA according to Danish national rules.

3. The Minister of Transport has not subjected the project to such procedures, before consent to implementation of the project was given.

The arguments stresses art. 1.5 of the EIA Directive as an exemption from the Directive's main rule in art. 2.1 that can only be granted under certain circumstances. The concrete obligations that must be fulfilled in order to qualify for the art. 1.5 exemption cannot be extracted clearly from a simple reading of the article.

The question of legal standing was opposed by the Minister of Transport with the argument that since there remained a choice between different projects and their final positioning this could not be considered a case of actual interest to Greenpeace. Furthermore the minister stated that the choice between different projects and their positioning was a result of ongoing investigations and administrative hearings - the latter only in Sweden. The minister stated that the conductance of investigations was not in conflict with art. 1.5 of the EIA Directive since these investigations were merely focused on an attempt to optimise the environmental performance of the project eventually chosen.

Article 1.5 of the EIA Directive

As mentioned, the wording of art. 1.5 is very ambiguous, not only because it mentions "the details of which ..." but also because it in the beginning of the second sentence uses the word "since ...". The questions that arises from the wording are first of all what details of the given project must be adopted by specific act, and furthermore how detailed an adoption of these details qualifies a project for the exemption granted. Secondly, does the word since mean that the parliamentary procedures automatically supplies Parliament and the public with the necessary information.

An interpretation of art. 1.5 must take its beginning from the most basic facts that can be read from the wording of the article. First of all it is stated that there must be an adoption of the project by law. It must be stressed that a decision must be taken and that the decision must be relevant for the implementation of the proper project. One could argue that the demand for a decision in form of a law is the only interpretation possible in this context. On the other hand it could be argued that more informal decision forms could be applied as long as these more informal forms are the culmination of a formalized procedure. If e.g. parliamentary procedures stated in the Constitution or in parliamentary codes of conduct provide for other decisions than adoption of law through procedures comparable to procedures undertaken before the adoption of a law, such decision forms might be within the legal boundaries of art. 1.5.

The Danish Constitution prescribes a three-step procedure undertaken before a law is adopted in accordance with the Constitution. Other decision forms do not require the same formalized procedures undertaken for the adoption of a parliamentary resolution that requires the relevant Minister to act in accordance with the contents of the resolution. It could be argued that it is not just a question of a formalized procedure but a question of putting forward information and that such information might be presented orally in a one-step procedure. (In fact a similar presentation would be in accordance with the detailed provisions of the EIA Directive). The crucial point in this respect must be whether the procedure undertaken is suitable for channelling the information on environmental impacts arising from the proposed project and that on the basis of this information the Parliament is convinced that a decision to carry the project out can be taken in which the details of the project can be settled. In fact comparable procedures have been undertaken in the Danish Parliament in the case of the Oeresund bridge. In as far as there were a number of unsolved environmental questions linked to the adoption of the *Act on the Oeresund bridge*, these unsolved questions and their consequential solutions sought by the administration have been presented for approval in Parliament in later procedures. The crucial point in this respect is of course whether such procedures satisfies the demand in art. 1.5 for a final decision in the Act in order to qualify for the exemption.

The conviction of Parliament that a decision can be taken and that such decision settles the details of the proposed project is the core of art. 1.5. It leaves Parliament with the discretion to decide the details, but excludes a decision where the details of the proposed project can be left for later administrative decision. In fact art. 1.5 excludes the delegation of decisive powers on the details of the proposed project to any administrative level. The duty posed on Parliament - in case the exemption in art. 1.5 can be granted - is of a profound nature, that obliges the Parliament to demand for extensive documentation on the proposed project. Only decisions that justify that the project documentation does not leave any discretion to settle vital details of the project to any other body than Parliament and that Parliament does not take any final decision on the project before the details can be settled in the Act qualifies for an exemption according to art. 1.5. Of course there are a vast number of details of lesser importance with regard to environmental impacts, that might be settled in following procedures, but in as far as the vital environmental problems have been documented and decided in parliamentary procedures such decisions might be within the legal boundaries of art. 1.5.

Concluding my very brief and only partial interpretation of art. 1.5 it can be summed up that the primary nature of obligations under art. 1.5 is of a procedural character. In order to qualify for the exemption Parliament must take a decision where the details of the project is decided upon excluding any kind of discretion left for administrative authorities to hold decisive powers with regard to settle details of the proposed project that concerns details of the project other than mere trivialities.

The Factual Arguments for Litigation

Since the adoption of the *Act on the Oeresund bridge* in 1991, the consortium that stands behind the implementation of the bridge has drafted eight different variants of the project. These variants have all been drafted in order to satisfy the concerns brought about in the Swedish consent procedure. Each of these variants represents an advancement in environmental performance, where the last variant was the only variant that satisfied the Swedish authorities with regard to scientific proof for not affecting the ecological balance of the Baltic Sea. Each variant was drafted successively after renewed investigations and modellisation of the in- and outflow of water through Oeresund. This development was to some extent foreseen in the Danish Act on the Oeresund bridge, where it was stated in the *travaux préparatoires* that:

> "The possibilities to enhance the environmental performance of the project must be examined closer in the near future, including the shape of the artificial island, and further investigations to calculate the projects impacts on the Baltic hydrography must be conducted, including the consequences concerning the extreme in- and outflow situations and the ecological consequences hereof must be assessed. Only after these investigations have been conducted it will be possible to make an assessment of the question of compensatory dredgings."

Furthermore it is stated:

> "The influence on the aquatic environment of the Baltic Sea can be neutralised through compensatory dredgings, in order to leave the salinity of the Baltic Sea unaltered."

> "Compensatory dredgings will have a negative impact on the aquatic environment of Oeresund ..."

In the conclusion of this subject it is stated that:

> "The Act *does not decide* how the balancing of concerns related to the aquatic environments in the Baltic Sea and Oeresund should be made." (emphasis added)

In conclusion hereof it is stated that:

> "Further progress in the question of the aquatic environment of the Baltic Sea and the question of compensatory dredgings can only be done through a special investigation programme."

As a consequence hereof it has not been possible to decide on these vital details of the project in the Act. As a sort of compensation for these shortcomings it was envisaged in the Act to establish an International Expert Panel to review the future investigations of this problem. The Panel has delivered four different reports on the progress of these investigations. In their second report[8] the Panel is given the opportunity to answer question put forward to the Panel in an open hearing. One of the questions was:

> "Is the Panel satisfied that the EIA presented gives a sound enough presentation of the environmental consequences of building a bridge across the Oeresund ?"

The answer to the question was:

> "No, we are not satisfied."

As late as in February 1995, the Panel stated that it still did not feel convinced that the investigations and modellisations sufficiently presented the problems of the project not-influencing the aquatic environment in neither the Baltic Sea nor the Oeresund.

Court Decision No. 1

In May 1994, the High Court made a preliminary ruling on the question of standing, which was separated from the main questions of the case. In a very clear ruling Greenpeace was given standing in the case.

In the decision the High Court expressed that:

> "The question of legal standing is to be settled by assessing if the plaintiffs interest in having the case tried at the courts is considered tangible, individual and essential, so that the case can be proceeded with.
>
> The High Court finds this an actual and tangible dispute, in as much as the case concerns the question of the procedure before the passing of the bill on construction. The circumstance that the layout of the project is subject to changes at the planning level cannot lead to any other conclusion. ...
>
> After an overall assessment of the plaintiff´s claim and of the proceeding organization´s structure and aim, the High Court finds that in connection with these proceedings the organization Greenpeace has shown sufficient legal interest in conducting a case, that the organization has the necessary power of action."

The ruling shows that the minister's argumentation has actually put himself in a deadlock, because on one hand he argued that there did not exist a final project and on the other hand he was forced to argue that the *Act on the Oeresund bridge* settles the details of a project that does not exist. The deadlock the minister was caught in was a consequence of the minister's will to have the case dismissed on the grounds of legal standing.

Injunction

The natural development in the case seen from Greenpeace's point of view was therefore to seek the legal interest they were given by the court decision protected by an injunction. This step was not only inspired by the perspective of the case pending in national courts for at least two more years - and probably one could add two more years if the case eventually would be presented to the ECJ in Luxembourg. It was also inspired by a press release from the Minister of Transport where the minister stated that the case would not in any way affect the continuous building of the bridge.

The question of injunction took its outset on the basis of the ECJ's ruling in the *Factortame* case[9] wherein the ECJ stated that:

> "It is for the national courts ... to ensure the legal protection which persons derive from the direct effect of provisions of Community law."

The ECJ also made it clear that such procedural conditions must not be less favorable than those relating to similar actions of domestic nature. Furthermore the ECJ stated that these procedural conditions must not under any circumstances make it impossible in practice to exercise the rights which the national courts have a duty to protect.

According to a recent decision of the Danish Supreme Court[10] the question of injunction should be considered on the basis of the following:

> "... a balancing of the need for public authorities not to delay the implementation of their decisions against the nature

and extension of damages the applicant may suffer, as well as it may be considered whether a preliminary judgement is in favour of the applicants claim for unlawful action."

On the background of these principles the High Court was to decide whether the *Act on the Oeresund bridge* qualified for the exemption in the EIA Directive and furthermore decide that if this was not the case would the nature and extension of the interests that Greenpeace purports to favour in litigation suffer irreparably from not being injuncted.

The High Court decided in a ruling in February 1995[11] that Greenpeace had not convinced the Court that their claim would be successful. The court stated in this connection that the nature of obligation in the EIA Directive was merely of a procedural character and did not prescribe particular results from the procedures undertaken. Furthermore the Court stated that the Danish Parliament in any case would be able to repair the legal "deficit" with regard to qualify for the art. 1.5 exemption by passing a new bill on the project. Finally the Court stated that it had put emphasis to the fact that the EC Commission in 1992[12] had decided to dismiss any legal action against the Member State Denmark because the Commission had judged that Denmark could invoke the exemption in art. 1.5 of the EIA Directive.

The decision is remarkable in several respects. First of all, the Court seems to deprive procedural rules of any legally binding effect as long as they do not prescribe any particular result from procedures undertaken. Such a judgement will in fact deprive the main part of environmental regulations of any legally binding effect and as such render these regulations meaningless. Secondly, the Court is exceeding its competences by referring to the fact that the Danish Parliament can repair the legal "deficit" with regard to the art. 1.5 exemption by passing a new bill on the project. The question of the power to pass laws and the declared will amongst a majority in Danish Parliament is not an argument that contradicts Greenpeace's claim in the main question of the case. It may be an argument in favour of not filing an injunction in the case, because it can be argued that an injunction would be meaningless when it is in the powers of Parliament to repeat the action that is sought an injunction for. Finally the Court seems to confine the EC Commission's informal press releases with legally binding effects and thus neglect the fact that the Commission in their assessment of taking legal steps towards a Member State or not must balance such action between political and legal needs. In this context it is very likely that the Commission's decision to give up legal proceeedings against Denmark was a consequence of the Danish government putting pressure on the Commission to refrain from any further action in the case. Such considerations must be emphasised even more since it is impossible to get access to the considerations inside the different divisions of the Commission with regard to legal action in the case[13].

The decision of the High Court has been appealed to the Danish Supreme Court, where Greenpeace has repeated its claim for an injunction. A decision can be expected during spring 1995 unless the Supreme Court refers the case to the ECJ.

Conclusion

The Oeresund litigation contains a number of very interesting problems with regard to environmental litigation. Seen from a Danish perspective, the case is breaking up frontiers with regard to the question of legal standing. It is now widely believed in Denmark that environmental organisations will get easier access to court litigation when challenging decisions of public authorities. Such a development must be welcomed since it is a step in the direction of a more active participation of organisations and individuals in the enforcement of environmental regulations. In a regional perspective it divides the Nordic countries into two categories - a Western-Nordic division comprising Norway and Denmark where organisations and individuals probably will be admitted in courts when the question comes to the enforcement of environmental regulations. The Eastern-Nordic division comprising Sweden and Finland does generally not recognize these interests in the courts - which was demonstrated in the Supreme Swedish Court for administrative affairs. A number of fishermen that would be directly affected by the building of the bridge had their cases dismissed by the Court.

The Oeresund litigation also points to the fact that judiciaries in some cases are very badly skilled in these matters. Court cases in environmental matters are often extremely complicated and require a lot of attention from the judiciaries because they are not familiar with the techniques involved in these cases. Nevertheless there is a growing need to involve ordinary courts in such cases in order to enforce the regulations. The problem could be solved in two ways - either it could involve the establishment of special courts with profound competences in such matters or it could involve the building up of competences amongst the judiciaries of the ordinary courts.

Above all it must be emphasized that the further development of environmental regulations and the confinement of procedural rights to citizens in general in the regulations must be followed up by a more liberalised approach to the question of legal standing, because a meaningful participation of individuals must comply the right to enforce these rights. If such a liberalisation in court practices does not evolve it may have the effect that the participation of citizens and organisations is experienced a meaningless activity because the non-respect of their rights cannot be sanctioned. In the long run the environment is the responsibility of all citizens and the individual's will to change behaviour in the light of the ongoing environmental degradation is also enhanced by the experience that participation in societal decision making is a meaningful activity.

Notes

[1] Case no. B-783/93 before the High Court of Copenhagen, 13 dept, Greenpeace, *DK v. The Minister of Transport.*

[2] Directive 85/337/EEC, OJ 1985 L175/40.

[3] Act no. 590 of 19 August 1991 on the establishing of a fixed link across the Oeresund.

[4] Miljø-Øresund 1991 (Environment-Oeresund 1991), which is the non-technical summary (110 p.) and technical background reports annexes 1-6.

[5] Governmental decisions nos. 38 & 39 of 16 June 1994.

[6] Miljøskyddslagen (Env. Protection Act) no. 1969:387.

[7] Act on the Use of Natural Ressources no. 1987:12 as amended by Act no. 1991:650 (provisions on EIA).

[8] Report from the International Expert Panel's second meeting, Copenhagen, April 1993.

[9] Case 213/89 ECR 1990, I p. 433.

[10] Supreme Court Decision of 24 August 1994, (U 1994, p.823.) (U refers to the weekly report on Court decisions in Denmark).

[11] High Court decision of 7 February 1995 in case B-783/93 *Greenpeace v. The Minister of Transport.*

[12] Press release from the EC Commission of 11 November 1992. The press release was the termination of a complaint procedure that had run for more than 1 year.

[13] Greenpeace tried in November 1994 to get access to the documents of the case by way of a formal application to the Commissions DG XI and the General Secretary succesively. Both applications were turned down on the grounds that these papers were internal documents not accessible to any outward person or organisation. It should be mentioned that Greenpeace was one of the complainants in the case decided upon by the Commissions press release. (Decision of the DG XI of 21 November 1994 in case no. XI/025067 and decision of the General Secretary of the Commission of 23 January 1995 in case no. SG(95) D/145102.)

Chapter 12

Transboundary Enforcement: Free Movement of Injunctions

by Gerrit Betlem

1. Introduction to International Civil Litigation

In the 19th century, international contacts were an exclu sive privilege of a small group of wealthy upper class people. In this day and age, air plane travel, computer networks and large scale migration are turning the world into a 'global village' for people of all walks of life. The internationalisation of the economic and social spheres requires the law to cope with an increasing amount of both factual situations connected with more than one jurisdiction and legal rules emanating from other bodies than the national legislature. The challenge to the traditionally national oriented legal community is profound and can only gradually be accommodated.[1] As far as private international law is concerned, the cited development has been phrased in terms of a 'proletarisation' of the field:[2] international cases no longer only concern barons, dukes and multinational corporations, but also feature 'the woman in the street'.[3]

At this grass roots level, environmentalists as well have been appearing on the stage of international litigation. For example the Dutch farmer Mr. Hamers, supported by environmental protection groups, challenged the licence of a German nuclear plant in Lingen before the German administrative courts.[4] This case deals with the issue of access to judicial review proceedings under German nuclear law, the *Atomgesetz*, for appellants not based in Germany. Although the Dutchman's action was held to be admissible, the decision of the *Bundesverwaltungsgericht* (the supreme administrative court) does not secure such access under other environment-related public law.[5] By contrast, under Dutch environmental law, appellants based outside the Netherlands do have general access to the administrative courts.[6] Legal protection against acts of Dutch public authorities frequently also involves the civil courts. For instance the Belgian local authority of Lanaken successfully brought suit for an injunction against the Dutch state. The court of appeal The Hague ordered the defendant, on penalty of a period payment of 10 million guilders, to enter into consultations with the plaintiff about the extension of an airport near Maastricht.[7]

However, this article will not be concerned with cases brought by foreign plaintiffs against Dutch-based defendants. Instead it will focus on actions for an injunction before the Dutch civil courts against defendants based outside the Netherlands. Although a prominent feature of most recent Dutch cases, the issue of standing of environmental protection organisations will not be examined either;[8] rather, the emphasis is on various aspects of the availability of civil remedies in international disputes. Before looking in detail at Dutch case law involving so-called extraterritorial injunctions, it is useful to outline some more general aspects of civil litigation in international cases and to look at recent developments in other fields of law where the impact of the internationalisation of legal life has been strong.

Foreign Defendant and/or Foreign Plaintiff

There is nothing unusual about defendants having to appear before the courts of another country.[9] As long as an acceptable head of jurisdiction provides the court with international competence over the defendant who is based outside the jurisdiction, public international law objections do not arise.[10] The most international variant is the position where both the plaintiff and the defendant are domiciled outside Holland; from a jurisdictional point of view, the domicile and nationality of the plaintiff is irrelevant.[11] Such a situation occurs frequently in intellectual property disputes.[12] It follows that environmental suits brought by a non-Dutch based plaintiff against a non-Dutch based defendant before the civil courts in the Netherlands are conceivable.

Two Interesting Adjacent Legal Fields: Consumer Law and Intellectual Property

When discussing actual and possible developments in civil international environmental litigation it is worthwhile to examine two other fields of law where similar questions arise:

consumer law[13] and intellectual property. The former is interesting because, like environmental law, there is a strong public interest element, in particular in the notion of protection of the economically weaker party. As regards the cooperation between national enforcement agencies the International Marketing Supervision Network is noteworthy.[14] It was established, in the framework of the OECD, in order to combat difficulties in the enforcement of, in international situations, the laws on misleading advertising and distance selling, due to disparities between the various national legal systems. Members include the U.S. Federal Trade Commission, the German *Verbraucherschutzverein*, the French *Direction Générale de la Concurrence, de la Consommation et de la Répression des Fraudes* and similar agencies from countries like Australia, Japan, Scandinavia and Switzerland; the Commission of the European Communities enjoys observer status. The principal aim is to organise informal cooperation between the participants of the Network in preventing cross-border marketing malpractices.

As a matter of European self-regulation, of interest is the Cross-Border Complaints Procedure of the European Advertising Standards Alliance (EASA).[15] It envisages mutual recognition of the Codes of Practice applicable in each EASA Member State and the decisions made thereunder. As for the question of the 'applicable law' (read: the applicable Code of Practice), it adopts the principle of home-country control; in other words, the advertisement in question must comply with the rules in force in the country where the media are located. But it requires compliance with rules of another country as well, if adverts are targeted to it as a specific market. Complainants are to apply to the relevant EASA body in their own country. The application is then forwarded to its counterpart in the country of origin (the question of the competent 'court'), where it is 'adjudicated' upon. This investigating organisation also takes care of the translation of the complaint. Finally, each national EASA organization shall apply its own sanctions, that is publicise the outcome of the dispute.

Another instance of self-regulation at Community level is The European Convention on Cross Border Mail Order and Distant Selling of the European Mail Order Trader's Association (EMOTA). This somewhat misleadingly termed 'Convention', an instrument of self-regulation, indicates in the preamble, next to the advantages of distant selling for the consumer, the need for a European-wide Code of Practice. It contains both substantive 'law' provisions, such as requirements for the contents of an offer, and 'private international law' provisions. For example Article 4 states that the applicable consumer protection law shall be the law of the country where the offer is made. Transposed to environmental cases, such a rule can be read strictly in that it applies to the place where the polluter acted. It could also be interpreted more widely so as to include the places of damage: after all, both types of locations can be seen as *loci delicti*. Like the EASA procedure, 'adjudication' takes place before the 'court' of the country of the seller. In my view, in the light of the principle of protection of the economically weaker party, it is preferable to leave the selection of the *forum* to the consumer; given the complexities of distance-litigation, it is likely, provided enforcement abroad is guaranteed, that consumers will opt for the court of their own state. Inevitably one of the parties will have to cope with litigating abroad; a choice must be made.

Finally on consumer law, the European Commission's Green Paper on Consumer Access to Justice warrants attention.[16] This discussion document surveys the legal situation in the member states, lists provisions on remedies in existing Community law and identifies two main problems: *locus standi* for consumer organisations and transfrontier disputes. As for this second procedural stumbling block, it advocates discussion of 'the free movement of actions for an injunction' (p.77). What kind of legal problems does the international consumer encounter? As with all international litigation, legal complexity is increased: what laws apply to the dispute, which courts are competent, where is the judgment enforceable? But the difficulties pertain especially to questions of law enforcement in the light of the various legal areas existing within the European Union (the Single Market is not accompanied by one common judicial area). A national enforcement agency is unable to take action, by its usual public law powers, against traders domiciled outside its territory; also, it may find itself unable to take action against a trader who is based in its territory but whose activities are targeted exclusively to consumers elsewhere.[17]

An illustrative case study is the *Home Vertrieb* litigation: a veritable legal horror story.[18] A German based trader sent misleading advertisements to consumers in France. Under German law, neither an offence nor a tort had been committed; there was criminal liability in France, but the French convictions were unenforceable in Germany. 'The resultant stalemate amounted to a victory for the unscrupulous trader'.[19] The central questions in this regard are whether enforcement bodies/private organisations are able to take legal action outside their own country and/or whether they are able to take action in their own country on behalf of consumers domiciled abroad. In technical legal terms, the *Home Vertrieb* case produced a Catch 22 situation where French plaintiffs were unable to act in Germany because standing to sue was reserved for German organisations alone, whilst these German organisations could not sue because they were deemed to be insufficiently interested in acting on behalf of consumers domiciled outside Germany. Under French law, only criminal action could be and was taken, but these judgments were not enforceable in Germany.

How to remedy this problem of remedies? As the Green Paper itself already points out (at p. 67), a first line of attack is based on Article 6 EC Treaty (the general prohibition of discrimination based on nationality).[20] Access to national law remedies would be available, under this provision, for foreign as well as domestic organisations. Recently, the European Court has given two far-reaching rulings on this provision which confirm this view, one in the field of intellectual property - the *Phil Collins* case[21] - and the other - the *Mund & Fester* case[22] - dealing with the relationship between Article 6 EC and the Brussels Convention on Jurisdiction and the Enforcement of Judgments. To a large extent, the application of Article 6 EC would produce mutual recognition of standing to sue. A more fundamental solution would be to harmonise the right to institute legal proceedings by a Community law directive[23] In order for the latter to be politically feasible, EU legislative action is likely to be limited to specific areas on a modest scale. For, in the words of the Economic and Social Committee: '[There are] legal and political obstacles, at this stage of European Union, to significant progress towards general standardisation in the area of access to justice'.[24]

The second adjacent legal field that may provide fruitful analogies with environmental civil litigation in international cases is intellectual property law, namely: the Community Trade Mark Regulation[25] and the Community Plant Variety Rights Regulation.[26] They merit attention because of the highly international character of this area and as an example of harmonisation of the law of civil remedies. The Community Trade Mark Regulation establishes the possibility, alongside the various national trade marks, of applying for the registration of a unitary Community-wide trade mark at the Community Trade Mark office in Alicante, Spain. Of interest to the environmental litigator may be Title X 'Jurisdiction and Procedure in Legal Actions Relating to Community Trade Marks'.[27] It refers to the Brussels Convention on Jurisdiction and Enforcement (below § 2) for most of these issues, but excludes its applicability as far as the environmentally most relevant heads of jurisdiction are concerned: the place of the harmful event, the so-called *forum delicti* and the arrangement for provisional measures; otherwise this Brussels Convention applies as the *lex generalis*.

Three notable features of the Community Trade Mark Regulation's jurisdictional scheme are: (i) its explicit inclusion of the possibility for a plaintiff to commence legal proceedings 'in respect of threatened infringement relating to Community trade marks', if such actions are permitted under national law (Article 92),[28] (ii) its provision on the extraterritorial reach of injunctions and (iii) its inclusion of actions for a negative declaration. The opportunity to sue to prevent an infringement altogether extends, under the conditions laid down by the Regulation, to all the available *fora* of the Regulation (Article 93):[29] the *forum rei* (place of domicile of the defendant), the *forum actoris* (place of domicile of the plaintiff), seat of the Community Trade Mark Office (Spain), the chosen court (prorogation) and the courts of the state in which an infringement has occurred or will occur (a more specific form of forum delicti). As will be seen in § 2, the availability of suing in cases of threatened harm at the *forum delicti* of the Brussels Convention is as yet a matter of uncertainty.

The second noteworthy issue tackled by the Community Trade Mark Regulation is that it contains a provision dealing with the territorial scope of the courts' competence (Article 94).[30] In addition to listing specific heads of jurisdiction, the Regulation stipulates that a Community trade mark court of a member state has competence to adjudicate (threatened) infringements occurring in the whole territory of the European Union. However, one court is denied such Union-wide jurisdiction: the *forum delicti*. The court of the place of infringement is only competent with respect to acts committed or threatened in its own state. That means that it does not have jurisdiction over infringements occurring outside its country, despite the fact that trade mark infringements often take place in more than one country at the same time. In order to be able to deal with this in one procedure the plaintiff has to turn to other courts, such as the *forum rei*.

The third special feature of the Community Trade Mark Regulation is that it envisages negative declarations. This unusual form of declaratory relief involves a suit brought with the object of having the court declare that no infringement has occurred. Such a suit is brought by the alleged infringer, the defendant in a 'normal' suit for an injunction or damages lodged by the trade mark holder against the infringer. Under Article 92, however (cited above), and like the action in cases of threatened wrong, the Regulation itself does not create this possibility. Instead, negative declarations are only available 'if they are permitted under national law'; this is the case, among other countries, in the UK and Germany.[31] One may apply for a declaration of non-infringement at all the *fora*, except at the Regulation's *forum delicti*. The ultimate form of international civil litigation combines the action for a negative declaration in country X with an action for an anti-suit injunction in country Y.[32] The objective of the anti-suit injunction in country Y is to restrain the defendant (the plaintiff in the other proceedings) from continuing its legal action in country X. A rather spectacular example concerns the enforcement of a choice of court clause by the English Court of Appeal involving a suit for damages in Greece.[33] The judgment has not exactly been well received in the legal literature, however; according to Briggs, it is 'bold, attractive and hopelessly wrong'.[34]

If environmental civil litigation would go down the same path as international business law, one can expect potential defendants to rush to the nearest court to obtain a negative declaration. If and when jurisdiction would be based on the Brussels Convention, that would prevent a second court, under Article 21, from being able to adjudicate the same cause of action in a suit subsequently brought by a 'normal' plaintiff such as victims of environmental damage and environmental protection organisations. Although this may sound rather far fetched, the European Court in the cited *Tatry* case has already decided that the rule of 'first come, first served' (that is, a second court must of its own motion stay proceedings before it in favour of the first court seized of the same cause of action) applies just as much where negative declarations are involved.[35] Such a vision of the future may be called Legal Darwinism - Survival of the Fastest; or in the words of Briggs: 'The Brussels Convention . . . contains one rule which, for most contentious purposes, transcends all others: do not wait to be sued, but sue first'.[36]

Having referred to all these rather complex private international aspects of the Community Trade Mark Regulation, discussion of its counterpart, the Community Plant Variety Rights Regulation,[37] can be brief. In essence it provides for a similar jurisdictional scheme in 'Part Six Civil Law Claims, Infringements, Jurisdiction'. As for the question of the territorial extent of a court's jurisdiction, Article 101(3) expresses the concept of the *forum delicti* in exactly the same terms as the Brussels Convention, i.e. 'the courts for the place where the harmful event occurred'. Like The Community Trade Mark Regulation, the competence of this *forum* is limited: 'In such cases, the court shall have jurisdiction only in respect of infringements alleged to have been committed in the territory of the Member State to which it belongs'. The other competent courts, by contrast, enjoy Union-wide jurisdiction, for Article 101(2) says: 'The competent courts [except the *forum delicti*] shall have jurisdiction in respect of infringements alleged to have been committed in any of the Member States'. As a final exercise in 'spot the difference' with the Community Trade Mark Regulation, it may be noted that none of the available *fora* under the Community Plant Variety Rights Regulation have jurisdiction in cases of threatened infringement.

Three Main Issues of Emerging European Remedy Law:

In the previous section some examples of European remedy law in the fields of consumer protection and intellectual property have been outlined. Before concentrating the discussion on the international civil (environmental) litigation which has taken place before Dutch courts, it should be stated that this article shall not deal with the question of the applicable law in detail, because all the environmental suits were adjudged under Dutch tort law. Dutch law was the law governing the dispute or so-called *lex causae*. Grossly simplified, the conflict of laws in these cases involves a choice between applying the law of the country of destination versus home-country control.[38] Under Dutch private international law, first of all parties are able to select the applicable law. Indeed this happened in the well-known French Potassium Mines litigation where it was recognised by the Rotterdam district court in its first (interlocutory) judgment on the merits.[39] In the absence of a choice of law, the main rule is the *lex loci delicti* rule.[40] There is no unambiguous case law to date which applies this rule in a situation of transfrontier pollution, where a solution of the conflict of laws cannot be provided by a simple application of this rule because there is more than one relevant *locus delicti*.[41]

The rest of this contribution examines the question of the international jurisdiction of the Dutch courts, the geographical extent of their competence and the kinds of injunction that have been granted over the past few years. Such an exercise may contribute to the development of a European Law of Remedies.

2. International Jurisdiction or Competence of Civil Courts

This is not the place for a more general introduction to the private international law question of jurisdiction of civil courts. Suffice it that it is principally a matter for the procedural law of the state of the court before which the case has been brought to decide this matter (private international law is national law). However, the role of domestic law is more and more limited in this respect due to the increasing importance of conventions dealing with both the question of jurisdiction and recognition and enforcement of foreign judgments. As reflected in the frequent citing in § 1, a pivotal role is played by the so-called Brussels Convention.[42]

The Brussels and Lugano Conventions' *Forum Delicti*

The 1968 Brussels Convention, as amended,[43] was concluded in the framework of the European Communities, namely in the context of Article 220 EEC Treaty.[44] Whether one may formally call this Convention 'Community law' or not is, for present purposes, an academic question for the European Court insists on the close relationship between the E(E)C Treaty and the Brussels Convention. In construing the one, regard must be had to the other.[45] This Convention is a necessary adjunct to the common market and every member state of the European Union is obliged to accede to it.[46] It 'seeks to determine the jurisdiction of the courts of the contracting states in the intra-Community legal order in regard to matters of civil jurisdiction'.[47] The regime of the Brussels Convention has been extended to the EFTA countries by the 1988 Lugano Convention.[48] Whenever defendants are domiciled in a state which is a party to one (or both) of these conventions, they may only be sued in accordance with the scheme laid down in these instruments. Since the provisions particularly relevant to environmental disputes are identical in the Brussels and Lugano Conventions and the Dutch cases under examination involved litigants domiciled in Brussels Convention states, I shall deal with this convention alone.

The principally competent court to sue a defendant not based in one's own country is the *forum rei* of Article 2:[49] the courts of the country of domicile of the defendant. According to Article 3(1), 'persons domiciled in a Contracting State may be sued in the courts of another Contracting State only by virtue of the rules set out in Sections 2 to 6 of this Title.' An important alternative forum for the environmental plaintiff is provided for in Article 5(3). It states: 'A person domiciled in a Contracting State may, in another Contracting State, be sued: in matters relating to tort, delict or quasi-delict, in the courts for the place where the harmful event occurred.' It follows that the connecting factor between the dispute and the competent court is encapsulated in the terms 'place of the harmful event' or *locus delicti*; hence the shorthand term '*forum delicti*'.

There is a problem of interpretation of this phrase in the situation where more than one place can qualify for the position of 'place of the harmful event'. This occurs in the environment sector where an emission of harmful substances takes place in one country and the resultant damage arises in another (or others). Consequently, the 'classical' case of transfrontier water or air pollution triggers this very question into practical significance. It was answered by the European Court in the *Bier* case, one of the judgments in the noted 14-year French Potassium Mines litigation saga.[50] The ECJ held that:

> Where the place of the happening of the event which may give rise to liability in tort, delict or quasi-delict and the place where that event results in damage are not identical, the expression 'place where the harmful event occurred', in Article 5 (3) of the Convention ... must be understood as being intended to cover *both* the place where the damage occurred and the place of the event giving rise to it.
>
> The result is that the defendant may be sued, *at the option of the plaintiff*, either in the courts for the place where the damage occurred or in the courts for the place of the event which gives rise to and is at the origin of that damage.[51] (Emphasis added.)

Consequently, Dutch environmental plaintiffs are able to sue defendants based in state parties to the Brussels Convention such as Belgium, France and Germany before those Dutch courts where their activities abroad have caused damage in the Netherlands (such as in *Bier* itself). The most important of the two *loci* encompassed by the Convention phrase 'place where the harmful event occurred' is the 'place where the damage occurred', as introduced by *Bier*. It is this place which significantly adds to the availability of competent courts because the place where the defendant carries out the damaging activities will frequently coincide with her domicile; indeed, in *Bier* itself the ECJ took this aspect into account where it considered that restricting the *forum delicti* to the place where the defendant has acted would, in many cases, merely duplicate the *forum rei* of Article 2 and thus deprive Article 5(3) of its effectiveness (*effet utile* argument).[52] The Convention, within the confines of these two terms (place of damage as a subcategory of place of harmful event), thus envisages the possibility of *forum* selection by the plaintiff.

Even if the outcome of *Bier* is pro-environmental-plaintiff, that does not mean that it is a 'green judgment', for the reasons the court gave for its construction of the *forum delicti* provision are based on considerations of procedural efficacy. That is that in its view all the special heads of jurisdiction of Article 5 Brussels Convention, and thus including the courts of the place of the harmful event, are justified solely because 'of a particular close connecting factor between the dispute and [such a court]' in the light of aspects of 'evidence and the conduct of the proceedings'.[53] Notably the Court did not follow the line suggested by Advocate General Capotorti to take into account the factor of protection of the weaker party. In the tort context of *Bier*, he argued that: 'The injured party, who must establish the unlawful act, is automatically deemed the weaker party and as such worthy of protection in the choice of the court having jurisdiction'.[54] One might slightly amend this position to protecting the weaker interest; such an approach would mesh with the fact that environmental protection has now been recognised, in the context of sustainable development, post-Maastricht, by Article 2 EC Treaty, as one of the objectives of the Community.[55] (In the same vein, pursuant to Article 3k EC Treaty, the Community is required to develop 'a policy in the sphere of the environment'.)

Why should it matter whether procedural or substantive grounds justify the plaintiff's option to sue at the courts of the place of damage (*forum damni*)? The answer is that the procedural line of reasoning combines with a more restrictive interpretation of Article 5(3) in 'hard cases' than one would adopt in a substantive plaintiff-protection approach.[56] The ECJ conceptualizes the *forum delicti* (and the other *fora* of Article 5) as exceptions to the general rule of Article 2, the *forum rei* (place of domicile of the defendant)[57] This baseline position invites the Court to adopt a restrictive reading of the Article 5 provisions; a kind of 'basic legal instinct' demands that exceptions are interpreted narrowly. However, it is doubtful whether, in the words of Briggs, 'the Pavlovian insistence upon a restrictive interpretation of Article 5'[58] is capable of producing a balanced system of available *fora* under the Convention, giving due regard to the legitimate interests of the plaintiff[59].

On two occasions the ECJ has had to consider the concept of the place of damage within the meaning of *Bier*. The first is the 1990 *Dumez* case,[60] where it held that '[this] concept can be understood only as indicating the place where the event giving rise to the damage, and entailing tortious, delictual or quasi delictual liability, directly produced its harmful effects upon the person who is the immediate victim of that event' (para. 20; emphasis added). A double limitation has thus been established: the link between the tortuous act and the ensuing damage must be direct and only immediate victims can sue at the place where such direct damage occurs. Making an 'Environmental Impact Statement' on *Dumez*, one would not expect real adverse consequences from this judgment for environmental plaintiffs. Both limitations should be seen against the background of the particular facts of that dispute, where a French parent company claimed to suffer loss in France, place of its domicile, due to allegedly unlawful behaviour of the German defendant vis-à-vis subsidiary companies also based in Germany. In other words, we are dealing with ricochet damage to a ricochet plaintiff. There is little analogy with a straightforward cross-border pollution case.

The second judgment in which the ECJ interprets the concept of place of damage, the 1995 *Shevill* case,[61] however, signals a more restrictive reading of Article 5(3) across the board. The facts concern a defamatory publication in a French newspaper suggesting the involvement in drugs-related money laundering of a 'Bureau de Change' in Paris; the name of a temporary employee, Ms. Fiona Shevill of Yorkshire (UK), was also mentioned. Copies of the litigious issue were sold throughout Europe. Together with a Belgian, an English and a French company, she brought a libel suit against the newspaper before the English courts, seeking damages. The defendant argued that the English courts have no jurisdiction because no harmful event within the meaning of Article 5(3) had occurred in the UK.

Like in the 1976 *Bier* case,[62] the central legal question is the assessment of the loci delicti in the situation of a ramified tort. In answer to a series of questions of the House of Lords, the ECJ introduced a new restriction to the availability of the *forum delicti*. It first cited both *Bier* and *Dumez*[63] and reiterated the main decisions of those cases. Then there takes place a compartmentalisation of the damage. The place where the tortuous act was initiated, in casu the domicile of the publishers of the newspaper, is competent to deal with the entirety of the damage; this place, the Court points out, will frequently coincide with the *forum rei*. The place where the damaging impact takes place extends to all the states where a victim alleges to be affected by the publication; however, these courts are only competent to deal with the damage caused in their own state (paras. 30 and 33). The Advocates General involved in this case, Mr. Darmon and Mr. Léger, had proposed an even stricter solution: in cases of defamation by a newspaper article circulated in more than one country, the courts of the places where the newspaper is distributed should 'have jurisdiction solely in respect of the damage arising ... within their judicial district'.[64]

This judgment is a case of 'the one hand giveth and the other taketh away': Article 5(3) is construed generously in that the courts of all the places where the newspaper has been distributed and damage has been caused are competent, but it is construed narrowly in that these courts are restricted to judging only the damage arising in their state.[65] The Brussels Convention thus contains two classes of *fora*: a first class, such as the court of the place of domicile of the defendant (Article 2) and the place where the tortfeasor has acted (Article 5(3)), having full fledged jurisdiction over all the damage produced by the tort; and a second class, the courts of the place where the damage occurred of Article 5(3), having limited jurisdiction over the damage located in its state alone.

The decision by the ECJ to curtail the extent of the jurisdiction of the *forum damni* is similar to French but contrary to German law; under the former the courts of the places where the effects of a defamatory publication take place have jurisdiction for the harm located in their district alone, under the latter these courts are competent to deal with all the damage, even where it is located outside their state.[66] It also reflects, as we have seen in § 1, the jurisdictional scheme of the Community Trade Mark Regulation. Probably, although this is not mentioned in the judgment, the ECJ was persuaded by the insistence of the Advocates General on preventing 'forum shopping'.[67] This possibility for a plaintiff might also be called 'forum selection',[68] instead of the pejorative allusion to shopping around (typically, the phenomenon is presented as if one refers to some unspeakable perversion). It is a matter of evaluation whether the selection options open to a plaintiff under the Convention should be restricted or not. Admittedly, striking a compromise in cases like *Shevill* between the *effet utile* of the *forum delicti* and the undue proliferation of competent courts is no easy matter.

However, there are three less consistent strands of reasoning in *Shevill*. First, centralization of suits in that the entirety of the damage is adjudged in proceedings before one court is possible only, post-*Shevill*, before two *fora*: the place of domicile of the defendant and the place where the tortfeasor has acted.[69] This approach ignores possible centralization before the court of the place of impact in that multiple plaintiffs bring one suit, involving one tort causing damage at various places, before one court of a place of damage (as happened in *Shevill* itself); such a suit would also benefit the defendant, who has to come to one foreign court dealing with the whole of the damage rather than several foreign courts dealing with parts of the damage.

Second, the attribution of jurisdiction to several *fora* as established in *Shevill* is based solely on considerations of a proper administration of justice (paras. 19 and 31). But it is difficult to see why the court of the place where the defendant has acted and the court where she is domiciled (the *forum rei*) should be better equipped to assess damage occurring in another country than one of the courts of the place of damage is. If an emission from country X produces harm in countries Y and Z, assessing the damage suffered in country Y is equally difficult or easy for the courts of country X and country Z. It follows that the application of the single criterion 'proper administration of justice' cannot be the decisive factor. Substantive factors dealing with the nature of the dispute and the position of the parties should be taken into account, in my view. For example, in the situation of defamation by a publication a relevant factor should be, not taken into account in *Shevill*, the defendant's right to freedom of expression. It is guaranteed by Article 10 of the European Convention on Human Rights, which is a main source for the Community law counterpart in the form of a general principle.[70] Clearly, there is no equivalent 'freedom to pollute' applicable in environmental disputes. It would be right and proper for the ECJ to develop subrules which would accommodate the idiosyncrasies of different torts.[71]

Finally and more fundamentally, I wonder whether the question of the extent of the jurisdiction of a court is a matter for the Brussels Convention at all. In *Shevill* the question of assessing whether certain facts give rise to liability was, rightly, considered to be a matter for the substantive domestic law governing the dispute.[72] Indeed, whether certain conduct may constitute a tort is a matter of substantive tort law, not a question for a Convention on jurisdiction to decide. (Life for the modern Euro-lawyer is rather complicated, however, because whether such an alleged tort constitutes non-contractual liability for the Convention purpose of establishing jurisdiction of the *forum delicti*, is, in turn, not a question for the applicable domestic law but is decided by the autonomous Convention concept of 'delict' etc. within the meaning of Article 5(3)).[73] Implicitly, the ECJ has decided that the issue of the extent of a court's jurisdiction is a question of jurisdiction law and not one of remedy law. As we shall see in the next paragraph, this is not the view taken by Dutch law in the context of actions for injunctions: there this issue is decided by the substantive (and procedural) law which governs the issue (*lex causae*). This is the better view, for the essence of this issue is the spatial extent of the remedy; in an action for damages that is the particular that has to be compensated. The question of international competence properly so called only concerns a relevant head of jurisdiction indicating the connecting factor between the dispute and the *forum*, such as the place of damage. Before examining this point in more detail, a final topic of Euro-jurisdiction law warrants attention.

The Forum Delicti and the Threatened Wrong

The relevance of the libel case *Shevill*[74] to environmental disputes especially concerns one as yet unresolved difficulty: does Article 5(3), and in particular the jurisdiction of the court of the place of the impact of a tort, also apply in situations of threatened harm? On a literal interpretation it would not, for the provision speaks of 'the place where the harmful event occurred'. In fact, in a situation of imminent environmental harm in the border region of Belgium and the Netherlands, a Dutch court held that it indeed lacked jurisdiction under Article 5(3)[75] (and also under Article 24 of the Brussels Convention, dealing with provisional measures; this provision will not be further examined presently).[76] However, such a grammatical approach to the Convention is not in keeping with the European Court's emphasis on teleological interpretation.[77] Also, most of the commentators favour a wide interpretation of Article 5(3) in this respect. According to Cheshire and North, for instance, it is 'a serious omission' that the threatened wrong has not been explicitly included; therefore the plaintiff is forced to sue in the country of the defendant instead of 'the obvious and appropriate country, the one where he is under threat'.[78]

Since March 1994, the issue of the applicability or not of the *forum delicti* in threatened tort situations is pending before the ECJ in *Beta-Film v Beta-Television*.[79] In the light of the developments so far, in particular the Community Trade Mark Directive and *Shevill*, it is quite conceivable, although an *effet utile* approach would point in the opposite direction, that the ECJ opts for a restrictive interpretation of Article 5(3). However, a wholesale exclusion of the threatened wrong from the scope of the *forum delicti* would, in my view, be contrary to secondary Community law, i.e. the Misleading Advertising Directive.[80] According to Article 4 of the Directive, member states must 'ensure that adequate and effective means exist for the control of misleading advertising in the interests of consumers as well as competitors and the general public.' Such means must include the right to take legal action for interested parties. In this context, 'Member States shall confer upon the courts or administrative authorities powers enabling them', to order discontinuation of the advertisement 'or - if misleading advertising has not yet been published but publication is imminent, to order the prohibition of ... such publication, even without proof of actual loss or damage or of intention or negligence on the part of the advertiser' (emphasis added). It follows that this provision presupposes that the courts have jurisdiction and thus also, in international cases of misleading advertising, international jurisdiction.

Since the Misleading Advertising Directive, unlike the

Community Trade Mark Regulation, does not provide for its own rules on competence (or indeed any reference to questions of private international law), the *lex generalis*, i.e. the Brussels Convention, applies. If the Convention were to be so construed as to exclude all situations of threatened wrong from the scope of Article 5(3) the effectiveness of this Directive would be impaired. This view is supported by the fact, noted in § 1, that an international network has been established in order to deal with just this type of case. Therefore the Court should, in the light of the close connection between the Convention and the E(E)C Treaty,[81] take this wider Community law context into 'Convention-account'. Moreover, in Article 57(3),[82] the Convention itself provides a supremacy rule in the event of a conflict between the general Convention and a more specific provision on jurisdiction laid down in a directive (and other acts of the EU legislature): the rules of secondary Community law take precedence; that is they may not be affected. By the same token, one could argue, implicit arrangements of jurisdiction in directives should be treated likewise. However, insisting upon the prevention of *forum* shopping combined with a restrictive construction of the 'exception' of Article 5, like in *Shevill*, would of course tip the balance the other way. 'To *Shevill* or not to *Shevill*, that is the question.'

3. Territorial Extent of Injunctions: The Dutch Approach

In *Kuunders*,[83] the Dutch supreme court killed two birds with one stone when it ruled that (i) environmental protection organizations have *locus standi* to bring suit for an injunction in order to promote ecological interests as such (ecosystems have standing) and (ii) that:

> 4.1.2 ... It further follows that in the event these [ecological] interests are harmed by violations of norms which protect them, this constitutes unlawfulness towards legal persons whose object and purpose according to the articles of association is to promote these interests; therefore, the groups are entitled in any event to apply for a prohibition of further breaches.[84]

It follows from this passage that any breach of a written or unwritten rule of environmental protection law constitutes tortious liability of the defendant vis-à-vis interested third parties, including an organization with the 'right' object under its articles of association; this legal position reflects not only the question of standing, but also the so-called relativity requirement or, in German: *Normzwecklehre* (doctrine of protective scope of the statute).[85] Put differently, as for the question of unlawfulness, Dutch law explicitly recognizes a relative concept of unlawfulness. An act may be unlawful as against one person but not as against another. This principle is expressed in Article 6:163 of the Civil Code (the *Burgerlijk Wetboek*, hereinafter: BW), which provides as follows: 'There is no obligation to repair damage when the violated norm does not have as its purpose the protection from damage such as that suffered by the victim'.[86] We see here formulated in negative terms the same principle as stated in positive terms in the *Kuunders* judgment.[87]

One might further observe in this provision that it talks about the remedy 'damages' alone. In an historical perspective, this is not surprising; for, as the development of the common law in England indicates,[88] damages is the older remedy. During the course of time, the protective scope of the law of torts has been extended to injunctive relief, including the prevention of a tort altogether. Or, in the words of the Dutch supreme court: 'the protection offered by [the law of torts] is not exhausted by the . . . explicitly formulated right to damages after an injustice has been done, but also covers preventive measures in the event of a serious threat that a wrong will take place'.[89] In the light of this case law and the relevant Civil Code provisions, the requirements for an action for an injunction founded on tort (domestic or international) may be summed up as follows:

- the violated obligation in question is owed to the plaintiff (relativity requirement);

- the relevant interests are of a kind protected by the law of torts;

- the plaintiff has a sufficient interest in the injunction.

Let us examine in more detail how Dutch law deals with the combination of injunctive relief and non-contractual liability;

then we shall examine the position in international disputes.

A Powerful Pair: Articles 3:296 and 6:162 Dutch Civil Code

Unlike English law where the granting of an injunction is a matter of discretion for the courts,[90] the Dutch Civil Code, subject to certain conditions, provides for a right to injunctive relief.[91] This right is formulated as follows in Article 3:296(1) BW:

> Unless the law, the nature of the obligation or a juridical act produce a different result, the person who is obliged to give, to do or not to do something vis-à-vis another is ordered to do so by the judge upon the demand of the person to whom the obligation is owed.[92]

This provision codifies the older case law of the supreme court, like the judgment cited above, where it recognized the plaintiff's right in general to injunctive relief. Next to the three possible exceptions, the provision contains two crucial elements: a duty of some kind (unlawfulness aspect), which must be owed to the plaintiff (relativity aspect).

The next step therefore is to analyze the grounds of unlawfulness recognized by Dutch tort law. They are contained in Article 6:162 BW, which reads:

1. A person who commits an unlawful act toward another which can be imputed to him, must repair the damage which the other person suffers as a consequence thereof.

2. Except where there is a ground of justification, the following acts are deemed to be unlawful: the violation of a right, an act or omission violating a statutory duty or a rule of unwritten law pertaining to proper social conduct.

3. An unlawful act can be imputed to its author if it results from his fault or from a cause for which he is answerable according to law or common opinion[93].

In a comparative perspective, the conceptualization of tortious liability in Dutch law is similar to the French approach, one all-singing, all-dancing general principle to be fleshed out by the courts, but contrary to the English approach of a system of separate torts.[94] In this paper, we can restrict ourselves to looking at one ground of unlawfulness, breach of statutory duty, because it is in this context that successful environmental litigation in international cases has taken place before the Dutch courts. In essence, Section 2 of the cited provision quite simply recognizes all possible forms of unlawfulness: breach of written law, both as breach of statutory duty and as infringement of a right, and breach of unwritten law (negligence or breach of the duty of due care). 'Written law here includes statutes in the strict sense but also by-laws of subordinate "legislators" as far as they establish regulations of a general binding character'.[95] For the purpose of establishing unlawfulness within the meaning of Article 6:162 BW not only breach of domestic statutes and subordinate legislation is pertinent, but also 'superordinate legislation': under the Dutch monist system, a violation of a directly effective provision of international law constitutes breach of statutory duty.[96]

It goes without saying that this category of unlawfulness is particularly relevant to environmental disputes, given the almost pervasive coverage of environment-related activities by public law environmental statutes and the like. The practical importance of the combination of Articles 3:296 and 6:162 BW is all the more pronounced after the Dutch supreme court had ruled that breach of the conditions of a licence has the same effects, 'tortwise', as breach of the underlying statute itself. In the context of the then applicable Nuisance Act, it ruled in 1981 that:

> 3. ... Conditions lawfully attached to a licence under the Nuisance Act, with a view to protecting those living in the neighbourhood, must be given a similar meaning than norms of conduct adopted by the central or local legislature, the violation of which in principle constitutes a tort in relation to those whose protection is sought by those norms, for the purpose of applying Article [6:162] BW in the concrete situation for which they have been written. In both cases, it must be understood that the relevant interests have been weighed as against each other by the public authorities. When a person is

affected by a breach of a condition of a licence under the Nuisance Act in an interest protected by that condition and that interest has been damaged, the offender by whose fault the damage has been caused shall be liable under Article [6:162] - except in the event of a justification ground which does not apply to the present case - for the damage caused by the breach.[97]

The operation of breach of statutory duty in the environment sector may be illustrated by the *CNC* case.[98] A group of both local and national environmental protection organizations sued the operator of a plant which emitted large doses of ammonia and SO_x. The court of appeal Den Bosch points out that it had been operating without the required licences for more than twenty years without any action taken against it by the competent authorities. Applying *Kuunders*,[99] it held the action by the environmentalists to be admissible and the conduct of the defendant unlawful; injunctions were granted ordering the defendant, after a certain period, to take measures to reduce the nuisance and to monitor the level of emitted substances.

The *CNC* litigation indicates the usefulness of civil action as a means of enforcement of (public) environmental law; such a supplement is particularly welcome where the public authorities refuse to take action.[100] Likewise, where public authorities are unable to act due to territorial restrictions to their powers, a civil suit may be the only remedy; for instance the use of public law enforcement powers is limited to the authority's own state.[101] Private enforcement both by public authorities and public interest groups does not require extensive international negotiations in order to provide new public law remedies but can make use of the available arsenal of private international law.[102]

Extraterritorial Injunctive Relief

One weapon available under Dutch law is an extraterritorial injunction: a court order with which the defendant has to comply outside the Netherlands. In a 1989 landmark judgment this possibility has been recognized by the supreme court.[103] This *Interlas* case involves a suit for an injunction in a dispute concerning a trade mark under uniform Benelux law. Joint plaintiffs were an American parent company and two of its subsidiaries, based in France and the Netherlands, suing a Dutch-based defendant accused of infringing the plaintiffs' trade mark. In a single suit it was sought to obtain a prohibition of further marketing of the infringing goods not only in the territory of the Netherlands but in Belgium and Luxembourg as well (the litigious trade mark also covered these three countries). In the summary proceedings before the President of a district court the plaintiffs further claimed that the defendant should be ordered to pay a periodic penalty payment of 1 million guilders. This so-called *astreinte* is also based on uniform Benelux law and is the 'normal' means of enforcement of injunctions in Holland; in the event of non-compliance, the penalties are due to the plaintiff not to the state.[104] Before the supreme court, it was argued that the Dutch court lacked jurisdiction to issue an injunction regarding the infringement of a trade mark outside the national territory. The court disagreed for it held as follows:

> 4.2.4 ... Unless the law, the nature of the obligation or a juridical act produce a different result, the person who is obliged to give, to do or not to do something vis-à-vis another, is ordered to do so by the court upon the demand of the person to whom the obligation is owed. In general there is no reason to accept that such an order cannot be given when the obligation - *possibly an obligation under foreign law* - is to be complied with outside the Netherlands. A more restrictive view as upheld in the cassation pleadings has no basis in law and would have, in a time of increasing international contacts, the undesirable effect on legal practice that, in international tort cases- such as infringement of intellectual property rights, unlawful competition involving several countries and *transfrontier pollution* - the Dutch victim might be compelled to apply to a court in all the countries involved.[105] (Emphasis added.)

In many subsequent judgments of the lower Dutch courts this ruling has been applied.[106] The following three comments may be made. First, this judgment is of general application and not limited to the infringement of Benelux trade marks. This follows from the fact that the first sentence of the cited passage is nothing else than Article 3:296(1) BW[107] and from the reference by the court to all forms of international torts, including cross-border pollution.

Second, The case does not involve jurisdiction as such but, as just said, an interpretation of Article 3:296 BW: that is, its territorial scope or application in international cases. In *Interlas* itself, the question of international jurisdiction of the Dutch courts was not problematic at all, for the defendant was based in the Netherlands, the competent court therefore was the *forum rei*. It follows that the characterization of the central issue in *Interlas*, territorial scope of an injunction, although related to the question of jurisdiction, should be distinguished there from and is best treated as a separate category of private international law: remedy law.[108] The most important consequence of this characterization question - jurisdiction v. substantive remedy law - is that it is the *lex causae* that decides what remedies will be available and not, therefore, a Convention dealing with jurisdiction law;[109] it will be remembered that this aspect was my main critique of the ECJ's Shevill judgment (§ 2 above). Given this substantive law characterization under Dutch law, the effect of *Shevill*[110] on *Interlas* is limited to cases where the jurisdiction of the Dutch courts is based on Article 5(3) of the Brussels Convention. Whenever their competence is based on other heads of jurisdiction, extraterritorial injunctions remain undoubtedly available. Assuming that the *Shevill* reasoning, involving an action for damages with respect to harm arising outside the state of the court ruling on the dispute, would equally apply to actions for an injunction involving (imminent) harm outside the jurisdiction, the result is the following.

An extraterritorial injunction is fully available for all plaintiffs, wherever they may be based, against defendants based in the Netherlands; the same applies to defendants not domiciled in a Contracting State of the Brussels Convention;[111] it is no longer available as against a defendant domiciled in a Contracting State of that Convention if the jurisdiction of the Dutch court is based upon the place of damage under Article 5(3) Brussels Convention; it is uncertain whether such injunctions will remain available as a provisional measure under Article 24 Brussels Convention. The impact of *Shevill* in the environmental context will be further considered below.

Third, an injunction against a non-Dutch based defendant may be granted in enforcing an obligation under non-Dutch law, according to the cited passage of *Interlas*. In other words, breach of foreign statutory duty can constitute a tort within the meaning of Article 6:162 BW just as much as breach of a Dutch statute will. This is exactly what happened in an international environmental dispute involving water pollution.

- Green *Interlas*

The judgment by the court of appeal The Hague in the *Sopar* case is testimony to the relevance of the supreme court's reference, in Interlas, to transfrontier pollution cases.[112] Here we have a suit of Dutch environmental protection groups against a Belgian based company which discharged PAHs into a waterway allegedly causing environmental damage in the Netherlands. The plaintiffs applied for a prohibition of the discharges, or alternatively, for an injunction, in combination with an *astreinte* of 500,000 guilders for each day of non-compliance, ordering the defendant to take measures to reduce the discharges to the technically lowest achievable level. At first instance, the plaintiffs had relied on breach of unwritten law; during the proceedings it became apparent that the defendant had not and did not comply with its Belgian law licence. Consequently and as seen above,[113] a breach of statutory duty was established. The court of appeal The Hague therefore ordered the defendant to comply in full with its licence on penalty of an *astreinte* of 500,000 guilders per day. The application of the 'normal' rules of Dutch tort law in this cross-border pollution context thus produced the following legal result: a breach of a Belgian statutory duty by a Belgium based defendant was sanctioned by a Dutch court on application by Dutch public interest groups.

But what about the precedent value of this judgment in the post-*Shevill* era? It is recalled that in *Shevill*[114] the European Court has ruled on the extent of the jurisdiction of the court of the place of damage within the meaning of Article 5(3) Brussels Convention in a libel suit for damages. It held that this *forum*'s jurisdiction is limited to dealing with the harm which occurred in its own state. I should think that for Dutch plaintiffs combatting environmental damage in the Netherlands the '*Shevill*-restriction' will not affect their possibilites to bring suit against defendants based elsewhere. The reason is that in practice an injunction in an environmental dispute ordering a defendant to take measures to reduce polluting emissions, even where it is limited to the effects of the discharges in the country of impact (the Netherlands), affect the source of the discharge (Belgium in *Sopar*) just as much as if the injunction also sought to prevent damage there. After all, operators will usually be unable to simply divert discharges; in practice, the only feasible option is a reduction of emissions at the point source. (In parenthesis, it is precisely in this respect where pollution cases differ from infringements of intellctual property rights: such torts are compartmentalized in that they involve, unless a unitary Community-wide right is in issue, separate territorially limited subjective rights; the impact of *Shevill* in this field is thus stronger.)[115]

This proposition may be illustrated by a 1992 judgment involving 'transfrontier racism', the *Verbeke* case.[116] Pamphlets by so-called revisionists, who claim that the holocaust had never happened, had been issued in Belgium and 'accidentally' ended up in the letter boxes of people with Jewish sounding names in a number of cities in the Netherlands. Anti-racism organizations sued the responsible Belgian group and its director before the President of the district court The Hague for an injunction, under penalty of an *astreinte*, restraining the defendants from further dissemination of these or similar leaflets. Judgment was given for the plaintiffs in so far as the director was forbidden to distribute - directly or indirectly - the pamphlets in question in Holland; he was also ordered to refrain from promoting the revisionistic views in the future in such a way as would grieve Jewish inhabitants of the Netherlands. Although the order is limited to occurrences within the Netherlands, indeed the court explicitly states that an exception to the possibilities of *Interlas*[117] is warranted in the case in hand, it nevertheless has extraterritorial effect in that the defendant is ordered to refrain from activities which produce their injurious effects on Dutch territory. In other words, the scope of the injunction encompasses acts occurring outside Holland. In fact, it is held that: 'This case concerns a duty to prevent discrimination which (also) must be complied with outside the Netherlands' (consideration 6.12).

The conclusion of all this is that extraterritorial injunctions remain available, notwithstanding *Shevill*, to Dutch based plaintiffs even where the competence of the Dutch court is found on Article 5(3) Brussels Convention as the place of harm. However, the restrictive scope of this *forum* does seem to curb possible legal development in that non-Dutch based plaintiffs cannot concentrate in one suit before this court a claim dealing with a ramified tort causing damage both in the Netherlands as elsewhere.[118] So in this regard *Shevill* is a step backwards in the environmental context, yet it does not affect the status quo for Dutch based plaintiffs.

4. Types of Injunction

What kinds of injunction have been issued in international disputes by the Dutch courts? Invariably the injunction is accompanied by a period penalty payment or *astreinte*. As seen above, in the environmental sector, this happened in the international *Sopar* case[119] and the domestic *CNC* case.[120] As to the type of order, from the case law on negligence in general, the following list of possibly required measures has been extracted:

- duty to warn (and/or consult);

- duty to monitor and to carry out maintenance;

- duty to investigate or research;

- duty to take residuary safety measures.[121]

In addition, in intellectual property cases, alongside a prohibition of (further) infringements of the right in issue, the plaintiffs frequently obtain an injunction ordering the defendant to submit a list of traders who are selling the litigious products (the courts have here carefully balanced the need for effective enforcement of the injunction with legitimate interests of non-disclosure of corporate information).[122]

Prohibition/Duty to Take Measures

It will come as no surprise that the primary court order sought by environmental plaintiffs has been the prohibition (of emissions of substances). It is perhaps equally unsurprising that the courts have been reluctant to issue such an injunction. In the cases just cited, the courts settled for the alternative claim: ordering the defendant, within a certain period of time, to take measures to reduce emissions.

Information

Another injunction of especial interest to environmental plaintiffs is that the plaintiff is ordered to monitor its emissions for the presence of certain (levels of) substances and submit the information to the plaintiffs, again, on penalty of an *astreinte*. An example in the domestic sphere is the cited *CNC* case. Yet such an order is not limited to Dutch defendants, for a like injunction has been issued by the President of the district court Maastricht against a Belgian based company in the *Cockerill Sambre* case.[123] To be exact, this is the operative part of the judgment:

> The President of the district court Maastricht, ruling in summary proceedings: Orders Cockerill [the defendant], within four weeks after notice of this judgment, to determine the daily amount of PAHs (Borneff's six [a certain laboratory measuring mode]), respectively on the first and the 16th of every month, in the effluent emitted by both the plants in Charleroi and Seraing, and to submit these analyses to the plaintiffs without delay; Cockerill shall forfeit an astreinte of 10,000 guilders for each day of non-compliance with this order.

However, this judgment of the first instance court was quashed on appeal, albeit not for the reason that such an order is not possible.[124] Indeed, such a right to information has received statutory recognition in both German law and an international convention. In Germany, the Environmental Liability Act 1990 (*Umwelthaftungsgesetz*) provides for a plaintiff's right to information as against the operator of a listed facility allegedly responsible for environmental damage (known as *Auskunftsanspruch*). Like the noted Dutch case law in the intellectual property field - the duty to provide of list of traders in infringing goods - a balance is struck between corporate confidentiality and procedural fact finding.[125] Unlike the Dutch court ruling in *Cockerill* though, public interest groups are not entitled to apply for this information.

At European level, a similar duty to disclose environmental information is incumbent on operators 'in respect of a dangerous activity' within the meaning of the Council of Europe Convention on Civil Liability for Damage Resulting from Activities Dangerous to the Environment.[126] According to Article 16 'Access to specific information held by operators', only persons who have suffered damage have such access and not public interest groups; the provision thus resembles the German Environmental Liability Act in this respect; furthermore, this 'right' does contain a rather wide range of exceptions.[127] In particular the opportunity for the operator to refuse disclosure of information that would be self-incriminating greatly limits the scope of this right to access; after all, many civil environmental wrongs will constitute criminal offences too. The provision ignores the possibility of distinguishing between civil and criminal proceedings and the difference between private parties and public authorities. The ECJ, by contrast, did just this in the field of competition law in *Otto*.[128]

Sanctio non conveniens

Finally in this context, some specific problems with transnational remedies may be noted. Professor Polak has suggested, in analogy to '*forum non conveniens*', a doctrine of '*sanctio non conveniens*' in order to cope with the idiosyncrasies of certain injunctions in a cross-border dispute.[129] Starting point is the geographically unlimited extent of the jurisdiction of the Dutch courts (the national court as 'world court', similar to the English law notion of world-wide *Mareva* injunctions). These wide powers should be balanced by taking into account a number of counterweighing factors. For instance, suppose that the *lex causae* of a dispute before a Dutch court would be English law, could the court than award punitive damages? This would be highly unlikely, for, according to Polak, this would be contrary to Dutch public policy (*ordre public* exception).[130] Under acknowledgment of restrictions of this kind, judicial development of international remedy law would be desirable.

5. Some Persistent Problems for Environmental Plaintiffs

It follows from the above that effective instruments of private international law for dealing with cross-border pollution are developing at the level of Dutch domestic law; hopefully, there will not be too much countervailing force from the Community law level.

Also under Dutch law there remain some items on the 'environmental wish list'. The courts have demonstrated reluctance in two respects: the development of unwritten duties of environmental due care and applying a kind of double actionability test in the international disputes. In other words, instead of judging the defendant's conduct on the basis of Dutch law alone, the courts were worried about whether there would also be unlawfulness under the law of the place where the defendant had acted. This is detrimental in that the plaintiff gets the worst of both worlds.

Last things last, what about executing an extraterritorial injunction? If and when the Brussels Convention applies, the machinery for recognition of the order and, in case of non-compliance, of enforcement of forfeited periodic penalty payments is in place. Whether it also works in practice is under examination by the European Commission.[131] But let me finish on an optimistic note. Robesin has pointed out that,[132] in the *Cockerill Sambre* case,[133] a Belgian court, even when the appeal was still pending, had already issued an enforcement order following the Dutch injunction. So there actually was free movement for *that* injunction.

Abbreviations

AB	Administratiefrechtelijke Beslissingen
BIE	Bijblad bij De Industriële Eigendom
BVerwG	Bundesverwaltungsgericht
BVerwGE	Entscheidungen des Bundesverwaltungsgericht
BW	Burgerlijk Wetboek
C.A.	Court of Appeal (UK)

Ch.	Law Reports (UK), Chancery Division
C.L.J.	Cambridge Law Journal
C.M.L.R.	Common Market Law Reports
CMLRev.	Common Market Law Review
CRW	Conclusies Rechtspraak van de Week
ECJ	Court of Justice of the European Communi ties
ECR	European Court Reports
E.H.R.R.	European Human Rights Reports
EIPR	European Intellectual Property Review
E.L.Rev.	European Law Review
Hof	Gerechtshof
HR	Hoge Raad
I.C.R.	Industrial Cases Reports
I.L.M.	International Legal Materials
I.L.Pr.	International Litigation Procedure
IPRax	Praxis des Internationalen Privat- und Verfahrensrechts
KG	Kort Geding
L.M.C.L.Q.	Lloyd's Maritime and Commercial Law Quarterly
L.Q.R.	Law Quarterly Review
M en R	Tijdschrift voor Milieu en Recht

NJ	Nederlandse Jurisprudentie
NYIL	Netherlands Yearbook of International Law
NILR	Netherlands International Law Review
O.J.	Official Journal of the European Commun ities
OLG	Oberlandesgericht
Pres. Rb.	President van de rechtbank
Q.B.	Law Reports (UK), Queen's Bench Division
Rb.	Rechtbank
RECIEL	Review of European Community & Interna tional Environmental Law
RIW	Recht der Internationalen Wirtschaft
RvdW	Rechtspraak van de Week
TMA	Tijdschrift voor Milieu Aansprakelijkheid/ Environmental Liability Law Review
Trb.	Tractatenblad

Notes

[1] See, e.g., Thijmen Koopmans, 'The Future of Legal Systems', Presidential Address to the David Hume Institute. Hume Occasional Papers No. 13 (Edinburgh 1990), cited from Juridisch stippelwerk (Deventer 1991), 114 and New York University's initiative to start a 'Global Law School Program', see 22 International Journal of Legal Information 209 (1994).

[2] H.U. Jessurun d'Oliveira, 'De proletarisering van het internationaal privaatrecht', in: Roel de Lange et al. (eds.), De dubbelzinnigheid van het recht (Nijmegen 1985).

[3] Such as in *Haughton v Olau Line* [1986] I.C.R. 357 (C.A.): a case of 'Transfrontier Sexism'. An female employee working on the ferry between Sheerness and Vlissingen complained of harassment on board ship before English courts. Jurisdiction was declined, because the relevant statute was regarded not to confer competence on English courts in the circumstances.

[4] BVerwG 7 C 29.85, 17 December 1986, BVerwGE 75, 285; TMA 1987, 70 note by Lammers. See also Jan Hendrik Jans, Grenzüberschreitendes Umweltrecht (Köln etc. 1990), para. 6.3.2. and Jan H. Jans, 'The Effect of a Licence on Liability in Cases of Transboundary Pollution,' in: Jan M. van Dunné ed., Transboundary Pollution and Liability: the Case of the River Rhine (Lelystad 1991), 53, 55.

[5] See the case note on Hamers, written in English, by Lammers: TMA 1987, 70 at 76 and the literature cited there.

[6] J.H. Jans, Europees Milieurecht in Nederland, 1st ed. (Groningen 1991), 220.

[7] Hof Den Haag 3 May 1990, NJ 1991, 194; AB 1991, 620; M en R 1991, p. 498 note by Jans (Lanaken/Staat).

[8] See my articles: 'Environmental *Locus Standi* in the Netherlands', (1994) 3 RECIEL 238 and 'Standing for Ecosystems - Going Dutch', [1995] C.L.J. 153; cf. Niels Frenk, 'Collective action in consumer affairs. Some recent developments', in: Th. Bourgoignie, ed., Group Actions and Consumer Protection (Brussels 1992), 101.

[9] See generally Peter Schlosser, 'Extraterritoriale Rechtsdurchsetzung im Zivilprozeß', in: Festschrift für Werner Lorenz (Tübingen 1991), 497-510.

[10] See generally I. Brownlie, Principles of Public International Law, 4th ed. (Oxford 1990), Chapter 14; and see M.V. Polak, Civiele Sancties in het Internationale Geval voor de Nederlandse Rechter, Studiekring "Prof.mr. J. Offerhaus", No. 3 (Deventer 1995), para. 8.

[11] Lawrence Collins (gen. ed.) et al., Dicey and Morris on the

Conflict of Laws, 12th ed. (London 1993), 353 (there are some exceptions but they are not relevant for present purposes); and see on choice of *forum* by the parties J.M.J. Chorus et al. (eds.), Introduction to Dutch Law for Foreign Lawyers, 2nd ed. (Deventer 1993), 224.

[12] J.J. Brinkhof, 'Overzicht van de octrooirechtspraak in eerste aanleg in 1992', BIE 1994, 113, 114.

[13] Cf. Economic and Social Committee, 'Opinion on the Green Paper on access of consumers to justice and the settlement of consumer disputes in the Single Market', O.J. 1994 C 295/1, 2, criticising the Commission's failure to refer to 'parallel situations where the same types of problems are assuming similar importance - such as environmental protection'.

[14] Office of Fair Trading, International Marketing Supervision Network, Report of First Meeting, London, October 26-27, 1992.

[15] Coordinated at the Brussels headquarters, 10A Rue de la Pépinière, 1000 Brussels; source: Europe No. 6195 (20/21 March 1994), 16.

[16] Commission of the European Communities, 16 November 1993, Green Paper, 'Access of Consumers to Justice and the Settlement of Consumer Disputes in the Single Market', COM(93) 576 final. See also Marco Gasparinetti, 'Accès à la justice et règlement des litiges de consommation dans le Marché unique: le coût des frontières "judiciaires"', Revue du Marché Unique Européen 1994/4, 83.

[17] Office of Fair Trading, op.cit., note 14, at 10.

[18] Id.; Green Paper, note 57; Hans W. Micklitz, 'Cross-Border Consumer Conflicts - A French-German Experience', 16 Journal of Consumer Policy 411 (1993).

[19] Id., at 11.

[20] Article 6(1) EC states: 'Within the scope of application of this Treaty, and without prejudice to any special provisions contained therein, any discrimination on grounds of nationality shall be prohibited.'

[21] Joined Cases C-92 and C-326/92 *Phil Collins* v *Imtrat Handelsgesellschaft* [1993] ECR I-5145; [1993] 3 C.M.L.R. 773.

[22] Case C-398/92 *Mund & Fester v Hatrex Internationaal Transport* [1994] ECR I-467; cf. Comment: Paul Matthews, 'Security for Costs and European Law', [1994] L.M.C.L.Q. 454.

[23] See for such a suggestion in the environment sector, Öko Institut/FIELD, 'Legal Standing for Environmental Associations in the European Community and Draft Proposal for a Council Directive', 3 RECIEL 261 (1994).

[24] Opinion on Green Paper, op.cit., note 13, at 13.

[25] Council Regulation 40/94 of 20 December 1993 on the Community trade mark, O.J. 1994 L 11/1; see also the Proposal for a European Parliament and Council Regulation on Community design, O.J. 1994 C 29/20.

[26] Council Regulation (EC) No 2100/94 of 27 July 1994 on Community plant variety rights, O.J. 1994 L 227/1.

[27] It is modelled on the Protocol on the Settlement of Litigation concerning the Infringement and Validity of Community Patents, O.J. 1989 L 401/34.

[28] French law does not recognise this possibility, see André Huet, 'La marque communautaire: la compétence des juridictions des Etats membres pour connaître de sa validité et de sa contrefaçon (Règlement (CE) n 40/94 du Conseil, du 20 décembre 19993)', *Journal de Droit International* 1994/3, 623, 633 (footnote 40).

[29] Article 93 International Jurisdiction reads as follows: '1. Subject to the provisions of this Regulation as well as to any provisions of the Convention on Jurisdiction and Enforcement applicable by virtue of Article 90, proceedings in respect of the actions and claims referred to in Article 92 shall be brought in the courts of the Member State in which the defendant is domiciled or, if he is not domiciled in any of the Member States, in which he has an establishment. 2. If the defendant is neither domiciled nor has an establishment in any of the Member States, such proceedings shall be brought in the courts of the

Member State in which the plaintiff is domiciled or, if he is not domiciled in any of the Member States, in which he has an establishment. 3. If neither the defendant nor the plaintiff is so domiciled or has such an establishment, such proceedings shall be brought in the courts of the Member State where the office has its seat. 4. Notwithstanding the provisions of paragraphs 1, 2 and 3: (a) Article 17 of the Convention on Jurisdiction and Enforcement shall apply if the parties agree that a different Community trade mark court shall have jurisdiction; (b) Article 18 of that Convention shall apply if the defendant enters an appearance before a different Community trade mark court. 5. Proceedings in respect of the actions and claims referred to in Article 92, with the exception of actions for a declaration of non-infringement of a Community trade mark, may also be brought in the courts of the Member State in which the act of infringement has been committed or threatened, or in which an act within the meaning of Article 9(3), second sentence, has been committed.'

[30] Article 94 Extent of Jurisdiction states: '1. A Community trade mark court whose jurisdiction is based on article 93(1) to (4) shall have jurisdiction in respect of: - acts of infringement committed or threatened within the territory of any of the Member States, - acts within the meaning of article 9(3), second sentence, committed within the territory of any of the Member States. 2. A Community trade mark court whose jurisdiction is based on article 93(5) shall have jurisdiction only in respect of acts committed or threatened within the territory of the Member State in which that court is situated.'

[31] See Helmut Rüßmann, 'Negative Feststellungsklage und Leistungsklage sowie der Zeitpunkt der endgültigen Rechtshängigkeit im Rahmen des EuGVÜ - Entscheidungs- und klärungsbedarf durch den EuGH', IPRax 1995, 76, case note on OLG Hamm, 3 December 1993, IPRax 1995, 104; and Lawrence Collins, 'Negative Declarations and the Brussels Convention', (1992) 109 L.Q.R. 545, case note on the (UK) Court of Appeal's judgment in *The Tatry*; see also the ECJ's judgment in this dispute: Case C-406/92, [1994] ECR not yet reported (judgment of 6 December 1994), paras. 37-45.

[32] See generally George A. Bermann, 'The Use of Anti-Suit

Injunctions in International Litigation', 28 Columbia Journal of Transnational Law 589 (1990).

[33] *Continental Bank v Aeakos Compania Naviera and Others* [1994] 1 W.L.R. 588; [1994] 2 All ER 540; [1994] Lloyd's Rep. 505 (C.A.).

[34] Adrian Briggs, Case and Comment: 'Anti-European Teeth for Choice of Court Clauses', [1994] L.M.C.L.Q. 158, 159. See also Rogerson, [1994] C.L.J. 241 and Bell, (1994) 110 L.Q.R. 204; but see Hartley, (1994) 19 E.L.Rev. 549.

[35] Case C-406/92 The Tatry [1994] ECR not yet reported (judgment of 6 December 1994), para. 43.

[36] Briggs, op.cit., note 34, at 158.

[37] Cited in note 26.

[38] See e.g. J.J.C. Kabel, 'Transborder Advertising and Unfair Competition: The Country of Origin or the Country of Destination? Clarification of the Resolution of the International League of Competition Law', in: D. Kokkini-Iatridou & F.W. Grosheide eds., Eenvormig en Vegelijkend Privaatrecht 1994 (Lelystad 1994), 285.

[39] Rb. Rotterdam 8 January 1979, 11 NYIL 326 (1980); NILR 1981, p. 63 note by Duintjer Tebbens. Affirmed in cassation by the Dutch supreme court: HR 23 September 1988, 21 NYIL 434 (1990).

[40] Chorus, op.cit., note 11, at 234; HR 19 November 1993, NILR 1994, 363 note by Duintjer Tebbens.

[41] See for an ambiguous decision HR 14 April 1989, NJ 1990, 712 CJHB and JCS, discussed in English in: Gerrit Betlem, Civil Liability for Transfrontier Pollution (London/Dordrecht/Boston 1993), 171.

[42] See generally Court of Justice of the European Communities, Civil Jurisdiction and Judgments in Europe (London 1992), Proceedings of the Colloquium on the Interpretation of the Brussels Convention by the Court of Justice considered in the

context of the European Judicial Area, Luxembourg, 11 and 12 March 1991; also available in French, German, Italian and Spanish.

[43] The Brussels Convention of 27 September 1968 on Jurisdiction and the Enforcement of Judgments in Civil and Commercial Matters, consolidated version in: O.J. 1990 C 189/1.

[44] Which states, as far as is relevant here: 'Member States shall, so far as is necessary, enter into negotiations with each other with a view to securing for the benefit of their nationals: . . . the simplification of formalities governing the reciprocal recognition and enforcement of judgments of courts or tribunals and of arbitration awards.'

[45] See Case C-172/91 Volker Sonntag [1993] ECR I-1963, para. 24; Case C-364/92 *SAT Fluggesellschaft v Eurocontrol* [1994] I-43, [1994] 5 C.M.L.R. 208, para. 28; Case C-398/92 *Mund & Fester v Hatrex Internationaal Transport* [1994] ECR I-467, passim.

[46] Alan Dashwood et al., A Guide to the Civil Jurisdiction and Judgments Convention (Deventer 1987), 4.

[47] Case 25/79 *Sanicentral v Collin* [1979] ECR 342, para. 5.

[48] Lugano Convention of 16 September 1988 on jurisdiction and the enforcement of judgments, O.J. 1988 L 319/9.

[49] It reads as follows: 'Subject to the provisions of this Convention, persons domiciled in a Contracting State shall, whatever their nationality, be sued in the courts of that State. Persons who are not nationals of the State in which they are domiciled shall be governed by the rules of jurisdiction applicable to nationals of that State.'

[50] Case 21/76 *Bier v Mines de Potasse d'Alsace* [1976] ECR 1735; [1977] 1 C.M.L.R. 284; [1978] Q.B. 708.

[51] [1976] ECR 1748, 1749.

[52] See para. 20 at [1976] ECR 1747 and the Opinion of A-G Capotorti at 1758; Case C-68/93 *Shevill* [1995] ECR not yet

reported (judgment of 7 March 1995), para. 26 and the Opinion of A-G Léger, No. 13.

[53] Paras. 11 and 17 at [1976] ECR 1746. See the consistent line of subsequent cases from Case 33/78 *Somafer v Saar-Ferngas* [1978] ECR 2183 at 2191 to Case C-68/93 *Shevill* [1995] ECR not yet reported (judgment of 7 March 1995), para. 19.

[54] [1976] ECR 1758.

[55] This codifies Case 240/83 *Procureur de la République v ADBHU* [1985] ECR 531, para. 13.

[56] Cf. the Opinion of A-G Darmon in C-68/93 *Shevill* [1995] ECR not yet reported, No. 65.

[57] To be exact: Case 73/77 *Sanders v Van der Putte* [1977] ECR 2383 at 2390; Case 33/78 *Somafer v Saar-Ferngas* [1978] ECR 2183 at 2191; Case 56/79 *Zelger v Salinitri I* [1980] ECR 89 at 96; Case 34/82 *Peters* v *ZNAV* [1983] ECR 987 at 1001; Case 9/87 *Arcado v Haviland* [1988] ECR 1539 at 1554; Case 189/87 *Kalfelis v Schröder* [1988] ECR 5565 at 5585; Case 32/88 *Six Constructions v Humbert* [1989] ECR 341 at 364; Case C-220/88 *Dumez France and Tracoba* [1990] ECR I-49 at 79; Case C-365/88 *Hagen* [1990] ECR I-1845 at 1864; Case C-261/90 *Reichert II* [1992] ECR I-2149, para. 10; Case C-26/91 *Handte* [1992] ECR I-3967, para. 14.

[58] Adrian Briggs, 'The Brussels Convention', in: A. Barav & D.A. Wyatt eds., 13 Yearbook of European Law 1993 (Oxford 1994), 511, 514.

[59] Cf. Court of Justice, op.cit., note 42, at 39 and 257, 258.

[60] Case C-220/88 *Dumez France and Tracoba* [1990] ECR I-49.

[61] Case C-68/93 *Fiona Shevill and Others v Presse Alliance* [1995] ECR not yet reported (judgment of 7 March 1995).

[62] Cited in note 50.

[63] Cited in note 60.

[64] Opinion of A-G Darmon of 14 July 1994, No. 111; confirmed by A-G Léger on 10 January 1995 (Case C-68/93).

[65] This possibility had also been noted by Briggs, op.cit., note 58, at 524.

[66] See the Opinion of A-G Darmon, C-68/93 *Shevill*, Nos. 30-34.

[67] Id., No. 67; and Opinion of A-G Léger, Nos. 17, 56 and 57.

[68] Cf. in the context of the question of the applicable law in contractual relations, Article 3(1) of the Rome Convention on the Law Applicable to Contractual Obligations, O.J. 1980 L 266. It reads: 'A contract shall be governed by the law chosen by the parties. The choice must be expressed or demonstrated with reasonable certainty by the terms of the contract or the circumstances of the case. By their choice the parties can *select* the law applicable to the whole or a part only of the contract' (emphasis added).

[69] Opinion of A-G Darmon, C-68/93 *Shevill*, Nos. 66 and 79.

[70] Case C-260/89 *ERT* [1991] ECR I-2925, 2963; [1994] 4 C.M.L.R. 540. Article 10 European Convention on Human Rights applies equally to expressions of a commercial nature: European Court of Human Rights 20 November 1989, Markt Intern Verlag, Publ. E.C.H.R., Series A, Vol. 165; (1990) 12 E.H.R.R. 161.

[71] See also D. Lasok & P.A. Stone, Conflict of Laws in the European Community (Abingdon 1987), 232. The ECJ has previously done so in the context of Article 5(1), see Case 133/81 *Ivenel* v *Schwab* [1982] ECR 1891; confirmed in Case 266/85 *Shenavai v Kreischer* [1987] ECR 239, Case 32/88 *Six Constructions v Humbert* [1989] ECR 341 and Case C-125/92 *Mulox* [1993] ECR I-4075.

[72] Paras. 34-41; Case C-365/88 Hagen [1990] ECR I-1845 applied.

[73] Case 189/87 *Kalfelis v Schröder* [1988] ECR 5565.

[74] Case C-68/93 *Fiona Shevill and Others v Presse Alliance*

[1995] ECR not yet reported (judgment of 7 March 1995).

[75] Pres. Rb. Middelburg 24 April 1987, *De Stichting Natuur en Milieu and others v Verenigde Energiebedrijven van het Scheldeland EBES* [1990] I.L.Pr. 246.

[76] See generally Lawrence Collins, 'Provisional and Protective Measures in International Litigation', in: 234 Collected Courses of the Hague Academy of International Law 1992-III (Dordrecht/London/Boston 1993), 9-238 (reprinted in Essays in International Litigation and the Conflict of Laws (Oxford 1994)); and in the context of environmental disputes Betlem, op.cit., note 41, at 144 et seq.

[77] See generally L. Neville Brown & Tom Kennedy, The Court of Justice of the European Communities, 4th ed. (London 1994), 304 and 316-321.

[78] Cheshire and North, Private International Law, 12th ed. by P.M. North & J.J. Fawcett (London etc. 1992), 300.

[79] Case C-136/94, O.J. 1994 C 188/7; preliminary question of the Bundesgerichtshof: BGH 17 March 1994, RIW 1994, 591.

[80] Council Directive 84/450/EEC of 10 September 1984 relating to the approximation of the laws, regulations and administrative provisions of the Member States concerning misleading advertising, O.J. 1984 L 250/17.

[81] See the cases cited in note 45.

[82] It states: 'This Convention shall not affect the application of provisions which, in relation to particular matters, govern jurisdiction or the recognition and enforcement of judgments and which are or will be contained in acts of the institutions of the European Communities or in national laws harmonized in implementation of such acts.'

[83] HR 18 December 1992, NJ 1994, 139 MS and CJHB.

[84] Cited from Betlem, op.cit., note 41, at 376.

[85] Cf. for the counterpart in Community law: Joined Cases 5, 7

and 13-24/66 *Kampffmeyer* v *Commission* [1976] ECR 245 at 262, 263.

[86] Cited from: P.P.C. Haanappel & Ejan Mackaay, New Netherlands Civil Code: Patrimonial Law (Deventer/Boston 1990), 298.

[87] See most recently, regarding environmental liability, HR 30 September 1994, RvdW/CRW 1994, 185; M en R 1994, 112 note by Kottenhagen-Edzes; TMA 1994, p. 159 note by Van Dunné; Bouwrecht 1995, p. 42 note by Bauw (Staat/Shell), on breach of unwritten law. And HR 30 September 1994, RvdW/CRW 1994, 188; TMA 1995, p. 31 note by Bierbooms (Van den Brink) on breach of written law.

[88] Konrad Zweigert & Hein Kötz, Introduction to Comparative Law, Tony Weir trans., 2nd ed. (Oxford 1994), 196.

[89] HR 18 August 1944, NJ 1944/45, 598 (Alkmaar/Noord-Holland).

[90] Margaret Brazier, Street on Torts, 9th ed. (London/Dublin/Edinburgh 1993), 517; Philip S. James, Introduction to English Law, 11th ed. (London 1985), 407.

[91] See Chorus, op.cit., note 11, at 99.

[92] Haanappel/Mackaay, op.cit., note 86, at 137.

[93] Id., at 298.

[94] Zweigert/Kötz, op.cit., note 88, at 662.

[95] Chorus, op.cit., note 11, at 104.

[96] Id., at 219 and 264-266; Asser-Hartkamp III, 9th ed. (Zwolle 1994), No. 34.

[97] HR 9 January 1981, NJ 1981, 227 CJHB; AB 1981, 264 JRSt (Van Dam/Beukeboom); cited from Betlem, op.cit., note 41, at 353.

[98] Summary proceedings: Hof Den Bosch 26 April 1994, KG

1994, 235; first instance: Pres. Rb. Roermond 3 June 1993, M en R 1993, 67. Final judgment on the merits: Rb. Roermond 24 November 1994, Milieurechtspraak 1995, 3; M en R 1995, 11K.

[99] Cited in note 83.

[100] See also M.A. Robesin, 'Procedeerlust Opwekkend en Remmend Privaatrecht', in: R.J.J. van Acht & G.C. Sicking eds., Privaatrecht en milieu (Zwolle 1994), 49-70.

[101] Brownlie, op.cit., note 10, at 307. Cf. for a recognition of this fact by the ECJ in the context of free movement of services: Case C-55/93 Van Schaick [1994] ECR I-4837, paras. 16 and 21.

[102] Cf. Dennis Crighton, 'Pantell (No. 1) Mareva Injunctions: Isolated Incursion into the Field of Public Law or Part of a Strategic Plan?' [1994] Journal of Business Law 8: a critical discussion of *Securities and Investments Board v Pantell S.A.* [1990] 1 Ch. 426, [1989] 2 All ER 673 (Ch.D.); and the Dutch *Benckiser* case, cited in note 41; Gerrit Betlem, 'Private Enforcement of Environmental Law in International Cases', in: Faure/Vervaele/Weale eds., Environmental Standards in the European Union in an Interdisciplinary Framework (Antwerpen/ Apeldoorn 1995), 231-250.

[103] HR 24 November 1989, NJ 1992, 404 DWFV (Focus Veilig/ Lincoln Electric Company), usually cited as the *Interlas* (or diesel welding-generators) case.

[104] Chorus, op.cit., note 11, at 99.

[105] Cited from Betlem, op.cit., note 41, at 123.

[106] See Jan J. Brinkhof, 'Could the President of the District Court of The Hague Take Measures Concerning the Infringement of Foreign Patents?' [1994] EIPR 360; Charles Gielen and Richard Ebbink, 'First Europe-wide Biotech Patent Injunction', [1994] EIPR 243.

[107] Cited above, text accompanying note 92.

[108] As suggested by Polak, op.cit., note 10, Part VI.

[109] Id.

[110] Case C-68/93 *Fiona Shevill and Others v Presse Alliance* [1995] ECR not yet reported (judgment of 7 March 1995).

[111] See Article 4 of the Convention and Case C-318/93 *Brenner and Noller v Dean Witter Reynolds* [1994] ECR I-4275.

[112] cf. Den Haag 19 November 1992, KG 1993, 15; [Belgian] Tijdschrift voor Milieurecht 1993-3, p. 153 note by Faure; TMA 1993, p. 131 note by De Vries; affirmed by the supreme court: HR 25 February 1994, unpublished, No. 15.251 (Rütgers/Sopar v. Stichting Reinwater et al.).

[113] Note 97 and accompanying text.

[114] Cited in note 110.

[115] See also Polak, op.cit., note 10, paras. 20 en 22.

[116] Pres. Rb. Den Haag 4 November 1992, KG 1992, 399 (CIDI et al./Verbeke et al.); affirmed, with minor modifications, on appeal: Hof Den Haag 14 June 1994, KG 1994, 330.

[117] Cited in note 103.

[118] See for a more elaborate discussion of this aspect Betlem, op.cit., note 41, at 130.

[119] Note 112.

[120] Note 98.

[121] R.J.J. van Acht et al., Milieuprivaatrecht (Zwolle 1992), 42.

[122] See HR 27 November 1987, NJ 1988, 722 LWH (Chloé/Peeters) and HR 23 February 1990, NJ 1990, 664 DWFV (Hameco/Smith Kline & French Laboratories).

[123] Pres. Rb. Maastricht 3 February 1993, Milieurechtspraak 1993, 17; [Belgian] Tijdschrift voor Milieurecht 1993-3, p. 155 note by Faure; TMA 1993, p. 135 note by De Vries.

[124] Hof Den Bosch 31 May 1994, Milieurechtspraak 1994, 43; KG 1994, 236; M en R 1994, 105 note by Van Acht. See further Gerrit Betlem, 'Cross-Border Pollution: Two Paradigmatic Dutch Cases', European Review of Private Law, forthcoming.

[125] See § 8 of the Act which states: '(1) If there are facts justifying the assumption that a facility has caused the damage, then the injured party may demand information from the operator of the facility insofar as this is needed to determine the existence of a claim for damages pursuant to this Act. The demand shall be limited to data about the structures used, the nature or concentration of the substances used or emitted, and other effects issuing from the facility ... (2) The right to disclosure pursuant to paragraph (1) shall not exist to the extent that the events must be kept secret pursuant to legal norms or the countervailing interests of the facility operator or of a third party require secrecy. (3) The injured person may demand from the facility operator an opportunity to review existing documents insofar as the assumption is justified that the information provided is incomplete, incorrect, or insufficient, or if the information is not provided within a reasonable time ...', cited from The Cologne Re's Liability Insurance Report 1A/93, 16.

[126] Lugano, 21 June 1993, European Treaty Series, 150; Trb. 1993, 149; 32 I.L.M. 1228 (1993); not (yet) in force.

[127] Article 16 provides as follows: '(1) The person who has suffered the damage may, at any time, request the court to order an operator to provide him with specific information, in so far as this is necessary to establish the existence of a claim for compensation under this Convention. ... The operator shall be required to provide information ... concerning the elements which are available to him and dealing essentially with the particulars of the equipment, the machinery used, the kind and concentration of the dangerous substances or waste as well as the nature of genetically modified organisms or micro-organism. ... (5) The court may refuse a request which places a disproportionate burden on the operator, taking into account all the interests involved. (6) In addition to the restrictions under Article 14, paragraph 2 of this Convention,* which shall apply mutatis mutandis, the operator may refuse to provide information where such information would incriminate him. ...' *

Article 14(2) reads: 'The right of access may be restricted under internal law where it affects: - the confidentiality of the proceedings of public authorities, international relations and national defence; - public security; - matters which are or have been sub judice, or under enquiry (including disciplinary enquiries), or which are the subject of preliminary investigation proceedings; - commercial and industrial confidentiality including intellectual property; - the confidentiality of personal data and/or files; - material supplied by a third party without that party being under a legal obligation to do so; or - material the disclosure of which would make it more likely that the environment to which that material related would be damaged. Information held by public authorities shall be supplied in part where it is possible to separate out information on items concerning the interests referred to above.'

[128] Case C-60/92 *Otto v Postbank* [1993] ECR I-5683; 31 CMLRev. 1375 (1994) note by Kerse. See for the common law approach: Gerard McCormack, 'Self-Incrimination in the Corporate Context', [1993] Journal of Business Law 425.

[129] Polak, op.cit., note 10, at paras. 20 and 29.

[130] Id.

[131] Commission of the European Communities, 'The Operation of the Community's Internal Market after 1992 - Follow-Up to the Sutherland Report', SEC(92) 2277 final (2 December 1992), No. 35.

[132] Op.cit., note 100, at 67.

[133] Cited in note 124.

Chapter 13

La Protection Pénale de l'Environnement en Droit Français

par Marie-José Littmann-Martin

Valeur fondamentale comme la vie ou la propriété privée et publique, l'environnement doit être protégé au même titre par le droit pénal: à côté du meurtre ou du vol, chaque code pénal doit comprendre une ou plusieurs incriminations de pollution, de nuisance, de destruction, de dégradation ou d'autres atteintes à la nature".[1]

Cette résolution, adoptée en 1977 par le Conseil européen du droit de l'environnement, traduit la dimension éthique qu'il convient d'attacher à la préservation d'un environnement de plus en plus menacé.

Confrontée, comme tous les Etats, à des facteurs de déséquilibre telles l'industrialisation, les nouvelles techniques agricoles particulièrement agressives, l'urbanisation accélérée, la France s'est dotée d'une législation qui permet de règlementer les activités humaines les plus perturbantes et de réprimer certaines atteintes aux éléments de l'environnement.

Elle le fit sous la pression conjuguée du droit international, et surtout du droit communautaire particulièrement incitatif, sous la pression aussi de l'opinion publique, des associations de protection de la nature, du monde scientifique aussi dont les cris d'alarme favorisèrent la nécessaire prise de conscience des politiques et des pouvoirs publics.

Ainsi s'est développé un droit de l'environnement, nouvelle branche du droit, et, à sa suite, un droit pénal de l'environnement, très fourni, composé d'une multitude d'infractions soumises à des régimes répressifs différents.

Plusieurs rapports, sérieux et argumentés, mirent en évidence les faiblesses de ce droit pénal de l'environnement et proposèrent des solutions dont la plupart sont restées sans lendemain.

Deux évènements firent espérer une clarification et une mise en ordre de ce droit pénal qui mérite à la fois pleine reconnaissance et présentation rigoureuse: la rédaction d'un nouveau code pénal et le projet de code de l'environnement.

La France vient de se doter d'un nouveau code pénal, entré en vigueur le 1er mars 1994. Le code pénal de 1810 avait cessé d'exprimer l'éthique de notre société dans ce vingtième siècle finissant et il semblait indispensable qu'un nouveau code pénal, à l'instar d'autres codes modernes, prit en compte les valeurs sociales nouvelles telle la protection pénale des éléments de l'environnement. Un livre spécial devait regrouper les délits d'atteinte à l'environnement et les compléter. Le nouveau code pénal devait s'enrichir d'autres livres consacrés au droit social, au droit de la consommation, de l'urbanisme, etc. Le projet, pourtant justifié, a été abandonné. Le contenu du nouveau code pénal recouvre, à quelques exceptions près, celui du code de 1810.

Certes, l'article 410-1 qui énumère les intérêts fondamentaux de la Nation fait référence "à l'équilibre de son milieu naturel et de son environnement", mais cette déclaration reste sans suite car ce livre IV, intitulé maladroitement "Des crimes et délits contre la Nation, l'Etat et la Paix Publique", ne contient aucune infraction d'atteinte à l'environnement à l'exception d'un crime de terrorisme écologique. L'article 421-2 du nouveau code pénal déclare: "constitue également un acte de terrorisme, lorsqu'il est en relation avec une entreprise individuelle ou collective ayant pour but de troubler gravement l'ordre public par l'intimidation ou la terreur, le fait d'introduire dans l'atmosphère, sur le sol, dans le sous-sol ou dans les eaux, y compris celles de la mer territoriale, une substance de nature à mettre en péril la santé de l'homme ou des animaux ou le milieu naturel". Ce crime est sanctionné de 15 ans de réclusion criminelle et de 1. 500.000 Francs d'amende, de réclusion criminelle à perpétuité si l'acte a entraîné la mort d'une ou de plusieurs personnes (art. 421-4 C.P.). La responsabilité pénale des personnes morales peut être retenue (art. 422-4 C.P.).

Le nouveau code pénal est donc profondément décevant. Qu'en est-il du projet de code de l'environnement? Nous étions nombreux à penser qu'une codification du droit de l'environnement simplifierait, harmoniserait et rendrait lisible cet amas de normes juridiques. Madame Ségolène ROYALE lança le projet en juillet 1992, lequel continua sous le ministère BARNIER. Malheureusement, la codification effectuée se fait à droit constant. Il s'agit en fait d'une compilation des textes législatifs, charcutés et ordonnés, selon un plan préétabli. Aucune modification ne peut être apportée aux dispositions législatives. Pour le pénaliste, le résultat dépasse les prévisions les plus pessimistes. Mon seul espoir est que la Commission des lois rejette l'ensemble.

En résumé, ces naissances espérées d'un droit pénal de l'environnement logique, clair, d'utilisation aisée, se soldent par deux échecs, du moins dans l'immédiat. Le droit pénal français de l'environnement reste donc imposant,complexe, souvent incohérent et, paradoxalement, peu appliqué.

Nous présenterons les grandes lignes de ce dispositif répressif (I) et proposerons ensuite quelques explications à son échec relatif (II).

1. Les grandes lignes du dispositif repressif

Un inventaire des infractions serait particulièrement lassant pour l'auditoire. Nous nous bornerons à présenter quelques infractions qui nous semblent caractéristiques (§1). Nous indiquerons ensuite quelques sanctions représentatives des possibilités répressives offertes au juge pénal (§2). Il conviendra aussi de mentionner rapidement les conséquences de certaines dispositions du nouveau code pénal sur la responsabilité pénale du pollueur. Nous évoquerons enfin le rôle des associations de protection de la nature que la loi Barnier du 2 février 1995 vient renforcer (§4).

1.1 §1 - De quelques infractions relatives à la préservation de l'environnement

Précisons que le droit pénal français classe les infractions en trois catégories: les crimes, les délits et les contraventions. Il n'existe pas d'autre crime que celui de terrorisme écologique dont nous avons déjà parlé. Les délits et les contraventions sont, par contre, extrêmement nombreux, d'où la nécessité de les définir. Le délit est l'infraction punie d'un emprisonnement maximum de dix ans, la peine d'amende ne peut être inférieure à 25 000 Francs. La contravention est l'infraction punie d'une peine d'amende qui ne peut excéder 20 000 Francs (présentation volontairement sommaire).

Certaines infractions sanctionnent une atteinte effective à certains éléments du milieu naturel (A), d'autres, les plus nombreuses, répriment la transgression de prescriptions prises pour une protection préventive de la sécurité, de la santé publique et de l'environnement (B).

1.1.1 Infractions d'atteinte à l'environnement

1.1.1.1 Les délits de pollution de l'eau

Il existe, en droit français, non pas un mais trois délits de pollution des eaux. Le plus ancien, la mieux connu et le plus appliqué est celui prévu par l'article L.232-2 du code rural qui protège les eaux douces, de surface et non closes. Ce texte réprime "Quiconque a jeté, déversé ou laissé écouler ... des substances quelconques dont l'action ou les réactions ont détruit le poisson ou nui à sa nutrition, à sa reproduction ou à sa valeur alimentaire". La jurisprudence a privilégié une interprétation large des éléments constitutifs de ce délit qui est devenu l'instrument juridique le plus efficace pour lutter contre la pollution des cours d'eau, lacs, étangs et plans d'eau. L'autorisation administrative de rejet n'étant pas considérée comme un fait justificatif de cette infraction, le pollueur pouvait être condamné, alors que son activité polluante s'exerce conformément à la règlementation des installations classées, par exemple.

Les peines encourues sont un emprisonnement de deux ans, une amende de 120.000 Francs. Le pollueur peut bénéficier d'une transaction dont les conditions sont fixées par le Ministère de l'Environnement et doivent être approuvées par le Procureur de la République. La transaction est utilisée dans plus de quatre vingt pour cent des faits de pollution des eaux douces.

Un délit de pollution des eaux salées a été créé en 1986 et introduit, malencontreusement, dans un décret-loi de 1852 sur les pêches maritimes. C'est le frère jumeau du délit de pollution des eaux douces mais le pollueur n'encourt pas de peine d'emprisonnement, l'article 6-13° du décret de 1852 ne prévoit qu'une amende de 150.000 Francs.

Un délit général de pollution des eaux est prévu par l'article 22 de la loi du 3 janvier 1992. Le délit n'est réalisé que si l'un des dommages visés au texte est constaté: effet nuisible sur la santé - dommage à la flore ou à la faune à l'exception des dommages prévus par les articles L.232-2 du code rural et à l'article 6-13° du décret-loi de 1852 - perturbation du régime normal d'alimentation en eau -limitation d'usage des eaux de baignade. La transaction n'est pas prévue. En revanche, le pollueur ne peut être condamné si la pollution est liée à des rejets autorisés et conformes aux prescriptions fixées par l'administration. Les peines sont sévères: deux ans d'emprisonnement, 500.000 Francs d'amende.

Ce texte présente un intérêt certain pour réprimer la pollution des eaux souterraines, des nappes phréatiques si vulnérables car ces milieux ne pouvaient être protégés par l'article L.232-2 du code rural. Malheureusement, le rôle reconnu à l'autorisation administrative de rejet lui retire une grande partie de son intérêt.

Donc, trois délits de pollution des eaux, soumis à des conditions de réalisation et à des régimes répressifs différents, alors qu'un seul, correctement rédigé, eut suffi. Par contre, il n'existe pas de délit de pollution de l'air, ni de délit de contamination des sols. Ces atteintes ne seront sanctionnées que si le pollueur a transgressé les prescriptions administratives règlementant les activités humaines, sources de telles pollutions. Dans ces domaines, le vide juridique est incontestable.

1.1.1.2 Les atteintes à la faune, à la flore et aux fossiles protégés

1° - S'agissant de la faune protégée, l'article L.211-1-1° du code rural interdit "la destruction ou l'enlèvement des oeufs ou des nids, la mutilation, la destruction, la capture ou l'enlèvement, la naturalisation d'animaux de ces espèces ou qu'ils soient vivants ou morts, leur transport, colportage, leur utilisation, leur mise en vente, leur vente ou leur achat". L'article 56 de la loi n° 95-101 du 2 février 1995 ajoute à ces interdictions "la perturbation intentionnelle" et "la détention".

En apparence, toutes les activités néfastes pour l'animal sont prohibées mais, d'une part, elles ne concernent que les animaux d'une espèce figurant dans des listes limitatives souvent incomplètes par rapport aux directives européennes et Conventions Internationales et, d'autre part, les espèces faisant l'objet de protection partielle se multiplient contrairement aux exigences législatives.[2]

2° - S'agissant de la flore protégée soit par des listes nationales, soit par des listes régionales, l'article L.211-1-2° du code rural interdit: "la destruction, la coupe, la mutilation, l'arrachage, la cueillette ou l'enlèvement des végétaux de ces espèces, de leurs fructifications ou de toute autre forme prise par ces espèces au cours de leur cycle biologique (art. 56-III, loi du 02.02.1995), leur transport, leur colportage, leur utilisation, leur mise en vente, vente ou achat, et la détention de spécimens prélevés dans le milieu naturel (art. 56-III de la loi du 02.02.1995)".

Cette profusion d'interdictions devrait mettre la flore protégée à l'abri de toute atteinte même minime. La réalité est différente car la règlementation prise en application de ce texte ne reprend pas tous les interdits, telle la cueillette, et soustrait à ces prohibitions "les parcelles habituellement cultivées".[3]

Notons aussi l'incrimination de "la destruction, de l'altération ou de la dégradation du milieu particulier à ces espèces animales ou végétales" (art. L.211-1-3° du code rural).

La loi Barnier du 2 février 1995 a comblé une lacune souvent dénoncée en créant un délit d'introduction d'espèces dans le milieu naturel, activité gravement perturbatrice qui ne faisait pas l'objet d'une prohibition générale.

L'article L.211-3 (nouveau) du code rural déclare: "Afin de ne porter préjudice ni aux milieux naturels ni à la faune et à la flore sauvages, est interdite l'introduction dans le milieu naturel, volontaire, par négligence ou par imprudence:

1° de tout spécimen d'une espèce animale à la fois non indigène au territoire d'introduction et non domestique;

2° de tout spécimen d'une espèce végétale à la fois non indigène au territoire d'introduction et non cultivée;

3° de tout spécimen de l'une des espèces animales ou végétales désignées par l'autorisation administrative".

Des dérogations peuvent être prises par l'administration à "des fins agricoles, piscicoles ou forestières ou pour des motifs d'intérêt général et après évaluation des conséquences de cette introduction". Il est trop tôt pour apprécier l'impact de telles dérogations.

3° - L'article L.211-1 du code rural interdit aussi "la destruction des sites contenant des fossiles permettant d'étudier l'histoire du monde vivant ainsi que les premières activités humaines et la destruction ou l'enlèvement des fossiles présents sur ces sites" (art. 56-X de la loi du 2 février 1995). Cette disposition n'a jamais été appliquée, de telles activités étant poursuivies sous la qualification de vol ou de destruction volontaire de la chose d'autrui, infractions prévues par le code pénal dès lors que l'agent n'est pas propiétaire du site.

Les peines encourues par l'auteur de ces comportements interdits sont un emprisonnement de six mois et une amende de 60 000 Francs à l'exception des perturbations intentionnelles et des introductions de spécimens par négligence qui, à ce jour, ne sont pas pénalement sanctionnées.

Ajoutons à ces infractions d'atteinte effective à l'environnement, le délit de destruction de territoire classé en réserve naturelle et celui de modification de l'état ou de l'aspect de ces territoires effectuée sans autorisation.

Point faible de ces infractions: elles ne sont réalisées donc ne peuvent être poursuivies et sanctionnées que si le résultat prévu par la loi est effectivement constaté. La tentative de ces atteintes n'est pas incriminée et, de ce fait, n'est pas punissable. Ainsi, le tir manqué sur un aigle royal, espèce protégée, ne sera qu'une contravention à la police de la chasse, sanction notoirement insuffisante.

1.1.2 *Les manquements aux prescriptions administratives*

Le législateur est intervenu pour règlementer l'exercice d'activités humaines présentant des risques d'atteinte à l'environnement. Ces législations et règlementations spécifiques prévoient de très nombreuses infractions dont la réalisation est indépendante de toute atteinte effective à l'environnement.

La typologie de ces infractions est celle que l'on rencontre dans le droit pénal administratif. Sont généralement réprimés:

1 l'absence d'autorisation alors que l'activité est soumise à autorisation. Il s'agit généralement d'un délit.

2 l'absence de déclaration alors que l'activité doit faire l'objet d'une déclaration, la qualification est généralement contraventionnelle.

3 le non-respect des prescriptions administratives. Cette infraction, selon les textes, est un délit ou une contravention.

4 le non-respect des prescriptions d'un arrêté préfectoral de mise en demeure. La qualification est délictuelle.

5 la poursuite de l'exploitation malgré une interdiction administrative ou judiciaire. Il s'agit d'un délit.

6 l'omission d'information, l'information inexacte lorsque celle-ci est légalement obligatoire.

Ces infractions se rencontrent dans la loi du 19 juillet 1976 relative aux installations classées pour la protection de l'environnement, dans la loi du 3 janvier 1992 sur l'eau, et, partiellement, dans la loi du 15 juillet 1975 relative aux déchets (voir aussi la loi du 13 juillet 1992 concernant les organismes génétiquement modifiés et la loi du 31 décembre 1992, lutte contre le bruit).

La plupart de ces lois sont dotées d'un système répressif particulièrement élaboré assorti parfois de sanctions sévères.

La technique législative utilisée est toujours la même. Quelques articles de la loi fixent des sanctions corectionnelles, conformément à l'article 34 de la Constitution française, les peines et mesures complémentaires et évoquent, en termes souvent vagues, les comportements délictueux ainsi sanctionnés. Il appartient ensuite aux décrets et aux arrêtés de fixer plus précisément les éléments cosntitutifs des infractions. Cette pratique du "chèque en blanc" délivré à l'autorité administrative est critiquée car préoccupante pour le respect des droits et libertés individuels.

Des exemples concrets seront proposés lors de la présentation de cette intervention. Indiquons à présent quelques sanctions et/ou mesures dont disposent parfois les juridictions pénales.

1.2 §2 - De quelques sanctions ou mesures spécifiques

Il convient de distinguer peines principales et peines de mesures complémentaires, le but étant de donner quelques informations indicatives.

1.2.1 Les peines principales

Leur nature ne présente aucune originalité. Les délits sont sanctionnés de peine d'emprisonnement et de peine d'amende, les contraventions généralement de la peine d'amende prévue pour les contraventions de la 5è classe, soit un maximum de 10.000 Francs (art.131-13 C.P.)

Par contre, la hiérarchie des infractions résultant du choix des peines décidé par le législateur est souvent déroutante. L'impression dominante est la logique incertaine des options législatives.

Ainsi les trois délits de pollution des eaux sont sanctionnés de peines différentes (voir supra). La loi du 19 juillet 1976 relative aux installations classées pour la protection de l'environnement punit d'un an d'emprisonnement et de 500.000 Francs d'amende, l'exploitation sans autorisation lorsque celle-ci est exigée (art. 18), l'exploitation d'une installation nucléaire de base ou la cessation de cette exploitation sans autorisation sont des contraventions de cinquième classe (amende de 10000 Francs) (art. 12 du décret du 11 décembre 1963).

Le refus d'informer l'administration ou l'information inexacte concernant certaines catégories de déchets réalisent des délits prévus par l'article 24-1° de la loi du 15 juilllet 1975 relative à l'élimination des déchets et à la récupération des matériaux (peines encourues, deux ans d'emprisonnement et/ou 120.000 Francs d'amende); la non-déclaration d'un accident nucléaire reste une contravention (art. 12-4 du décret du 11 décembre 1963).

Ramasser un hérisson mort et le transporter est un délit (six mois d'emprisonnement, 60.000 Francs d'amende), tirer sur un ours et le manquer, une simple contravention.

Le délit d'obstacle au contrôle des agents et fonctionnaires habilités est prévu dans chaque loi relative à l'environnement et sanctionné de peines différentes.

L'indigence et souvent l'inadaptation des peines princpales peuvent être corrigées par la juridiction pénale grâce aux peines alternatives prévues par l'article 131-6 du code pénal, qui offre un large éventail de sanctions pouvant être prononcées à titre de peines principales telle l'interdiction professionnelle pour une durée de cinq ans au plus.

1.2.2 Les peines et mesures complémentaires

Dans certains secteurs, l'effort créatif du législateur est indéniable. Nous n'insisterons pas sur la suspension ou sur l'interdiction de l'activité irrégulière, sanction souvent prévue, mais sur la remise en état des lieux qui constitue la mesure la plus efficace pour prévenir de nouvelles atteintes à l'environnement et pour remédier aux conséquences d'une première infraction.

De nombreuses lois prévoient une telle mesure et permettent son prononcé dans un cadre innovant: l'ajournement de peine avec injonction de restaurer le milieu dégradé. Citons l'article 18 de la loi du 19 juillet 1976 relative aux installations classées, les articles 22 et 23 de la loi du 3 janvier 1992 concernant la restauration du milieu aquatique dévasté par la pollution, certaines dispositions de la loi "déchets" du 15 juillet 1975, malheureusement peu cohérentes, l'obligation de détruire l'ouvrage irrégulier ou de procéder à la réaffection des sols en vue du rétablissement des lieux dans leur état antérieur (art. L.480-5 Code de l'urbanisme qui ne prévoit pas l'ajournement de peine avec injonction).

Cette mesure devrait être généralisée et plus fréquemment utilisée par les juridictions pénales car elle constitue une réelle avancée.

1.3 §3 - La responsabilité pénale de l'agent et les innovations du nouveau Code pénal

Deux nous semblent notables: la suppression des délits matériels et la responsabilité pénale des personnes morales pour certaines infractions.

1.3.1 La suppression des délits matériels

Pour apprécier la portée de cette nouveauté, il convient de distinguer la situation avant le 1er mars 1994, date d'entrée en vigueur du nouveau code pénal, et après cette date.

1.3.1.1 Situation avant le 1er mars 1994

Le rôle joué par l'élément intentionnel pour retenir la culpabilité de l'agent ne cessait de s'amoindrir. De nombreux délits concernant l'environnement étaient considérés comme des "délits matériels". Le délit matériel est réalisé, et par conséquent punissable, "du seul fait de l'accomplissement matériel des faits incriminés et indépendamment de la constatation d'une volonté de transgression ou d'un comportement fautif". Cette qualification permet le déclenchement d'un mécanisme implaccable, l'agent étant déclaré coupable dès que les éléments matériels de l'infraction sont prouvés et qu'ils lui sont imputés. L'absence de faute n'est pas une cause d'exonération de sa responsabilité pénale.

La chambre criminelle de la cour de cassation, dans l'arrêt Ferrier du 28 avril 1977, avait attribué la qualification de délit matériel au délit de pollution des eaux douces réprimé alors par l'article 434-1 du code rural (devenu l'article L. 232-2 du même code). Une solution identique avait été implicitement retenue par le législateur pour le délit de pollution des eaux, prévu par l'article

22 de la loi du 3 janvier 1992. Malgré les réactions défavorables d'une doctrine majoritaire qui s'élevait contre la prolifération arbitraire des délits matériels, la généralisation de cette solution n'était pas à exclure, s'agissant des infractions relatives à l'environnement.

L'application du nouveau code pénal vient modifier cette situation.

1.3.1.2 Situation depuis le 1er mars 1994

Le nouveau code pénal supprime les délits matériels. En effet, l'article 121-3 déclare:

"Il n'y a point de crime ou de délit sans intention de la commettre. Toutefois, lorsque la loi le prévoit, il y a délit en cas d'imprudence, de négligence ou de mise en danger délibéré de la personne d'autrui. Il n'y a point de contravention en cas de force majeure".

Le principe général, posé par le nouveau code pénal, est qu'un délit ne peut être imputé à son auteur, que si son comportement a été volontaire et conscient selon la définition du dol général.

Exceptionnellement, le comportement fautif suffira pour engager la responsabilité pénale de l'auteur du délit mais il faudra que cette exception soit prévue par les lois spéciales et que la faute soit caractérisée. A défaut d'une telle précision législative, on retombe dans le régime général.

La solution est claire pour les délits créés postérieurement au 1er mars 1994. Le texte, en revanche, n'apporte pas de solution pour les délits créés antérieurement.

L'article 339 de la loi n° 92-1336 du 16 décembre 1992, dite "loi d'adaptation" énonce :

"Tous les délits non intentionnels réprimés par les textes antérieurs à l'entrée en vigueur de la présente loi demeurent constitués en cas d'imprudence, de négligence ou de mise en danger délibéré de la personne d'autrui même lorsque la loi ne le prévoit pas".

S'agissant des délits considérés comme matériels, la culpabilité de l'auteur devra se fonder sur un comportement fautif, puisque ces nouvelles exigences du code pénal sont favorables au prévenu et, de ce fait, doivent rétroagir. La jurisprudence s'est déjà prononcée en ce sens à propos du délit de pollution des eaux réprimé par l'article L.232-2 du code rural. Ainsi, des industriels, poursuivis pour pollution de rivière sur le fondement de l'article L.232-2 du code rural ont été relaxés au motif "que la preuve d'une imprudence ou d'une négligence qui leur serait imputable n'est pas rapportée" (Caen, 4 novembre 1994, Tb. Corr. Valenciennes, 30 juin 1994, confirmé par Douai, 14 février 1995, Droit pénal 1995, comm. 127).

Ces exigences nouvelles du code pénal mettent fin à la responsabilité pénale quasi automatique des dirigeants d'entreprises polluantes. Leur situation, désormais plus confortable, pourra encore être améliorée par l'innovation majeure concernant la responsabilité pénale des personnes morales.

1.3.2 La responsabilité pénale des personnes morales

Son principe a été adopté après des débats parlementaires acharnés.

Il ne s'agit pas d'une responsabilité pénale générale des personnes morales. Celle-ci ne peut être retenue que si le texte d'incrimination la prévoit expressément.

La loi du 16 décembre 1992 prévoit la responsabilité pénale des personnes morales pour de nombreuses infractions relatives à l'environnement. Citons les infractions à la loi du 2 août 1961 relative à la lutte contre les pollutions atmosphériques et les odeurs, les infractions à la loi du 15 juillet 1975 relative aux déchets, certaines infractions à la loi du 19 juillet 1976, les infractions à la loi du 3 janvier 1992 sur l'eau. Cette liste a été complétée par la loi "Barnier" du 2 février 1995 qui corrige certaines anomalies. Ainsi, tous les délits de pollution des eaux pourront être imputés à la personne morale (auparavant, seul le délit prévu par l'article 22 de la loi du 3 janvier 1992 pouvait lui être reproché). Cette extension concerne les infractions à la loi du 7 juillet 1976 relative à la prévention et à la répression de la pollution marine par des opérations d'immersion effectuées par les navires et aéronefs et à la lutte contre la pollution marine accidentelle, et les infractions à la loi du 7 juillet 1976 relative à la prévention et à la répression de la pollution de la mer par les opérations d'incinération (art. 81).

Des peines spécifiques sont prévues pour sanctionner les personnes morales. L'amende, notamment, peut être quintuplée par rapport à l'amende encourue par le coupable, personne physique.

A ces prévisions textuelles s'ajoutent des conditions particulières dont l'interprétation et la mise en oeuvre soulèveront de nombreuses difficultés qu'il serait inutile d'évoquer dans le cadre général de cette intervention. L'article 121-2 du code pénal exige que "l'infraction soit commise pour le compte de la personne morale, par son organe ou représentant". Des conditions plus strictes sont fixées pour engager la responsabilité des collectivités territoriales et de leurs groupements.Ces innovations sont trop récentes pour qu'il soit possible d'en mesurer l'impact. Leur potentiel répressif n'est pas négligeable, les risques de dérives ne doivent pas être sous estimés dans l'hypothèse où la responsabilité pénale du groupe se substituerait à celle du dirigeant. On assisterait alors à une dilution des responsabilités défavorable à toute prise de conscience lucide afin de concilier activités humaines et protection de l'environnement. Précisons que la responsabilité pénale du dirigeant peut être retenue cumulativement avec celle de la personne morale.

1.4 §4 - Le rôle des associations agréées de protection de l'environnement

Toute victime d'une infraction peut se constituer partie civile devant les juridictions pénales pour obtenir réparation. Cette constitution de partie civile peut mettre en mouvement l'action publique contre la volonté du ministère public qui aurait décidé de ne pas poursuivre. La victime peut saisir directement le tribunal de police, compétent pour juger les contraventions, le tribunal correctionnel, compétent pour juger les délits. Ce mode de saisine par citation directe suppose que la victime a identifié le ou les auteurs de l'infraction et réuni des preuves suffisantes quant à leur culpabilité. La victime de l'infraction peut aussi saisir le juge d'instruction, en matière criminelle ou correctionnelle, mais non en matière contraventionnelle. Ses pouvoirs sont donc considérables puisqu'ils peuvent porter atteinte au monopole du ministère public dans sa décision de poursuivre ou de classer, conformément au principe de l'opportunité des poursuites.

C'est pourquoi des conditions limitatives sont exigées par le code de procédure pénale pour que la recevabilité de l'action civile des victimes d'infraction soit déclarée recevable devant les juridictions répressives. Le préjudice invoqué doit être personnel et en relation directe avec l'infraction (art. 2 C.P.P.).

En conséquence, les associations qui poursuivent une mission d'intérêt général, telle la défense des milieux naturels, la protection de la faune et de la flore sauvages et prétendent qu'une infraction lèse leur intérêt associatif ou statutaire, se verront répondre "qu'elles ne justifient pas, en l'espèce, d'un préjudice personnel et direct, distinct du préjudice social dont la poursuite est confiée au ministère public"...[4]

Conscient du rôle déterminant joué par les associations pour une application effective des règles protectrices de l'environnement, le législateur les habilite à exercer l'action civile devant les juridictions répressives. Cette habilitation les dispense alors de démontrer la réalité d'un préjudice personnel et directement lié à l'infraction constatée. Le préjudice associatif est présumé découler de certaines infractions. L'action civile de telles associations est alors recevable et elles peuvent prendre l'initiative de déclencher des poursuites, palliant ainsi l'inertie du Parquet.

La plupart des lois récentes relatives à l'environnement prévoyaient de telles habilitations en faveur de certaines associations. Néanmoins, la situation était chaotique car les conditions fixées pour ces habilitations variaient d'une loi à l'autre. En outre, le domaine de l'habilitation était limité aux infractions propres à chaque texte[5].

La loi Barnier du 2 février 1995 apporte, enfin, la solution uniforme et générale souhaitée depuis de nombreuses années.

Toute association agréée de protection de l'environnement au sens de l'article L.252-1 du code rural "pourront exercer les droits reconnus à la partie civile en ce qui concerne les faits portant un préjudice direct ou indirect aux intérêts collectifs qu'elles ont pour objet de défendre et constituant une infraction aux dispositions législatives relatives à la protection de la nature et de l'environnement, à l'amélioration du cadre de vie, à la protection de l'eau, de l'air, des sols, des sites et paysages, à l'urbanisme ou ayant pour objet la lutte contre les pollutions et les nuisances ainsi qu'aux textes pris pour leur application" (art. L.252-3 du code rural). Cette innovation est pleinement satisfaisante car elle lève tout obstacle juridique à l'action des associations bénéficiant d'un agrément.

Certaines personnes morales de droit public bénéficient aussi, grâce à la loi "Barnier", d'une habilitation qui devrait leur permettre de saisir les juridictions pénales pour assurer la défense d'intérêts généraux souvent délaissés par le Procureur de la République (art. L.253-1 du code rural).

Ce panorama du droit pénal français se présente comme relativement complet, permettant, malgré certaines lacunes, de lutter correctement contre les atteintes portées aux éléments de l'environnement. Pourtant, son efficacité reste aléatoire.

2. Une efficacité aleatoire

"La loi pénale sera certainement jugée inefficace - et elle est doublement ineffective - si une infraction ayant été commise, une punition ne s'ensuit pas"[6]. Tel est souvent le cas en matière d'environnement, encore qu'une évolution s'amorce et que l'on constate depuis quelques années un certain frémissement.

Cette inefficacité se vérifie à deux niveaux:

- au niveau des poursuites, rares, parfois inexistantes dans certains secteurs,

- au niveau des sanctions, lorsque les juridictions pénales ont été saisies, trop modérées et (ou) mal adaptées.

2.1 La rareté des poursuites

Les magistrats du parquet en conviennent volontiers, se plaignant tout à la fois pour expliquer leur inertie: "de la multiplicité et de la trop grande technicité des textes" fixant les prescriptions et, de ce fait, les éléments constitutifs des infractions[7]. Ils avouent aussi ne pas toujours saisir la gravité sociale des comportements délictueux en matière d'environnement, faute d'une formation appropriée dans les sciences de la nature.

Des raisons sociologiques mais aussi juridiques expliquent donc une situation qui devrait évoluer avec l'arrivée de jeunes magistrats plus conscients des menaces graves qui pèsent sur notre planète.

Mais la décision de poursuivre prise par les magistrats du ministère public suppose qu'ils soient correctement informés des infractions commises, qu'ils soient persuadés que des poursuites sont nécessaires et qu'ils maîtrisent les textes applicables afin de qualifier correctement les comportements délictueux dont ils ont connaissance. Or, ces conditions ne sont pas toujours réunies: information et formation sont également défectueuses.

2.1.1 Le manque d'information

A l'origine de ce manque d'information, la non constatation des infractions par les fonctionnaires et agents habilités à cette mission, la non transmission des procès-verbaux par les administrations aux parquets au mépris des textes l'imposant, les transactions avec le délinquant qu'elles soient ou non prévues par la loi.

La non constatation des infractions est une évidence. Gendarmes et policiers n'ont ni le temps, ni la formation technique pour le faire. Agents et fonctionnaires spécialement affectés à cette mission se dérobent. Or, dans ce domaine, le comportement des corps spécialisés est déterminant tant pour l'établissement des procès-verbaux constatant les infractions que pour leur transmission au Procureur de la République. Mais la plupart n'ont pas la fibre répressive et ne perçoivent pas toujours l'intérêt de la voie pénale car ils ne sont pas systématiquement informés des suites que l'autorité judiciaire donne à leurs initiatives.

C'est pourquoi, l'inspecteur des installations classées par exemple, ne dressera procès-verbal que lorsque l'industriel en infraction aura refusé toute négociation. L'agent verbalisateur attend alors de la voie pénale un résultat qu'il n'a pu obtenir par le recours à des sanctions administratives. Certes, il arrive que la situation délictueuse fasse rapidement l'objet d'un procès-verbal. Elle concerne alors des délinquants dont le "profil" prive la négociation de tout intérêt (cas de ferrailleurs marginaux exerçant une activité de collecte et de stockage artisanale). Signalons aussi la pression des municipalités, de l'opinion publique lorsqu'elle est soutenue et amplifiée par les médias.

De nombreuses situations infractionnelles ne sont donc jamais officiellement constatées ou, lorsqu'elles le sont, ne parviennent pas à la connaissance du Procureur de la République, faute de transmission des procès-verbaux par la hiérarchie.

Un observateur particulièrement attentif des pratiques administratives constate: "Une mise en oeuvre pragmatique, faisant une large place à la négociation et utilisant les ressources fournies par le droit, en vue de l'obtention de certains résultats matériels. La recherche d'une efficacité concrète l'emporte ici sur le souci d'un légalisme strict. On peut dire dans ce sens que l'administration des installations classées gère pragmatiquement les risques industriels et constitue une sorte de "magistrature technique".[8]

Ces pratiques courantes expliquent la mauvaise information du Ministère Public. Elle explique aussi les réactions de méfiance des autorités judiciaires lorsque l'information leur parvient et sont un élément, parmi d'autres, des classements sans suite.

2.1.2 Les classements sans suite

L'impression dominante est qu'ils sont nombreux. Mais les statistiques dans ce domaine restent incomplètes et peu fiables.

Plusieurs facteurs concourent à cette situation qui influent aussi sur les décisions des juridictions répressives.

Nous évoquerons tout d'abord "la formation déficitaire des magistrats pour ce qui touche à l'environnement", formation qualifiée de "fragmentaire et de limitée"[9]. La gravité de ces infractions est sous estimée par rapport à la délinquance dite "classique". Le voleur sera plus systématiquement poursuivi que l'industriel qui empoisonne un cours d'eau ou stocke irrégulièrement des déchets toxiques. Le premier est un associal qui mérite un châtiment, le second, un chef d'entreprise, créateur d'emplois, souvent influent et respecté, qui parfois indemnise spontanément les victimes directes des nuisances qu'il provoque.

Le Ministère de la Justice ne fait rien pour infléchir cette vision rétrograde de la délinquance. Aucune circulaire n'a eu pour objectif de sensibiliser les magistrats à ces formes nouvelles de délinquance qui menace le patrimoine des générations futures et peut avoir des effets irréversibles. "Les bases ou les axes d'une politique répressive en la matière ne sont pas actuellement clairement définis, les actions des parquets étant abandonnées aux initiatives individuelles."[10] "La délinquance écologique n'est plus désignée comme un secteur prioritaire de l'activité pénale."[11]

Nous signalerons ensuite les réticences des magistrats à se transformer en gendarmes du droit administratif: "L'autorité judiciaire semble considérer qu'elle n'est saisie que de manière njustement sélective, dans des conditions et pour des finalités qui lui échappent."[12]

Surchargés de travail, les magistrats ne s'empressent pas de porter secours à une administration incapable de faire respecter les règles qu'elle édicte, qui dispose de pouvoirs coercitifs importants et qui, généralement, les tient à l'écart, préferant gérer seule ce type de situation.

A ces raisons psycho-sociologiques s'ajoutent des causes techniques de classement sans suite: procès-verbaux mal rédigés, incomplets, manque d'experts compétents, coûts prohibitifs des expertises.

Donc classer paraît plus simple surtout quand le pollueur propose de réparer les dommages résultant de l'infraction et/ou d'améliorer le fonctionnement de ses installations. Cette décision peut être prise dans un cadre légal: celui de la médiation pénale. En effet, la loi du 4 janvier 1993 prévoit que le Procureur de la République peut, préalablement à sa décision sur l'action publique et avec l'accord des parties, décider de recourir à une médiation s'il lui apparaît qu'une telle mesure est susceptible d'assurer la réparation du dommage causé à la victime, de mettre fin au trouble résultant de l'infraction et de contribuer au reclassement de l'auteur de l'infraction (art. 41 in fine, C.P.P.).

Les associations ne peuvent pas toujours pallier l'inertie du parquet malgré les habilitations dont elles bénéficient. Difficultés juridiques et financières sont souvent dissuasives.

On comprendra donc que le contentieux pénal concernant les infractions relatives à l'environnement soit rare. "Quelques miettes pour l'appareil judiciaire" selon l'heureuse formule de M.P. Lascoumes[13]. Lorsque les juridictions pénales sont saisies, les peines prononcées sont généralement indulgentes donc peu dissuasives et (ou) mal adaptées à ce type d'infraction.

2.2 Une répression souvent decevante

Indulgence des peines principales et manque d'originalité dans leur choix, utilisation trop rare des peines et mesures complémentaires, dommages et intérêts dérisoires accordés aux associations de protection de l'environnement, telles sont les principales caractéristiques qui se dégagent de la jurisprudence qui ne doivent pas occulter certaines prémices d'une évolution.

2.2.1 Des sanctions généralement peu dissuasives

Lorsque la pollution des eaux douces superficielles était sanctionnée par l'article 434-1 du code rural (devenu l'article 407 puis l'article L.232-2 du même code), la peine d'amende encourue ne pouvait dépasser 8 000 Francs. Ce maximum, pourtant dérisoire, n'a jamais été prononcé. Le montant moyen des amendes prononcées était de 2 000 Francs.

A ce prix, il s'agissait moins d'une sanction que d'un permis de polluer sans frais. En effet, il était plus avantageux pour le pollueur de courir le risque, très relatif, de nouvelles poursuites que d'entreprendre des travaux d'assainissement. En 1984, le législateur porta le maximum de l'amende à 120.000 Francs et la peine d'emprisonnement à deux ans. On constata alors une élévation significative des amendes prononcées, encore que les cours d'Appel marquent plus d'indulgence que les tribunaux correctionnels.

Ainsi, le tribunal correctionnel de Mont-de-Marsan, le 22 octobre 1991, avait condamné le directeur d'une coopérative pour infraction à l'article L.232-2 du code rural à 40 000 francs d'amende, la cour d'Appel de Pau, le 28 janvier 1992, prononça une amende de 50 000 francs dont 40 000 francs avec sursis (Juris-Data, réf. 040753). Les amendes de 10 000 francs restent fréquentes. Les peines d'emprisonnement sont rares et accompagnées de sursis.

Les condamnations prononcées pour manquement à la règlementation des installations classées offrent de nombreux exemples de curieuse mansuétude. Le tribunal de police de Trévoux, le 25 septembre 1980, condamna à 600 Francs d'amende l'exploitant d'une installation qui, depuis des années, ne respectait pas les prescriptions de l'arrêté préfectoral. Mécontent, le condamné fit appel! Le tribunal correctionnel de Bourg-en-Bresse, le 7 décembre 1983, reconnut coupable d'infraction à l'article 434-1 du code rural et d'infraction à la règlementation des installations classées, l'exploitant qui polluait les eaux et persistait à faire fonctionner une installation classée malgré une mesure de suspension prise par le Préfet. Sanction: dispense de peine.

L'indulgence est plus manifeste encore s'agissant d'infraction à la loi du 10 juillet 1976 relative à la protection de la nature. Alors que les peines encourues pour la destruction d'un animal d'une espèce protégée peuvent atteindre 6 mois d'emprisonnement et une amende de 60 000 francs, les amendes prononcées excèdent rarement 3 000 francs. Mais des sanctions plus fortes sont retenues à l'encontre des taxidermistes qui naturalisent des espèces protégées, encore que les amendes ne soient pas à la mesure des profits réalisés.

Mis à part quelques cas spectaculaires où les juges, manifestement scandalisés et soucieux de faire un exemple, décident de frapper fort[14], les peines choisies ne renforcent pas la crédibilité du droit pénal dans ce domaine.

Pourtant une évolution se dessine vers un traitement plus énergique de certaines atteintes à l'environnement. La cour d'Appel d'Agen, le 15 octobre 1990, a confirmé une amende de 50.000 francs, prononcée par un tribunal correctionnel à l'encontre d'un exploitant de gravières qui avait détruit une frayère d'esturgeons, espèce protégée[15].

2.2.2 L'utilisation trop rare des peines et mesures complémentaires

La remise en état des lieux, comme la démolition de l'ouvrage irrégulier, l'enlèvement des déchets stockés illégalement et la décontamination des sols, la restauration des milieux dégradés, l'ordre de mise en conformité avec la règlementation, sont des mesures beaucoup plus efficaces qu'une condamnation à une peine d'amende. De nombreuses lois relatives à l'environnement donnent pouvoir aux juges répressifs de les prononcer, parfois dans le cadre très nouveau de l'ajournement de peine avec injonction sous astreinte. Le sort du coupable sera alors fixé à l'occasion d'une nouvelle audience en fonction de la diligence mise pour exécuter la mesure.

Il est décevant de constater le peu d'empressement des juridictions pénales à les utiliser. L'encombrement des tribunaux, le manque de compétence technique des juges, la difficulté d'assurer le suivi et le contrôle de l'exécution de ces mesures expliquent cette situation regrettable. Depuis l'entrée en vigueur du nouveau code pénal "le juge de l'application des peines, dans le ressort duquel le prévenu a sa résidence, s'assure soit par lui-même soit par toute personne qualifiée de l'exécution des prescriptions énumérées par l'injonction de la juridiction" (art. 747-4 C. Proc. Pén.). Cette innovation devrait avoir des effets positifs quant à l'exécution des mesures destinées à corriger les conséquences de certaines infractions.

D'autres signes annoncent qu'une prise en compte plus sérieuse du droit pénal de l'environnement est perceptible.

Cycles de formation adressés aux magistrats, meilleure collaboration des parquets et des administrations concernées, accueil plus favorable fait aux associations bien que les dommages et intérêts octroyés restent toujours aussi dérisoires (2 000, 3 000 francs) et risquent de décourager ces bénévoles dans l'exercice d'une mission souvent ingrate.[16]

Certes, réprimer n'est pas le remède miracle qui sauvera l'environnement des maux qui l'accablent mais c'est un moyen de reconnaître qu'il a été porté atteinte à une valeur sociale essentielle qu'il faut défendre au même titre que d'autres, plus traditionnelles. L'évolution d'une politique criminelle jusqu'alors défaillante semble amorcée, encore timide mais encourageante. L'avenir dira s'il s'agissait d'un frémissement sans lendemain ou d'un véritable bouleversement des mentalités judiciaires face à la délinquance écologique.

Notes

[1] Cité par M. Delmas-Marty, préface à l'ouvrage de J.H. Robert et M. Remond-Gouilloud, Droit pénal de l'environnement, Masson, Collection Droit pénal des affaires, 1983.

[2] Ainsi le lynx, le loup, l'ours, espèces devant faire l'objet d'une protection intégrale, peuvent être détruits ou capturés (arrêté du 22 juillet 1993).

[3] J. Littmann-Martin, Juris-Classeur Pénal Annexes, Environnement, Protection pénale de la nature, Fasc. 10, n° 56 et ss.

[4] Cass. crim. 10 nov. 1976, J.C.P. 1977, II, 18709, note M. Delmas-Marty.

[5] Ainsi une association de protection des oiseaux pouvait exercer l'action civile en cas de destruction d'un spéciment d'une espèce protégée mais était irrecevable pour les infractions à la police de la chasse, faute d'habilitation.

[6] J. Carbonnier, "Flexible droit", L.G.D.J. 1969, p; 95.

[7] Rapport C. de Vilmorin, "La lutte contre les atteintes à l'environnement", Ministère de l'Environnement et du Cadre de Vie, 1980, p. 63 et ss.

[8] P. Lascoumes, "La justice de l'environnement industriel: une place à prendre et à inventer", Justice, novembre 1988, p. 34.

[9] Rapport Gallet, Commission "Ecologie et actions publiques", juin 1991, p. 31.

[10] X. Matharan et D. Mondon, "Parquet et protection de l'environnement: pour une politique volontariste", Rev. Sc. Crim., 1991, p. 301.

[11] Rapport Gallet, op. cit., p. 32.

[12] Rapport Gallet, op. cit., p. 35.

[13] Chiffres proposés par l'auteur: 1,3 % de l'ensemble des condamnations en 1988, 2,2 % de l'ensemble de ces dix dernières années.

[14] Le tribunal correctionnel de Strasbourg, le 11 mars 1983, a condamné à un an d'emprisonnement (avec sursis) et à 70 000 francs d'amende un importateur clandestin de déchets toxiques qu'il fit répandre dans des gravières en contact avec la nappe phréatique, Rev. Jur. Env., 1983, p. 244, note M.J. Littmann-Martin. Voir aussi Tb. Corr. De Saint-Quentin, 26 juin 1985, Rev. Jur. Env., 1985, p. 480, note M.J. Littmann-Martin.

[15] Rev. Jur. Env., 1992, p. 339, note M.J. Littmann-Martin.

[16] M.J. Littmann-Martin et Cl. Lambrechts, "La spécificité du dommage écologique", in, le dommage écologique, colloque SFDE, Nice 21 et 22 mars 1991, Economica, p. 73.

Crimininal Law in France

Summary

French criminal and environmental law provides for two types of offences against the environment. The first category seeks to protect particular media against certain kinds of polluting activities. The second type of offences is related to a failure to comply with regulatory licensing requirements.

1. Within the first category three different offences exist to protect different kinds of waters. Thus, art. L. 232 (2) of the Code rural seeks to protect fresh and generally speaking the internal waters of France and makes it an offene to throw, to pour, or to let trickle any substances into water the action or reaction of which has destroyed fish or has impaired the nutrition, reproduction, or nutritious value of fish. If charged with this offence, it is no defence that the act occurred in compliance with licencing requirements and was thus authorized by the administration. A similar offence was created in 1986 in relation to marine water pollution. A general offence of water pollution has been created by art. 22 of the Law of 3 January 1992. This offence is committed where water pollution has had harmful effects on human health, has caused damage to fauna and flora with the exception of the type of damage sanctioned by the other two water pollution offences or interferes with normal water supplies and the use of bathing water. While the criminal sanction provided in art. 22 is more severe than the one in the other water pollution offences, it is a defence under art. 22 if it can be shown that the act in question has been duly authorized by a regulatory agency. Since ground water is not covered by the offence laid down in art. 232 (2) of the Code rural, the offence created by art. 22 of the Law of 3 January 1992 would seem to be of interest primarily to protect ground water. Unfortunately, the defence of due authorization diminishes the practical relevance of the provision in large part.

While French law thus provides for three different kinds of water pollution when in fact a single, correctly drafted offence would be sufficient, no offence exists in relation to air pollution or soil contamination. The latter media are protected only to the extent that certain polluting activities are subject to licencing requirements and that failure to comply carries criminal sanctions.

The Code rural does, however, afford criminal protection to protected fauna and flora (art. 211 (1) (1) and 211 (1) (2). Although especially the latter provision would seem to lay down a host of prohibitions against even minimal interferences, reality is often different, since implementing regulations do not take up all of the prohibitions.

The Barnier Act of 2 February 1995 has closed a loophole in the law by creating a further offence in relation to the introduction of non-native species into the natural environment.

The weak point of these offences to afford criminal protection to protected species is that they do not cover an attempt to commit the offence. Thus, a missed shot aimed at a royal eagle could merely be prosecuted under regulations governing hunting, a situation notoriously insufficient.

2. A number of offences can be found in the law of 19 July 1976 concerning "classified installations", in the law of 3 January 1992 concerning water and, partially, in the law of 15 July 1975 concerning waste management. These offences are usually related to a violation of specific provisions contained in the various statutes and the regulations adopted thereunder, and can be committed quite irrespective of any actual damage to the environment. The legislative technique is usually the same: In accordance with art. 34 of the French Constitution a number of provisions in these laws lay down criminal sanctions for a certain type of conduct which is described in fairly general terms. The exact elements of the offence are then defined in specific decrees and administrative orders. This practice of handing a blank cheque to the administrative authorities is sometimes criticized in view of the threat it poses for civil liberties.

Generally speaking six types of offences can be distinguished:

1. Violation of a requirement to obtain a licence.

2. Violation of a requirement to notify the authorities of a certain activities. The failure to bring to the authorities' notice a certain activitiy constitutes as a rule, however, only a misdemeanor ("contravention" as opposed to a "délit").

3. Failure to comply with administrative requirements. This can be either a full-blown offence (délit) or a minor misdemeanor (contravention).

4. Failure to comply with an order served by a prefect.

5. Continuation of a certain activity in violation of an administrative or judicial order to cease the activity in question.

6. Failure to provide required information or furnishing inexact information.

3. Criminal sanctions are as a rule those provided for in other areas of French criminal law. Thus offences can carry prison terms and fines, misdemeanors only fines. The exact sentences, however, are marked by a large degree of variability. The three different types of water pollution offences discussed above, for example, each carry a different sentence. Here the dominant impression is that of an uncertain logic behind the legislative choices. In some sectors the legislature has made an effort to provide for more original criminal sanctions where additional or supplementary sanctions are concerned. The most effective of these is an order to restore the natural environment to its original state. A number of laws provide for this sanction to be applied, and this in an innovative context: the order to restore the environment is made as part of an injunction which also provides for the execution of the sentence should the defendant fail to comply with the injunction.

4. In the area of criminal corporate liability and the criminal liability of corporate executives a new situation has arisen as a result of the new Criminal Code of 1 March 1994 having come into force. The new provisions have abolished so-called substantive offences ("délits matériels") which could be committed solely on the basis of certain facts having occurred irrespective of criminal intent or negligence. Art. 121 (3) of the new Code now declares, however, that no offence can be committed where there was no intent to commit the offence.

The requirement of intent puts an end to the quasi-automatic criminal responsibility of business executives whose corporations have been found to pollute protected media or fauna and flora either in violation of administrative requirements or in contravention of the provisions of the Code rural. The situation of business executives could improve even further by a reform of provisions concerning the criminal liability of legal persons.

The latter can be held liable under criminal law for violation of environmental statutes following the extension of corporate criminal liability to most environmental laws by the Barnier Act of 2 February 1995. The law provides for specific penalties to be imposed on corporations. As a rule, fines can be increased five-fold to the amount an individual can be fined if found guilty of an environmental offence.

Furthermore, a new art. 121 (2) of the Criminal code now requires that the "offence be committed as an act on behalf of the legal person either by one of its organs or one of its representatives. The provision is too recent to measure its impact. While its potential for sanctioning criminal behaviour in the environmental area may be considerable, the risks should not be underestimated either where it is not inconceivable that corporate criminal liability is substituted for the individual criminal liability of corporate leaders. Such a development could only lead to blurred responsibilities with adverse effects on raising environmental awareness among corporate leaders.

5. Environmental groups with a status of an officially recognized association can be a party to a criminal law suit as "partie civile". Moreover, a "partie civile" can require the authorities to prosecute against a decision not to bring charges. French criminal law thus provides for private enforcement actions. Under the Barnier Act of 2 February 1995 any environmental association recognized under the Code rural can exercise the rights of a "partie civile" concerning any act which has infringed directly or indirectly those collectively held interests that the association under its constitution seeks to protect and which constitutes a breach of environmental law provisions.

6. Until recently most observers have characterized French

Criminal Law in the field of the environmental as largely ineffectual. This has been due to the scarcity of prosecutions and the leniency of sentences where prosecutions went forward.

The lack of criminal prosecutions has been attributed to a lack of information on the part of the prosecuting authorities which are largely dependent on relevant information being passed on to them by administrative officers within the regulatory agencies. The latter quite frequently do not see any point in bringing criminal charges, and, instead, prefer to negotiate directly with a pollutor. Frequently also proceedings are stayed because the gravity of the offences are underrated by comparison to classic criminal conduct such as theft, robbery etc. A stay of proceedings often appears the easiest solution when the polluter agrees to pay damages to victims and to restore the environment. In fact, the law of 4 January 1993 now specifically provides for criminal mediation between victim and offender where the public prosecutor finds that such a measure would be capable of restoring any damage caused to the victim.

As for sanctions, fines generally hover around FF 10,000 or less. Prison terms are rarely imposed and if so as a suspended sentence. As a rule, the judges' sentencing practices have not reinforced the credibility of criminal law in the environmental area.

Finally, injunctions to force the offender to restore the environment on the pain of suffering the execution of an otherwise suspended sentence are too rarely used. The new Criminal Code in its art. 747 (4) seeks to enhance the position of the judge when reviewing the implementation of a judicial order to restore the environment. The judges can rely on the technical expertise of qualified experts now.

Chapter 14

Liability Litigation in Italy

by Stefano Nespor

1. Environmental Liability in Italian Law: A Brief Overview

One of the basic principles of Italian Tort law is its open structure[1]. This means that there is no fixed determination of the types of unlawful activities which will give rise to claims for compensation for damage. Any unlawful behaviour may justify compensation if damage arises and the unlawful behaviour was undertaken with negligence or a more serious mental element.

Under this framework, since the late 1970, citizens associations, NGOs, environmental organisations and local authorities have made claims for environmental damage. For example, several cases arose from the Seveso disaster. The Regione, local authorities (*Comuni*), injured or displaced individuals and people forced to perform periodic sanitation measures all made claims. Some of these have been settled; others are ongoing in a seemingly endless process. The most recent outcome was the affirmation on appeal by the Appeal Court of Milano of an award of compensation for psychological damage to 21 Seveso residents.

The turning point in Italian law was in 1986, when Art. 18 of the Law no. 346 introduced a specific right to compensation for environmental damage. The law introduced several relevant changes in the Italian tort law tradition. Three are worthy of note:

a) Not everyone can make claims for compensation, using the Art. 18. Standing is limited to the state (through the appropriate Ministry) and to other local authorities (*Regione* and *Comune*). Environmental organisations, even those qualified[2], lack standing. They may only legally intervene, supporting a claim by the State or by another local authority.

b) Priority is given to the material elimination of the consequences of damage; this means the restoration of the environment to its pre-existing condition. In contrast, the general tort law gives priority to compensation with payment of money.

c) Compensation may exceed the value or amount of damage. This means that a kind of punitive damages has been introduced into Italian law, while in the general system of tort law, punitive damages do not exist, and compensation may never exceed the damage.

The new law has not been widely employed in its first eight years, as the summary below will show. There are several reasons why:

1. The denial of standing for citizens' groups which are usually more active in promoting and supporting claims than government and official institutions (who often have contributed in some way - for example, by giving the necessary authorisations - to the causation of the damage).

2. The legal costs associated with bringing claims, which small local authorities are often unable to afford.

3. Technical problems associated with bringing a claim under Art. 18.

There are two main difficulties:

a) It is unclear what the relationship is between claims based on the general tort law system and those based on Art. 18: can a claim be based on both grounds, or does the specific claim of Art. 18 exclude the possibility of using the general tort law for claiming compensation for environmental damage?

b) It is not clear what period of time Art. 18 claims cover: how should environmental damages effected prior to 1986 be treated?

Nonetheless, the number of cases is growing slightly and some of these legal uncertainties are being resolved.

2. Claims for Environmental Damages: A Quantitative Summary

In the seven years since the right for environmental compensation was introduced (1986), through the first semester of 1993) there have been judgements in approximately 60 cases.

Courts of first or second instance have solved 40 cases; criminal courts, 30; civil courts, 10; the supreme court (*Corte di Cassazione*) 14; the Constitutional Court, 2.

Who brings these cases to the courts? Of the civil cases, local authorities brought six, environmental organisations (including both those organisations certified by the Ministry of the Environment, and committees without automatic standing) brought 4. The Ministry of the Environment has never claimed compensation for damages to the environment in a civil case.

In criminal cases the situation is different. Here the Government has made claims on seven occasions; four were made by the Ministry of the Environment; one by the Ministry for the Protection of National Monuments; and two by the Ministry of the Sea and the Navy (the latter for pollution of the sea near Sicily, caused by a ship's accident, following the Convention of Bruxelles).

Certified environmental organisations have claimed compensation 25 times (with the Courts granting standing 19 times, and denying standing in six, on the ground that there were no relationship between the goal of the organisation and the specific damage). Unauthorised citizen's committees and associations have claimed compensation on three occasions (with standing being denied twice). As of 1993, elimination or remediation of environmental damages has not been granted, despite the fact that - as said - Art. 18 gives priority to this form compensation: Courts seem to be frightened to abandon the traditional compensation of money.

In only five cases have the Courts granted a specific amount of money as compensation (in many cases compensation has been granted generically, with the settlement of a specific amount being delayed to further proceedings or to a separate case).

Of these five cases, the Government has been granted compensation on three occasions ($3,5 million to the Ministry of the Sea and Navy, $300,000 as provisional compensation to the Ministry of Environment in a case involving illegal waste disposal into a river). On one other occasion, a certified environmental organisation (*Italia nostra*) was granted provisional compensation of $50,000, and on other occasion a citizen's committee (claiming compensation using the general tort law) was awarded $25,000 for moral damages in relation to consequences of the Seveso disaster.

Notes

[1] This principle is fixed in the Art. 2043 of the Civil Code.

[2] The principal environmental organisations are certified by the Ministry of Environment.

Chapter 15

The F-16 Case: An Effective Threat with Tort Action

by Luuk Boerema

Introduction

First I would like to thank the organisers of this Conference for allowing me to speak here. I do so on behalf of the Dutch Society for the Protection of the Wadden Sea.

Let me introduce myself. My name is Luuk Boerema and until 15 days ago, I was one of the three lawyers of the Wadden Society. Recently I have become lecturer of environmental law and the law concerning animal welfare at the Van Hall Instituut, Professional University for Food, Agriculture and Environment in the city of Groningen.

The structure of my speech is as follows:

After a short introduction to the Dutch environmental law system I will take a closer look at tort action, especially the "F-16 case", and I will end my speech with an evaluation of the use of civil litigation as an instrument for preventing environmental damage from occurring.

1. Dutch Environmental Law

The Dutch environmental law can be divided into administrative law, criminal law and civil law.

1.1 Administrative Law

If one has a personal and a direct interest (which can be objectively determined) in challenging a decision of a governmental body, the Dutch administrative environmental law system is quite accessible for individuals as well as for environmental organisations. For the latter an additional stipulation is that they must have a legal basis; they must be a corporate body, e.g. a foundation or a society. Since the mid-70, Dutch Administrative Courts have accepted environmental organisations as defenders of "public interests" such as the protection of the environment in court. Administrative law is frequently used by environmental organisations in Holland. Litigation is relatively cheap, and there is no need for hiring an expensive barrister. Instead, the lawyer of the environmental organisation can litigate him/herself. And (generally speaking) almost every decision made by a governmental body can be challenged in an administrative court.

But there are restrictions in the use of administrative law. The environmental organisation is always dependent on the actions (or the lack of them) of governmental institutions (local governments for example). The costs of environmental damage cannot be claimed, although the introduction of the General Bill on Administrative Law (1994) has brought some improvement.

1.2 Criminal Law

In some cases it can be very useful to enforce environmental law through criminal courts, though usually the role of criminal law is limited. An environmental organisation can provide the impetus for a criminal proceeding, by informing the Public Prosecutor of the offence which has been discovered by the environmental organisation. But almost always the damage has already been done the moment the Public Prosecutor is being informed ...

1.3 Civil Law

But the main object of today is to look for the possibilities tort action can provide in order to prevent environmental damage from occurring.

A closer look at the Dutch civil law is therefore required.

1.3.1 "Party Concerned"

First of all I will discuss the possibilities of tort action for Dutch Environmental Organisations.

In the Netherlands both the government and environmental organisations may initiate a tort action in defence of general environmental interests. Environmental organisations are in Dutch law accepted as plaintiffs in tort actions, with the right to stand up for the interest of the environment. A legal basis for environmental organisations to do so can be found in the Bill on the Right to Collective Actions, another bill which was accepted this year.[1] The basic idea reflected in this bill is that in the case of protecting a general interest, like for instance the environment, it is adequate and efficient to grant a corporation established for the explicit purpose of protecting the environment (an NGO, a society or a foundation) the right to litigate, if the environment is endangered by some act of a third party. This party can also be a governmental body.

1.3.2 The "Unlawful Act" as a Legal Basis

Most of the time the basis for the tort action is Article 6:162 Section 2 of the Dutch Civil Code, the so-called "unlawful act" (deed). This unlawful act is committed with respect to the plaintiff.

An unlawful act is, according to the Dutch Civil Code:

- "a violation of a right, or

- a failure to comply with, or an action contrary to, a legal duty, or

- a violation of what is, according to the unwritten rules of general behaviour in society, acceptable;

- anything else unless there exists a justification rule."

Most describe the unlawful act as a failure to comply with a general legal duty.

But before we can speak, in a judicial sense, of a completed unlawful act, there are certain elements which have to be fulfilled:

- The person (or body) committing the unlawful act must also be guilty (acting on purpose, doing wrong while he was in a position to know that what he was doing was wrong); and

- damage must be done or threat of damage must occur; and

- the (possible) damage must be the direct result of the unlawful act; and

- the legal norm that has been violated must have the purpose of protecting the injured person or the interests of the (environmental) group.

If all these conditions are satisfied, there is a good chance that a claim on the basis of an unlawful act will be successful.

1.3.3 Verdicts in (Dutch) Tort Action

When litigating on the basis of an unlawful act, an environmental organisation can ask for a prohibition of the continuance of the unlawful act and, in the case of a threatened unlawful act, for a judge's declaration in advance that the act is indeed unlawful. Finally, when loss has already occurred one can ask for (financial) compensation in the form of damages.

1.3.4 A Quick Verdict

When speed is required because of the nature or the severity of the environmental threat, one usually tries to instigate a so-called "summary proceeding" by the President of a District Court. Summary proceedings can be started every day of the week and even during evenings when the situation requires so, and the President agrees. A summary proceeding can be a very effective weapon in the hands of NGOs, because the judge usually decides within the week and sometimes even on the same day as the proceedings.

1.4 Relation between Administrative Law and Civil Law

In the Dutch system, before you can turn to a civil court, you have to make sure there is no possibility of going to trial in the administrative law. If an administrative procedure is still an option, e.g. presenting the case to an administrative court, the chances for a successful tort action are very slim.

2. Tort Action in Practice: The F-16 Case

The Dutch Wadden Sea is legally probably one of the best protected nature reserves in the world. The Conventions of Bonn, Bern and Ramsar are applicable to it, as is the European Bird Directive and the European Habitat Directive. Almost 95% of the area is protected by the Dutch Nature Conservation Act.

From August until the beginning of November many birds take a rest during their long trip to Africa in the Dutch Wadden Sea area. Hundreds of thousands of migrating birds a year pass the Wadden Sea during this time of year.

Almost one year ago on October 19th 1993, the Dutch Ministry of Defence announced in a press-release that NATO low-level flying[2] practice with F-16 Jet fighters would take place over the Dutch Wadden Sea from 22 - 29 of October. The Dutch Society for the Protection of the Wadden Sea immediately sent a telegram to the Minister of Defence in which he was asked to revoke his decision.

This NATO flying practice (called "Cold Fire")planned for October could not have had a more unpleasant timing. Scientific reports have shown how quickly migrating birds are disturbed by aircraft[3]. Not only do they get confused, but they also lose a lot of energy when flying off. During the time of disturbance they cannot feed and lose precious energy that they need for their flight to Africa.

When the Dutch Minister of Defence had not responded within 48 hours of the telegram being sent, time began to run short before the low-level flying would take place. So the Wadden Society decided that it was time to try and prevent the practice from taking place by judicial means.

The lack of a formal administrative decision made it impossible to instigate an action through the Administrative court. Tort action seemed the only solution.

Off course the media was very interested in this case and the Wadden Society got a lot of publicity when we announced that we were thinking of starting a summary proceeding against the

Minister of Defence. The Wadden Society, together with the Stichting Natuur en Milieu, de Vereniging Natuurmonumenten and Birdlife International Holland, considered the low-flying practice, at this time of the year over a very vulnerable and generally recognised bird-resting area, "a violation of what is, according to the unwritten rules of general behaviour in society, acceptable." All organisations together decided to take the case to court.

A specialist barrister at environmental law was quickly found and, together with the lawyer of the Wadden Society, a "last warning" to the Dutch Minister of Defence was written and faxed. Our message to the Minister was this: If he did not before 10 a.m. of the following day give an order to stop the operation of "Cold Fire", he would be summoned to appear before the President of the District Court of The Hague in a summary proceeding.

Three hours after sending this "last warning" I got a telephone call from a high-ranked public servant of the Ministry of Defence, telling me that our warning "was a matter of great concern to the Secretary of State of the Ministry of Defence" and that we would receive an answer before the next morning.

The next morning at 10 a.m. we received a fax from the Dutch Ministry of Defence. The Secretary of State wrote us that he had cancelled the low-level flying practice because of "the fact that some of the pilots were not sufficiently trained to be able to fly the difficult course"...

The F-16 flying-practice over the Wadden Sea area was called off.

3. Discussion: The Advantages and Disadvantages of Tort Action for Environmental Organisations

3.1 The Advantages:

- Tort action (summary proceeding) can provide a quick and satisfying solution to a direct environmental threat.

- Threatening with a civil action can be very effective, but never threaten if you can't carry out your threat.

- With civil law you have the possibility to litigate direct against the real offender.

- It is possible, also for environmental organisations, to claim a damages payment[4].

3.2 The Disadvantages:

- Not every potential threat can be dealt with by tort action. In environmental law you find yourself very often tied by the rules of administrative law.

- You need a barrister, so a simple tort action can cost an environmental organisation a lot of money. The F-16 case would probably have cost the Wadden Society about f 6000,— if the case had gone to court. And our lawyer charged us a special tariff. Environmental organisations in Holland mostly decide to take a case into civil court together, in order to keep costs as low as possible. This can be a useful solution.

- There is always a financial risk involved, so always view your factual information critically.

4. Conclusion

Tort action can be a very effective instrument in preventing environmental damage from occurring. It should, like every legal instrument, be used with care. A threat of using tort action can also be effective, if the timing is right and your factual information is correct.

The use of the instrument has been limited up to now.

In my opinion more organisations would go to court in a civil action if it was not so expensive. A solution to this could be to make local courts exclusively competent in environmental proceedings. When proceeding before a local court you do not need a barrister. Lawyers of environmental organisations would then be able to take environmental cases to court themselves. The use of tort action would probably increase.

Notes

[1] The new bill is more or less a codification of case law.

[2] Low-level flying means: flying at a low altitude, between 75 and 100 meters above ground-level.

[3] See e.g. "The disturbance of foraging knots by aircraft", by Theunis Piersma and others, NIOZ, Texel.

[4] In the *Borcea* case (a tanker that spilt oil in the North Sea) the Dutch section of Birdlife International claimed a damages payment for the cleaning of oil-smeared seabirds. The case was settled by an agreement: a large sum of money was paid to Birdlife.

Chapter 16

Citizen Rights and Litigation in Environmental Law An Antipodean Perspective on Environmental Rights

by Paul L Stein

The Lucky Country?

Visions of Australia conjure up dreams of an unspoilt landscape. A vast island continent cut off from the predatory instincts of the outside world. The sheer beauty of its diversity - the desert interior with red earth, deep blue skies and extraordinary flora and fauna. Cool temperate rain forests in Tasmania and sub-tropical rain forests in Queensland. Myriad white sandy beaches along an endless coastline. The Great Barrier Reef Marine Park and Kakadu National Park, the jewel of Australia's North. Indeed, natural wonders appear infinite. All this coupled with a unique and internationally appealing biological diversity.

Yet if we are to face the truth it must be admitted that in a little over 200 years of European settlement we have managed (by lack of proper management) to dramatically transform the landscape. Desertification due to farming and grazing practices has degraded enormous areas of land. Erosion and salinity are major problems and loss of an already thin and fragile topsoil is reducing its potential for production. Massive clearing of woodland and forest has exacerbated the process of land degradation.

Meanwhile, in the urban areas and cities, where most Australians live, the picture is equally disturbing. Some rivers, bays and beaches are off bounds to swimmers. Sewage has been a problem on many of our famed ocean beaches. Coastal and inland wetlands have been destroyed. Water and air pollution remain a problem in many locations. Past agricultural and industrial practices have left a legacy of thousands of contaminated sites.

The Legacy of the Past

While Australia's environmental difficulties may appear minor when compared to Europe or North America, many are realising that time may be running out, environmentally speaking, for the "lucky country"[1]. Much environmental damage over two centuries stems from the attitude of European settlers, mainly British, to the land. This immense, alien continent, vacant save the Aborigines, was seen by them as ripe to exploit and to conquer. The relationship of settlers to the land was engendered by fear which accentuated their desire to tame and mould it by consuming its natural resources.

White Australians have never been able to comprehend the intense feelings of Aboriginal peoples for their land. Indeed, it is only comparatively recently that many Australians have developed a loving, caring attitude to their environment. This relationship, however, is sometimes tinged with guilt, sadness and frustration ... guilt at its seizure, sadness at its desecration and frustration at the powerlessness to turn back what is perceived as a tide of destruction and deterioration.

Increasingly Australians are becoming angry at the policies of the past and the unwelcome changes that have been wrought. They are starting to reject unsustainable practices. In particular, the younger generations are vociferous in their disapproval. Young people want to do better than their forebears - to pass to their children an environment in better shape than it is today.

The Impact of the Federal System

At the heart of Australia's environmental problems is our Federal system of government. The Commonwealth of Australia evolved out of an unwilling union of semi-independent British colonies only 93 years ago.[2] English Colonial boundaries became State boundaries. The "reluctant nation"[3], as some call it, continued to cling to the Motherland, preferring to regard itself as a loose collection of fairly autonomous States, ceding only narrow powers to the Central Government.

Of particular importance to the States was land and power

over it. Until comparatively recently the States controlled almost all land-use decisions - some being assigned to local government councils, the third tier of government. The result was that until the last decade or so land was seen as a resource to exploit to its fullest with scant regard to sound land management practices. Long-term thinking was often absent and policies such as sustainability were seldom, if ever, considered. The country was seen as unending, partly because of its sheer size (relative to population), possessing unlimited natural resources - there to mine, quarry, dam, plough, graze, fell and into which to dispose of waste from expanding towns and cities.

The Commonwealth Enters the Field

However, as the Commonwealth Government started to exert its long dormant constitutional muscle, the clamour of Federal interference with "States' Rights" was repeatedly heard.[4] Slowly the Commonwealth, partly by virtue of ratification of International Treaties and Conventions affecting the environment,[5] World Heritage listings, (the external affairs power) and its power over corporations, started to erode the states' hegemony over the environment. Examples include the Franklin River (Tasmania), Fraser Island and the wet tropics of Northern Queensland.

In terms of power over land, the crunch came fairly recently (1992) when the High Court of Australia acknowledged in the *Mabo* decision[6] that Aborigines owned the land before white "settlement" and Native Title to land still existed. Hitherto, the land was seen as *Terra Nullius* from 1788 when England established the first penal colony in Sydney.

A Shift in the Balance[7]

Many Australians now believe that the States have failed, to varying degrees, in their duty as responsible land managers. True it is that some have upped their game over the last 10 to 15 years, but the legacy of past depredation and neglect persists to-day. The fact is that many environmental issues know no artificial State boundaries. For example, trans-border pollution, wind direction, water flow and climatic variations are beyond the reach of individual States. Native fauna habitats ignore State borders. It is a matter of embarrassment that the States cannot even agree on summertime![8] Indeed, there are many occasions when the integrity of the environment is threatened or compromised by competing regulation by 2, 3, 4 or even more governments and their bureaucracies, eg., the Murray-Darling River system and the Lake Eyre Basin.[9]

Australians are at last becoming exasperated with parochial interests which seem quite unable to provide rational solutions, environmental protection or sustainable policies. They seek leadership with vision - vision past the next election.

In this context it is probable that Commonwealth jurisdiction over the environment is poised to blossom over the next couple of decades. It is likely that the power of the States will continue to decline and ultimately they will become minor players in environmental decision-making and regulation. Not many citizens will rue this shift in power given the record and the fact that we are but one nation with one environment. Australians are also emerging from feelings of inferiority and becoming more "Australian", more assertive and confident and more aware of and careful with their national identity. Less liable to think of themselves as say, Queenslanders, Victorians or Tasmanians. In short, more likely to put the nation and environment first, before their State.[10]

True it is that the Commonwealth is still a considerable distance from acting decisively to preserve and protect the environment and ensure sustainable practices, or to protect Australia's unique biological diversity. The recently enacted Commonwealth *Endangered Species Protection Act* 1992 is a step in the right direction, albeit a small one. Much more needs to be done to ensure that species diversity is maintained and species loss halted.

Citizen Rights and Participation Required

But as the Federal Government extends its legislative reach it is essential that it open up procedures and decision-making to increased public participation and scrutiny. Much greater accountability will be needed. The Commonwealth must firmly put aside the temptation, acceded to in 1974 when it passed the *Environment Protection (Impact of Proposals) Act*, to make environmental decisions non-justiciable.[11] It must also resist the temptation to settle for the lowest common environmental denominator in an effort to resolve judisdictional differences.

To this end there is, in my opinion. a need to consider an Environmental Bill of Rights - rights to clean air, clean water, uncontaminated lands, guaranteed access to the "bush" (countryside), to implementation of the principles of Ecologically Sustainable Development (ESD),[12] to information about the environment and to participate in decision-making. It is imperative that such rights be enforceable in the courts through open-standing and other mechanisms. From my experience this would best be achieved by the establishment of an independent specialist Environmental Court where governments and decision-makers would be accountable to citizens for decisions affecting the environment and for its protection.

There is, of course, nothing novel about Environmental Rights. They are beginning to be recognised in many parts of the world, eg., the *Ontario Environmental Bill of Rights*[13] in Canada and the recent policy on Environmental Rights of Citizens of the United Kingdom Labour Party.[14] Other illustrations have been discussed at this Conference.

The Land and Environment Court Experience

My home State (New South Wales) has led the way since 1979 in access to the Land and Environment Court in order to seek to enforce environmental legislation and judicially review decisions through truly "open standing" provisions. Indeed, "any person" may challenge a decision claimed to be in breach of environmental law.[15] No particular interest, pecuniary or otherwise, is required and the rules of common law standing have been abolished. The popularity of these provisions is such that they have recently been expanded to new areas by the Parliament, rather than being narrowed.[16]

Nonetheless, this facilitation of access to the Courts must be accompanied by new procedures to overcome other barriers to participation. New attitudes by Judges and lawyers are emerging. These include attitudes to discovery and inspection of documents, to Crown (Government) and other privileges, to legal aid, to legal costs and to undertakings as to damages in interim injunction cases. Most of these rules or conventions grew up in an atmosphere of private, party/party litigation, inappropriate to Public Law situations where the public interest is at stake. If continued, they act only as barriers to access.[17]

Open or more liberal standing provisions are slowly extending to other Australian jurisdictions, as are specialist Environmental Courts.[18] Cases determined in the Land and Environment Court often influence the way in which environmental decisions are thereafter made. Generally the Court has sought to enhance citizen involvement. Judgments have also led, inter alia, to improved environmental assessment, revised forest logging policies and endangered fauna legislation requiring fauna impact statements when the environment of endangered fauna is likely to be significantly affected.[19]

One of the current challenges for the Court is how to apply and interpret the principles of Ecologically Sustainable Development in order to attempt to translate them into practical reality. This is starting to occur, for example in *Leach v National Parks and Wildlife Service*.[20] Civil, and indeed criminal, enforcement rights by citizens have brought about many changed decisions and more environmentally aware decision-making thus acting as a safeguard on the excesses of development (public and private).

Citizen participation in environmental decision-making, the ability to restrain breaches of the law by civil enforcement and to judicially review decisions, have the proven capacity to develop a new body of Environmental Law. Governments should not be nervous of this development. It is symptomatic of a healthy democracy, obedience to the Rule of Law and the separation of Powers between the Executive and the Judiciary.

Conclusion - Doom or New Dawn?

I hope my speech has not sounded too gloomy. In fact, I remain an optimist because it is possible to discern a rising tide of sentiment among Australians that unless positive action is taken to protect the environment, we will have failed in our stewardship and in our responsibility to future generations.

Notes

[1] The title of a best selling book on Australian Society by Donald Horne, Penguin Books, 1964.

[2] The *Constitution Act* 1901 (Commonwealth).

[3] The Reluctant Nation - Environment, law and politics in Australia, Phillip Toyne, former Director of the Australian Conservation Foundation, ABC Books, 1994.

[4] Protection of "States Rights" is not confined to the environment and has been important in the past in many clashes over issues such as education and health. Recently, it was raised in the context of homosexual intercourse in Tasmania when Federal legislation, the *Human Rights (Sexual Conduct) Bill* 1994 was passed to override State law and protect the sexual privacy of individuals.

[5] For example the Montreal Protocol on Substances that Deplete the Ozone Layer, the U.N. Framework Convention on Climate Change, the Convention of Wetlands of International Importance (Ramsar), the Migratory Birds Agreements with China and Japan, the Bonn Convention on Conservation of Migratory Species of Wild Animals, Convention on International Trade in Endangered Species of Wild Flora and Fauna (Cites), the Convention on Biological Diversity and the Rio Declaration on Environment and Development.

[6] *Mabo & Ors. v. State of Queensland* (No. 2) (1992) 175 CLR 1.

[7] A recent example of trans-boundary pollution was extensive fish kills in the Barwon River in Northern New South Wales caused by aerial spraying of pesticides on cotton farms in Queensland. The Queensland offender was successfully prosecuted in the New South Wales Land and Environment Court

[*State Pollution Control Commission v. Brownlie* (1992) 76 LGRA 419].

[8] To the chagrin of the tourist industry, and many others, the States vary in their rules as to summer-time. Queensland, Northern Territory and Western Australia have none. New South Wales, Victoria and South Australia have one hour and Tasmania starts and ends it summer-time out of kilter. The result is confusion and a standing joke, see Get Set for a Confusing Time, The Australian, 1 October 1994.

[9] The Murray-Darling River system is the longest in Australia, flowing from Queensland through New South Wales and Victoria entering the ocean in South Australia. The Lake Eyre Basin is an enormous inland desert wetland basin of ephemeral sale lakes 1.14 million kilometres square. It extends from Mount Isa in Queensland to Alice Springs in the Northern Territory, east to the western edge of New South Wales and south to Lake Eyre itself in South Australia. Five different governments attempt to administer it but fail to cope with the enormous environmental risks, see New Scientist 27 August 1994.

[10] This trend has become marked with the recent and continuing debate for Australia to cut its ties with the Queen of England and become a true Republic with an Australian Head of State.

[11] The policy of the legislation and the Common Law standing rule have hindered the development of Federal Environmental Law and even prevented the Australian Conservation Foundation, the peak environmental NGO, from taking action in the courts, see *ACF v Commonwealth of Australia* (1980) 146 CLR 493. However, the ACF was at least held to have standing by a Federal Court Judge in *ACF v Minister for Resources* (1989) 76 LGRA 200, a case concerning the south-east forests.

[12] The 1992 Intergovernmental Agreement on the Environment (IGAE) has included ESD principles. In addition, the *Protection of the Environment Administration Act* 1991 (New South Wales) and *Fisheries Management Act* 1994 (New South Wales) have included ESD principles to guide the New South Wales Environment Protection Authority and the conservation of

fishery resources respectively. The *Environment Protection Act* 1993 (South Australia) and recent Tasmanian Local Government legislation have also included the principles.

[13] *Environmental Bill of Rights*, 1993 (Ontario) claims to provide resident rights to participate in environmentally significant decisions, to provide increased accountability, to increase access to the courts for judicial review and enforcement in respect of environmental harm.

[14] United Kingdom Labour Party Policy Commission on the Environment, In Trust for To-morrow, London, July 1994.

[15] *Environment Planning and Assessment Act* 1979, *Heritage Act* 1977, *Wilderness Act* 1988, *Environmentally Hazardous Chemicals Act* 1985, *National Parks and Wildlife Act* 1974, *Local Government Act* 1993, *Fisheries Management Act* 1994 and *Environmental Offences and Penalties Act* 1989. Elsewhere, open standing provisions have been included in the *Local Government (Planning and Environment) Act* 1990 (Queensland), the *Development Act* 1993 (South Australia) and the *Environmental Management and Pollution Control Act* 1994 (Tasmania)

[16] From time to time open standing provisions are criticised as opening the "floodgates" of litigation. Judges have continually refuted this allegation as contrary to fact. In a report by Mr Gary Sturgess, Thirty Different Governments. Report on the Commission of Inquiry into Red Tape January, 1994, Sydney, the author demonstrates that the criticism is no more than myth. He concludes, "[At] a time when public scrutiny of government is expanding, it is unthinkable that the right of review ... should be repealed".

[17] The Land and Environment Court has developed the concept of costs in public interest litigation whereby a losing citizen or environmental group may not be ordered to pay the costs of the winner, see *Oshlack v Richmond River Council* (1994) 82 LGERA 236.

[18] In particular Queensland and South Australia.

[19] *Endangered Fauna (Interim Protection) Act* 1991 amending the *Environmental Planning and Assessment Act* 1979 and the *National Parks and Wildlife Act* 1974. Although intended as stop-gap legislation the statute is now current until at least October 1995.

[20] (1993) 81 LGERA 270 regarding the application of the precautionary principle to endangered fauna, namely the Giant Burrowing Frog and the Yellow-Bellied Glider.

Chapter 17

Voluntary Agreements for Environmental Protection

by Sanford Lewis

Lately there has been an explosion of "environmental volunteerism" in the U.S., exemplified by a growth in diverse voluntary arrangements and agreements within and among corporations, between corporations and government, and between nongovernmental organizations (NGOs) and corporations. The idea of voluntary corporate action is based on the evident lack of ability of our laws, either as currently written, or (some would say) by the very nature of law and the lawmaking process, to adequately address the need for continuous improvement and innovation toward environmental progress.

Given the limited time available, I can only begin to scratch the surface of this broad topic. So I will begin by briefly describing the types of arrangements that have been entered in the U.S., and follow this with some general observations and lessons from these arrangements.

1. Categories of Agreements

The following are some categories of agreements and arrangements, proceeding from those that are most voluntary to those for which some force of law has led to their establishment.

1.1 Corporate Codes and Other Corporate Volunteerism

One form of "voluntary agreement" is the corporate code of conduct, e.g. an industry-wide code of practices agreed to among certain members of an industry. The most well-publicized of these in the U.S. is the Responsible Care initiative, which the Chemical Manufacturers' Association (CMA) has required for all of it members. This code sets forth a requirement for members to abide by certain environmental and safety performance standards, to engage in management reforms, to undertake dialogue and information sharing with local communities and to perform annual self-reviews of progress in meeting the code's goals.

1.2 The CERES Principles

The CERES Principles are a ten point code of environmental ethics advanced by the Coalition for Environmentally Responsible Economies (CERES). CERES is an organization of investors, environmental groups, and religious organizations which was established after the Exxon Valdez oil spill disaster, to seek reform of corporate environmental performance. Originally known as the Valdez Principles, the CERES Principles contain ten points, each spelled out in a few sentences (attached).

1. Protection of the Biosphere;
2. Sustainable Use of Natural Resources;
3. Reduction and Disposal of Wastes;
4. Energy Conservation;
5. Risk Reduction;
6. Safe Products and Services;
7. Environmental Restoration;
8. Informing the Public;
9. Management Commitment;
10. Audits and Reports.

Notably, there is a disclaimer at the end of the principles, stating:

> **Disclaimer**: These Principles establish an environmental ethic with criteria by which investors and others can assess the environmental performance of companies. Companies that sign these Principles pledge to go voluntarily

beyond the requirements of the law. These Principles are not intended to create new legal liabilities, expand existing rights or obligations, waive legal defenses, or otherwise affect the legal position of any signatory company, and are not intended to be used against a signatory in any legal proceeding for any purpose.

Recently some large U.S. corporations have endorsed the CERES principles, such as the Sun Company, which is a major oil company, and General Motors, which is our largest automobile manufacturer.

1.3 Voluntary Corporate Agreements and Arrangements with the Government

The Environmental Protection Agency (EPA) has developed a number of cooperative initiatives with industry. An example is the Industrial Toxics Project, also known as "33/50", so named because companies who participate pledge to reduce their emissions of 17 EPA-designated toxic substances by 33 percent by 1992 and 50% by 1995. Nearly 1200 companies have taken part and have so far claimed at least a 40% reduction below 1988 levels (the baseline year.)

1.4 Voluntary External Audits for Specific Issues

Yet another type of arrangement between businesses and NGOs often involves no written agreement, but rather involves a hands-on, in-depth analysis by NGOs of corporate opportunities to achieve certain goals. The leading efforts among these are for toxics use reduction, and involve the Environmental Careers Organization in partnership with numerous organizations, including the Good Neighbor Project. The Environmental Careers Organization is a twenty year old organization which provides training and jobs placement on environmentally-related jobs. ECO has five regional offices across the country and 5,000 alumni. ECO's technical advisor for toxics use reduction program has retrained 18 career professional scientists, most of them retired, to become advisors to NGOs for evaluating industries' potential for toxics use reduction. These advisors are conducting assessments of toxics use reduction opportunities at numerous plants. The program is half way between a business service and a community empowerment initiative; many facilities are voluntarily submitting to toxics use reduction assessments under the program. The advisors' analyses have identified ways that companies can save money and prevent pollution.

Similarly to the ECO efforts, the Environmental Defense Fund and other organizations have also entered arrangements with specific industry sectors - e.g. automobile manufacturers and printers - to work cooperatively with industry to find toxics use reduction and other environmental opportunities and concerns on a sector-wide basis.

1.5 Innovative Settlements of Permit Challenges

Innovative agreements have been entered voluntarily by companies in settlements of citizens' challenges to water and air pollution discharge permits. Two examples will serve to demonstrate the range of these agreements.

1.5.1 Rhône-Poulenc, Manchester, Texas

In June 1992, a serious accident occurred at the Rhône-Poulenc (R-P) chemical plant in Manchester, Texas - a release of a cloud of sulfur dioxide. At least 27 people were sent to area hospitals. With the assistance of the environmental organization, Texans United, as well as my organization, the community won an agreement which gave the community specific rights never before recognized in Texas. R-P agreed to pay for an independent environmental audit by an expert selected and supervised by a panel of community residents and Texans United. Among the features of the agreement are:

- ***A broad audit***, which includes review of regulatory compliance, safety training, accident prevention, emergency response, waste analysis and information systems, monitoring programs, and waste minimization practices.

- ***Public disclosure*** of company documents, including hazard assessment and risk analysis, lists of accidents/upsets/near-misses/corrective actions, and waste minimization and reduction plans.

- *RP committed to "negotiate in good faith*" on the audit recommendations.

- Citizens are entitled to *accompany the auditor* and conduct *other inspections by appointment.*

- The agreement is l**egally binding** because it is integrated to the firm's operating permit under the hazardous waste law.

1.5.2 Chevron, Richmond, California

A second permit-challenge related agreement, involving the Chevron Corporation in Richmond, California (an oil company), took a very different form. This agreement, entered by the West County Toxics Coalition, Citizens for a Better Environment, and People Do!, resulted from a challenge to an air emissions permit for an expansion project. The agreement includes the following features:

- *Pollution Reduction*: The company agreed to install leakless valves to reduce fugitive emissions (350 valves in expansion project, 200-400 valves retrofitted in the existing refinery) and to take no pollution credits (emissions trading) for the resulting emission reductions. They agreed to fenceline air pollution monitoring to be piloted at the plant with community-suggested target chemicals. They agreed that other toxic emission reductions at the plant will continue.

- *Local Economy*: It makes this agreement most unique is the strong recognition that it gives to the link between ecotnomic and environmental concerns. The company agreed to give $5 million over five years to *the facility's near neighbors* (who are primarily low income African-Americans) through nonprofit service organizations. It also agreed to provide skilled job training to 100 fenceline neighbors, and to aggressively pursue of employment of people from the community.

These two agreements typify the *Good Neighbor Agreements* which my organization, the Good Neighbor Project, helps state and local organizations to promote. The local client groups vary. In many instances they are coalitions who include labor unions and religious organizations as well as environmental and civic organizations. Note the two different kinds of goals sought - substantive commitments (the Chevron agreement), and *processes* for long term, continuous improvement and participation rights (the Rhône-Poulenc agreement). It often seems easier to get firms to agree to substantive environmental commitments than to an oversight process with real rights and resources for ongoing public review.

1.6 Lawsuit Settlements

The Environmental Protection Agency has been entering special settlement agreements in its enforcement proceedings. Supplemental Environmental Projects (SEPs), as these alternative agreements are known, are currently in wide usage. What makes these agreements worthy of mention here is that the companies "volunteer" to take certain actions that they otherwise would not be legally required to do. In exchange, the amount of penalties that they owe for violations are reduced. Generally they must pay at least $2.50 in SEP expenditures for every $1 in penalty reduction that they are granted. In fiscal year 1992, EPA regions reduced penalties in 222 cases using SEPs valued at $50 million. One out of 10 EPA settlements now include SEPs and they are being quickly adopted by state environmental agencies as well.[1]

The largest portion of SEPs involve companies making direct expenditures for pollution reduction or prevention. Often these pollution prevention SEPs result from violations of Community Right to Know Act reporting - i.e. a failure to comply with requirements to report to the EPA the amount of toxic materials emitted to the environment. After being caught failing to report under the Community Right to Know Act an electric coil company spent $95,850 to eliminate the use of 12,000 pounds of 1,1,1 trichloroethane per year, allowing its proposed penalty to be reduced by $34,350. A plastics company agreed to install an acetone recovery system for $26,500, which allowed their penalty to be reduced by only $1,250. Other SEPs which are less desirable from a health and environmental standpoint involve pollution control rather than pollution prevention - e.g. installing wastewater or air emissions treatment systems which recapture pollutants (which may then lead to hazardous waste disposal, worker exposure to toxics and other types of undesirable secondary environmental impacts.)

Besides reducing pollution other forms of SEPs include: Environmental Restoration projects (2 percent of 1992 settlements) environmental audits (4 percent), public awareness projects (5 percent), and donations to Local Emergency Planning Committees for local emergency preparedness planning (4 percent).

In addition to the EPA settlements, there have been numerous private settlements of citizens suits by NGOs, particularly under the Federal Community Right To Know Act and the Clean Water Act. Many of these settlements require the company to study pollution prevention with a consultant auditor selected by the plaintiff NGOs, and then allow the firms to offset penalties for affirmative in-plant pollution prevention measures like the EPA SEPs.

Some of the private citizen suit settlements have also established funding sources for further environmental activism. Atlantic States Legal Foundation, probably the national leader in bringing citizens suits, recently settled a threatened suit against the Georgia Pacific company for violations of sewer discharge pretreatment requirements at a corrugated cardboard facility in Olympia, Washington. The settlement allotted $99,900 for environmental projects. The organization sent out requests for proposals from groups in the state, which resulted in the funding of educational projects and land conservation projects. Another ASLF case in Washington state, involving shipyard stormwater violations netted $67,500 for People For Puget Sound. The money will be used by the NGO recipient to look at other pollution discharge permits in the area and promote further water pollution prevention.

2. Trends in Voluntary Agreements

I would like to focus on three key patterns that can be seen at this point in these voluntary agreements. These are:

1. True volunteerism generally only occurs where there is an efficiency opportunity - a strong potential to boost corporate efficiencies and profits while advancing environmental goals.

2. Beyond the "efficiency factor," the strength of an agreement

or arrangement is generally inversely proportional to its voluntariness.

3. Volunteerism is making its mark on environmental law and policy.

2.1 True volunteerism generally only occurs where there is an efficiency opportunity - a strong potential to boost corporate efficiencies and profits while advancing environmental goals.

Fueling true volunteerism more than anything else is a "gold rush" mentality, based on evidence of a potential to boost industries' profits by discovering hidden cost cutting opportunities, primarily eliminating waste of materials, compliance costs and potential liabilities. The chemical industry and other industries are reporting significant reductions of pollution through more attention to materials efficiencies. In some cases, there are also product quality improvements or product marketing opportunities that draw firms toward environmentally progressive measures.

Yet at the same time that this volunteerism has been emerging, companies have been cutting corners at risk to health and environment. *Industrial Safety and Hygiene News* recently polled 850 readers in corporate safety departments regarding the impact of economic competitive pressures and downsizing of staff levels. Seventy-five percent of those surveyed said that their firms are cutting safety spending due to competition; one out of three acknowledged that reduced maintenance is actually creating safety risks at their facilities.[2] In an environment where action, studies and spending are voluntary, and where the choices made are not genuinely transparent to the affected stakeholders, we need to realize that internal corporate processes readjust to spend less as economic pressures mount. The foundation upon which volunteerism rests must be not be overestimated in its breadth.

While some companies volunteer for ECO toxics use reduction assessments based on the apparent potential for profit enhancement, others refuse. For instance, another Rhône-Poulenc plant, this one in Institute, West Virginia, is of concern to one of the Good Neighbor Project's key client groups, People

Concern About Methyl Isocyanate. R-P's Institute plant is one of the last plants in the world, if not *the* last plant, to continue storing large quantities of methyl isocyanate, the chemical that caused Union Carbide's Bhopal, India disaster killing thousands of people. The Institute plant (which was purchased from Union Carbide), actually stores up to five times the amount of MIC that was involved in Bhopal. The plant has had a number of accidents and the community is naturally quite concerned about all of the MIC. This year is the tenth anniversary of Bhopal, and the community group, the local college and several labor unions have been calling on the company to submit to a complete external safety review - like the Manchester plant's agreement.

The Good Neighbor Project has deployed an ECO advisor to evaluate the potential for finding creative solutions to reduce the inventories of MIC at the site. Our advisor is a retired R&D chemist who has worked for chemical companies for 35 years. He can help to evaluate the potential, for instance, for switching to a just-in-time production system where MIC is consumed as quickly as it is produced. But the trouble is, so far the company has refused to let him on the site, or to share relevant information. So our advisor's draft study of the Institute plant, which he just completed, was done based on a literature search. We are continuing to seek cooperation from the company, but are also beginning to think about forms of legal and political recourse. While there may be hidden efficiencies involved in making the transition to low or no inventory uses of MIC, this potential so far is not enough to win their cooperation. It is, after all, also possible that the solution to MIC inventory reduction could require costly process changes.

2.2 Beyond the "efficiency factor," the strength of an agreement or arrangement is generally inversely proportional to its voluntariness.

There is a lot of loose discussion these days about changing corporate culture through volunteerism. But the slow accretions of change within corporate culture seem to come much more quickly when there is the force of law to bring about concrete action and restructuring of corporate-community-environmental relations. It would be incorrect to say that all voluntary agreements are without merit. But in general, the more agreements entered are truly voluntary (i.e. entered without a threat of imminent legal or political force), the less legal teeth and enforceability the agreements tend to have.

2.2.1 EPA's Strong SEP Policies

In arguably the least voluntary of these agreements - lawsuit settlements by EPA - the EPA issued guidelines on settlements in 1991. EPA guidelines specify that to get an offset for pollution prevention studies it is not enough for the defendant to study issues of pollution prevention. The EPA settlement guidelines impose the strong requirement that in a settlement the EPA:

> must have the authority to review the completed study to decide whether it is technologically or economically feasible to implement the results. Should the U.S. decide that the results can be implemented but the defendant / respondent is unwilling to do so, the offset for the pollution prevention study will be rescinded and the final assessed penalty must be paid in full.[3]

2.2.2 CMA Self-Policing

In contrast, one of the weakest of the voluntary programs is the Responsible Care program. The weaknesses of this self-policing approach to improving corporate performance should be self-evident, but are perhaps best exemplified by what happens when corporations set up "advisory committees" under the program. These committees are typically the main forum for "dialogue" with the community. Corporate managers often hand-pick their friends, or other community members ideologically or financially aligned with the corporation, to fill most of the slots on these committees. At the same time, they often exclude or marginalize the community organizations and leaders with genuine concerns or grievances regarding the corporation.[4] Advisory committee members selected by these firms are not a random or representative segment of the populous. This point was driven home by a survey by the CMA, which found that while most of the public remains seriously concerned about the chemical industry, 86% of chemical firms' panel members surveyed viewed the industry favorably.[5]

The CMA has been very slowly developing a third party verification system to go along with Responsible Care. But they appear to be carefully steering towards a process of using consultants that the firms still choose and control, and veering away from a system of verification that would empower stakeholders to oversee the process and review the detailed content of plant audits.

Too often the volunteerism of corporations under Responsible Care seems to track the instructions of public relations mogul E. Bruce Harrison who suggests in his book, Going Green: How to Communicate your Company's Environmental Commitment, the following style of "dialogue" with environmental groups:

> Offer to meet with them. ... Your task is to try and deflate their balloon and get direct information about what's motivating them, how serious they are, who they are, what they will consider 'success'... Be friendly. Politely put off giving more direct information. Offer to meet with them again. As long as you are talking, you may not be fighting...

Some citizens groups' succumb to this style of community relations, holding out hope upon hope that being patient with companies using such tactics will eventually build trust and yield results. An example may be Citizens for a Better Environment in Minnesota, which identified the 40 worst toxic polluters in their state using the toxic release inventory, and then targetted 10 of them to seek Good Neighbor Agreements for pollution prevention, between the companies and their neighbors. Unlike NGO efforts elsewhere, CBE in Minnesota has taken the unusual position of stating that they will not resort to permit challenges or other adversarial recourse to win those agreements. As a result, they have been faced with a lot of coporate talk but little action. After three years of this effort, CBE has not secured any written commitments from companies. Indeed, they have seen just how far companies can go to manipulate environmental groups who have thrown down their weapons. In one instance, CBE and affiliated community groups proposed four different draft agreements to a foundry, which would require various types of pollution prevention measures. After being rebuffed each time, the groups asked the company to take their latest draft and revise it to the company's liking.

The company took out all the substantive content and returned a document of pure rhetoric, devoid of concrete actions or commitments.

2.2.3 The CERES Principles

There is some pressure on firms, (e.g. shareholder resolutions), to force companies to endorse the CERES Principles. But, by and large, the CERES principles are also voluntary in nature. In order to get large companies like Sun and GM to endorse the CERES principles, the sponsors of the principles had to bend over backwards - deleting some of the real teeth in the principles. When originally drafted, they would have required companies to submit eventually to annual *independent* audits which would be disclosed to the public. Now they only require an *internal* audit charting their progress in compliance with CERES (which can remain internal) and a report to the public that indicates certain companywide statistics. The report is stronger in format than a typical company public relations report, but lacks the details about specific plants that would be needed for localized accountability. The legal disclaimer clause was also added to appease potential corporate signatories and their legal departments.

What is the impact of a set of voluntary principles that are intended to have no legal force or effect? The intent is to set in motion forces of cultural change within large corporations. Yet the on-the-ground significance of CERES is yet to be proven. And as it matures, CERES is facing new tests.

2.2.4 The Body Shop

One of the endorsers of CERES was the Body Shop, a cosmetics company which built its empire of environmentally conscious and animal friendly product lines into 1,050 shops in 45 countries with annual worldwide retail sales of $700 million. But a recent article in Business Ethics magazine has put a severe damper on the company's public profile. According to the article, the company's "natural" cosmetics include numerous artificial colors, fragrances, synthetic preservatives and other petrochemicals. The company's quality control measures have sometimes indicated mold or bacteria in products, but the company has not had affected products taken off the shelves of the stores. The company's environmentally friendly record according to a former environmental attorney for the company is "window dressing", with several discharges of products to the sewer system and not nearly as extensive recycling as their literature implied. Their public position states that they are opposed to animal testing of products, but the fine print says that they will only decline cosmetic products tested on animals within the previous five years. Even that commitment has apparently sometimes been breached where the ingredients rather than the cosmetics themselves had been subject to animal testing within the prior five years.[6]

2.2.5 The Sun Company

The Sun Company, the first large endorser of CERES, is also under gathering clouds of scrutiny. Since their endorsement, the Environmental Protection Agency has fined them for numerous water and air pollution violations, amounting to millions of dollars in penalties. On top of this, their refinery in Philadelphia recently had an accident spewing "tons" of catalyst dust over the community, a substance known to pose both immediate and long term health concerns. The company has become elusive in its dealing with a community/labor coalition that is focused on the firm. Sun may soon try to fall back on the vagueness of CERES regarding informing the public:

> We will inform in a timely manner everyone who may be affected by conditions caused by our company that might endanger health, safety or the environment. We will regularly seek advice and counsel through dialogue with persons in communities near our facilities.

In contrast to this vague language the Community/Labor Refinery Tracking Committee of Philadelphia has asked the company to negotiate concrete, legally binding commitments on a wide range of specific safety and environmental concerns, and to provide the tracking committee with the rights and resources necessary for effective ongoing discussions with the groups, i.e. the kinds of information disclosure and technical assistance secured in Manchester, Texas.

In addition, it is unclear how aggressively Sun, as an oil company whose products are inherently environmentally damaging, can or will implement the strong requirement of CERES for endorsers to "reduce, and where possible, eliminate the use, manufacture or sale of products and services that will cause environmental damage or health or safety hazards." Sun Environmental Affairs Director Ted Grabowski, in an April, 1994 meeting at the Massachusetts Institute of Technology noted that when it comes to product changes, the company is a slave of the market. If consumers demand oil products, Sun has a duty to its shareholders to sell it to them. Sun's marketing department is researching the potential to sell biodegradable lubricants for marine boating applications. If consumers would be willing to buy these goods for twice the price of ordinary lubricating oil, then Sun would enter the market. Their business direction, he asserted, will be determined primarily markets, not by environmental considerations. Grabowski mentioned the benefits of the CERES endorsement in working with local communities, and in advertising to environment-conscious consumers. Sun advertising now mentions the CERES endorsement. But to what extent is any added credibility with the public justified?

***

The situations of both the Body Shop and the Sun Company raise a real question about the depth of commitment that companies make when they sign the CERES principles. A reappraisal among CERES Board members is underway. How will CERES endorsers be policed despite the acknowledged lack of legal effect to the endorsement? There may eventually be an internal CERES process for placing companies on probation for environmentally poor performance or refusal to comply with the letter or spirit of the principles.

2.3 Volunteerism is making its mark on environmental law and policy.

For better and for worse, all of this so-called volunteerism is having an impact on law and policy in the U.S. The corporate community likes these voluntary arrangements because it gives them flexibility as to how and when to meet environmental objectives. Many corporations are citing their voluntary actions, however weak they may be, to argue against new legislation and regulation. At the same time that Sun says it is a slave of markets, its lobbyists will lobby against new legislation that might cut into those markets. Sun official Grabowski noted that among the benefits to Sun from endorsing the Principles, would be the added credibility they gain lobbying Congress on environmental legislation that they find too costly.

Some changes in law to accomodate volunteerism make sense. For instance the Clean Air Act Amendments of 1990 contains a provision on Early Reductions of toxic pollutants giving an air polluter six years to come into compliance with future EPA established air emissions rules if the firm reduces their air toxics emissions by 90% prior to the EPA's proposal of an applicable rule. Many states have established technical assistance programs to aid companies in identifying opportunities for economically viable or advantageous pollution prevention measures. Also, the State of Minnesota has established a technical assistance program which expressly seeks to facilitate more Good Neighbor Agreements. Technical assistance engineers for the state separately advise both industries and community groups on technical options for reducing the use of toxic chemicals. Grants are available to community groups for independent technical advisors on toxics use reduction. A full-time government staffer works to educate the public on the importance of pollution prevention.

However, corporations are looking for more dubious changes in the law to encourage more volunteerism. A well-organized campaign of the corporate law community is currently underway, to create a right for firms to keep internal environmental audits secret from the EPA and the public. They claim creating an environmental audits privilege against disclosure in enforcement actions and all lawsuits would encourage firms to voluntarily undertake more auditing; better still, say the corporate lawyers, would be a national policy dismissing all penalties (or, in some proposals, all criminal penalties) against companies who voluntarily disclose violations identified in their audits. NGOs are responding that corporations have already had massive secrecy rights, and it has not led to improvements, but to cutting corners. Extending secrecy could extend the right of corporations to pick and choose among the violations and hazards that they will rectify - i.e., to ask whether a violation is well-hid enough that it will not be detected and thus need not be corrected. Secrecy of audits would encourage corporations to pack all internal studies into their protected internal audits, despite the fact that community groups and government inspectors need the documents to evaluate corporate performance. If corporations are able to disclose violations in order to avoid penalties, then the incentive will be great to disclose violations in anticipation of an inspection, thereby avoiding public penalties. There are few subtleties that can be added to the policy or legal framework that could genuinely protect against such abuses.

In closing I should note that the use of agreements and the encouragement of voluntary action by corporations is not likely to stop any time soon. Indeed, it is accelerating under President Clinton, a man known to be biased toward negotiation as a solution to public policy questions. A new EPA initiative, known as the Common Sense Initiative, has been launched by the EPA to encouraging dialogue among various stakeholders to identify strategies for "cleaner, cheaper and smarter" environmental protection. The initiative is beginning with an examination of several industrial sectors, among them oil refining, electronics and computers, printing, iron and steel, metal finishing and plating, and automobile assembly. This initiative launched this year will undoubtedly lead to changes in future rulemaking, permitting and industry-community relations.

There is a lack of clarity in discussions of voluntary measures as to what their appropriate place is in the overall schema of environmental law. Is the focus on these measures because government lacks the authority at the moment to get a particular job done? Because too much law strangles the ability of industry to both produce products and meet environmental goals? Because the environmental tasks that we face now cannot be achieved with the same types of mandates established in the past? Or is it because past lawmaking has gone overboard in the application of mandates so that a focus on volunteerism can counterbalance past legal and regulatory excesses?

The answer varies depending on who is speaking. What is clear is that the idea of stakeholders, government and corporations negotiating new ways of advancing environmental goals is here to stay.

For NGOs, the period ahead promises to be one of major policy and legal invention as we work to refine existing agreements and arrangements to gain more substantive results, and to expose sham agreements and arrangements. Clearer thinking will be needed about the potential and limitations of using the efficiency factor and other positive incentives to encourage voluntary action. We need to develop strategies which pay due respect to efficiency while also appropriately ensuring enforceability and rights. NGOs will need to develop more effective strategies for using the resources and authority of government to promote future arrangements which effectively empower stakeholders with rights and resources - arrangements which are more enforceable and more in the nature of rights, and thus are less voluntary in nature.

The Rhône-Poulenc Agreement, Manchester, Texas

Texas law directed the Texas Water Commission to adopt regulations on hazardous waste facility permitting imposing "at a minimum, a requirement that a waste facility owner or operator fund an independent inspector for the facility, a requirement for an independent annual environmental audit of the facility, a procedure for considering comments from affected parties on the selection of the independent inspector, a requirement that operational personnel at the permitted facility be certified by the state as competent to evaluate the size and type of hazardous waste management facility for which the permit has been issued, and a requirement that such facility provide for fenceline and ambient air quality monitoring." Texas Health and Safety Code 361.114 (1993)

In compliance with and expanding upon the resulting regulations, a settlement agreement between Rhône-Poulenc (RP), local residents and the statewide organization the Texans United Education Fund provided as follows (excerpts):

Community Advisory Council: RP agrees to recognize and

work with a Community Advisory Committee ("CAC"). The CAC shall be geographically representative of the local community surrounding the Rhône-Poulenc facility and consist of no more than 25 members, all whom shall be residents of the local community. Additional members or replacement, will be nominated and voted on by existing CAC members... RP agrees to the list of persons attached as Exhibit B as the original members of the CAC.

Audit Scope: The Audit Scope shall include, at a minimum, regulatory compliance, safety training, accident prevention, Emergency response and preparedness, waste analysis and information systems, monitoring programs, and waste minimization and reduction practices... RP will consider comments from the CAC concerning details of the Audit Scope. Texans United Education Fund shall communicate any comments it has concerning the Audit Scope through the CAC.

Citizen Participation: Consistent with applicable safety standards, designated CAC members and a representative of Texans United Education Fund will participate with the auditor in the physical inspection of the plant, interview with plant personnel and the review of documents, including: safety and emergency response manuals and training materials; existing safety and environmental agency inspections and nonconfidential safety and environmental records; documents associated with waste minimization and reduction plans or practices; documents associated with waste generation and disposal; hazard assessments and risk analysis; and lists of accidents, upsets, near misses and corrective actions.... RP will allow a RP worker representative of the CAC's choice to participate in the inspection. The CAC will allow a representative of RP's choice to be present during all phases of on-site audit.

Consistent with applicable safety standards, RP will continue to allow citizen inspections of its Manchester plant operations by appointment at all reasonable times.

All documents provided to the CAC by RP pursuant to this Settlement Agreement shall also be provided to the public library and be considered public information; however, RP reserves the right to consider certain materials provided to the CAC company confidential and proprietary and request that those documents not enter the public domain.

The CAC will control its own agenda and can make use of resource persons it chooses. RP will have representatives available to answer questions and concerns of the CAC as required. It is understood that the CAC and the Texans United Education Fund are independent of RP, and RP shall in no way be responsible for acts or omissions of the CAC or the Texans United Education Fund, their members, agents or other representatives. It is also understood that the CAC and the Texans United Education Fund are in no way responsible for the acts or omissions of RP which negatively impact the workers, community, or environment.

RP agrees to provide financial assistance to the CAC in an amount agreeable to both the CAC and RP to cover administrative costs of the CAC, if said financial assistance is requested by the CAC....The CAC will designate a member to receive communications from RP and to chair CAC meetings. Should an occasion arise where both the CAC and RP desire the services of a facilitator, said facilitator must be agreeable to both parties.

Audit Findings: The auditor will present a copy of the audit findings to RP, the GAO, and other affected persons as identified by the TWC. Additionally, Texans United Education Fund will be provided with a copy of the audit findings for the first annual audit conducted under this agreement. RP further agrees to consider recommendations, if any are forthcoming, from citizen participants in the audit and negotiate in good faith the implementation of these recommendations.

RP agrees to discuss and negotiate improvement of local emergency notification procedures agreeable to the CAC and City of Houston officials. RP agrees to allow the CAC to have input into the design of this system. This would include the use of the plant siren and a localized radio broadcast system.

RP ... agrees to split samples with the CAC or with representatives of the CAC when requested, allowing representatives, consistent with applicable safety standards and regulations, to be present during sampling procedures to receive split samples for independent analysis.

Health Survey: RP agrees to provide to the CAC a copy of its own employee health study prepared in January of 1992. RP agrees to work in conjunction with the CAC to review the feasibility of a citizens health survey... If RP and the CAC agree upon a citizens' health survey design and form, RP agrees to cover the administrative expense incurred by the CAC in performing a citizens' health survey in the local community ... in an amount not to exceed $4,000 ... Nothing in this Settlement Agreement shall be construed to require medical testing of individuals.

Notes

[1] "Use of Supplemental Environmental Projects by EPA, States Increasing as Familiarity Grows," BNA Environment Reporter, June 10, 1994, p.282.

[2] Dave Johnson, "Downsizing: Prelude to Safety's Next Catastrophe?" Industrial Safety and Hygiene News, May 1994, p.31.

[3] USEPA, Policy on the Use of Supplemental Environmental Project in Enforcement Settlements, February 12, 1991.

[4] Some advisory groups are full of well-meaning people who may look like average residents, except that they have an above-average financial stake in maintaining favorable status with corporate officers - e.g. owners of restaurants or hotels who benefit from having the firm send visitors to the plant their way for food or lodging. These panelists are unlikely to engage in very much criticism of corporate performance, since their personal income may hang tenuously in the balance. Also in order to avoid criticism over their committee selection processes, an increasing number of corporations are hiring consulting firms to screen advisory committee members. The firm's management can then shift the blame to the consultant when a key local activist is excluded from participation.

[5] CMA News, November 1992, p.4.

[6] "Shattered Image," Business Ethics, Sept./Oct. 1994, p.25.

Chapter 18

Les Accords Volontaires: un Exemple en France, l'Affaire de Marckolsheim

par Bernard Dyssli

Introduction

Marckolsheim est une petite ville située au bord du Rhin, au milieu de l'Alsace à environ une cinquantaine de kilomètres au sud de Strasbourg. Dès le début des années 1960, conformément à un schéma global d'aménagement du territoire ayant opté pour une industrialisation de la frange rhénane liée à la voie navigable, une grande partie de la forêt rhénane de Marckolsheim est classée en zone industrielle pour permettre la création d'une zone portuaire de près de deux mille hectares dont la réalisation et la gestion ont été confiées à un établissement public spécialisé, le Port Autonome de Strasbourg.

Le site de Marckolsheim devient au milieu des années 1970 l'un des hauts lieux de l'écologie en France. En effet les données de l'aménagement de la zone portuaire ont profondément changé. D'une part les objectifs ambitieux affichés dans les années 1960 n'ont pas été réalisés, la zone industrielle n'ayant même pas été aménagée et le site toujours boisé. D'autre part, en 1965, s'est créée en Alsace l'une des premières fédérations d'associations de protection de l'environnement, l'Association Fédérative Régionale pour la Protection de la Nature (A.F.R.P.N.) qui sensibilise la population alsacienne à la problématique de la protection des richesses naturelles de la région[1]. L'un des objectifs principaux de cette fédération qui regroupe environ deux cents associations de protection de l'environnement va notamment porter sur la protection de la forêt rhénane[2].

En 1974, le projet d'implantation d'une usine de fabrication de stéarates de plomb dans la zone industrielle se heurte à l'opposition farouche de la population qui craint les effets néfastes pour la santé de la pollution par le plomb[3]. Elle est soutenue par l'Association Fédérative Régionale pour la Protection de la Nature qui est elle opposée à la destruction de la forêt[4]. Le projet sera abandonné suite à l'occupation du site non seulement par les opposants français au projet mais aussi les associations badoises de protection de l'environnement.

Fin des années 1980, une société autrichienne désire implanter en Alsace une usine de fabrication, à partir de céréales, d'acide citrique[5]. C'est un terrain situé dans la zone industrielle de Marckolsheim qui lui est proposé car la société désire avoir un accès direct à la voie navigable du Rhin. Le projet se concrétise le premier trimestre de l'année 1989 et dès qu'il est connu il suscite à nouveau l'opposition de l'Association Fédérative Régionale pour la Protection de la Nature.

Pourtant contrairement au premier conflit, la seconde affaire de Marckolsheim va déboucher sur une solution négociée (I) et, au delà des raisons qui expliquent cette issue, il est intéressant de tirer les principales leçons de cette affaire (II).

1. La seconde affaire de Marckolsheim: du conflit à la solution négociée

Ce banal projet d'implantation d'une usine dans une forêt classée en zone industrielle va devenir, en quelques jours, un psychodrame national (A) mais conscientes de leurs faiblesses, les parties en conflit vont opter pour une solution négociée (B).

1.1 Un psychodrame national

Bien que le conflit dure depuis plusieurs mois, c'est au début de l'été 1990 qu'il prend une ampleur nationale[6]. Comme chaque début d'été, les médias n'ont pas de grandes informations à développer.

L'actualité, notamment politique, est faible même si le Président de la République vient de rappeler sa sensibilité aux problèmes d'environnement en affirmant son aversion pour les défrichements. Profitant de l'occasion, Antoine Waechter, l'un des chefs de file du parti écologiste "Les Verts", originaire de la région, interpelle le Président de la République et lui demande de bloquer le projet de défrichement de la forêt rhénane en cours d'instruction au ministère de l'Agriculture.

Mal informé des éléments de cette affaire (voir infra), le Président de la République répond au leader écologiste qu'il n'est pas opposé au défrichement et que l'Etat s'engage en compensation à protéger six mille hectares de forêts rhénanes. Dans la foulée, le Ministre de l'agriculture accorde l'autorisation de défrichement de la forêt. L'affaire prend une dimension nationale lorsque un grand quotidien national demande de façon quelque peu impertinente au Président de la République ami des arbres s'il aime également les arbres d'Alsace[7].

Par ailleurs, profitant d'une conférence de presse organisée par les promoteurs du projet et destinée à présenter l'autorisation de défrichement, les écologistes manifestent leur désaccord au projet. L'ensemble des médias nationaux s'empare alors de l'affaire qui lui permet de confronter directement le Président de la République aux mouvements écologistes et notamment au chef de file du parti des Verts.

Afin de trouver une solution politique au problème, le gouvernement décide alors de réunir les parties en présence au travers d'Etats généraux de la forêt rhénane destinés à mettre fin au conflit. Lors de cette réunion qui a lieu début août, le ministre de l'Agriculture s'engage à protéger très rapidement l'ensemble des forêts rhénanes, mais l'Association Fédérative Régionale pour la Protection de la Nature réitère son opposition à l'implantation de l'usine dans la forêt de Marckolsheim. Il est alors décidé de constituer un groupe de travail chargé de trouver un autre site d'implantation pour le projet. Un mois plus tard, le conflit s'achève par une solution négociée.

1.2 Les raisons du compromis

Mieux vaut un mauvais arrangement qu'un bon procès. Cet adage ne suffit pourtant pas à expliquer les raisons pour lesquelles les différentes parties au conflit ont préféré la solution négociée. En fait, le recours au compromis s'explique par les faiblesses des deux plus importants protagonistes du conflit, à savoir d'une part l'Etat et d'autre part la fédération des associations de protection de l'environnement.

1.2.1 Les faiblesses de l'Etat

1.2.1.1 Les faiblesses au plan politique

La position de l'Etat présente de grandes faiblesses au plan politique pour deux raisons:d'une part l'argumentation scientifique présentée par le mouvement associatif en faveur de la protection de la forêt rhénane est difficilement contestable, d'autant plus que l'Etat s'était déjà, par le passé, engagé à protéger ces forêts.

En effet, au plan scientifique, la nécessité de la protection de la forêt rhénane est difficilement contestable. La forêt alluviale du Rhin est considérée comme une des plus intéressantes d'Europe avec celle du Danube[8]. Il s'agit d'un écosystème très riche, au plan de la flore mais aussi de la faune, dont la valeur a été reconnue au plan international par le Conseil de l'Europe et l'Union Internationale pour la Conservation de la Nature.

Or, suite aux travaux de rectification du cours du Rhin et de l'aménagement du Grand canal d'Alsace, ainsi qu'au développement des gravières et des zones industrielles, la forêt rhénane a perdu près de 50% de sa superficie en 50 ans[9]. Alors qu'à l'origine elle constituait une bande continue le long du Rhin la forêt a été morcelée et le massif forestier de Marckolsheim-Schoenau est, avec ses 1800 hectares, le plus grand massif relictuel.

L'Etat pensait néanmoins pouvoir mettre l'argumentation des écologistes en défaut sur le site même de l'implantation de l'usine. En effet, en 1983, dans le but évident de contrer les mouvements écologistes, la municipalité de Marckolsheim avait organisé de façon originale le déboisement presque total du site[10]. Mais en une quinzaine d'années, le terrain avait été recolonisé par la forêt. Pour les promoteurs du projet, il n'y a plus de forêt rhénane mais un mauvais taillis sous entendu sans valeur écologique, les arbres les plus vieux ayant seulement une quinzaine d'années[11]. L'argumentation soutenue par l'administration en charge de la législation forestière n'était cependant pas fondée au plan scientifique car elle oubliait deux données fondamentales de écosystème de la forêt rhénane.

En premier lieu, malgré sa jeunesse, ce taillis constituait encore un substrat forestier et pouvait déjà être considéré comme une forêt rhénane en devenir. En second lieu, la forêt rhénane ne pouvait être affectée par un déboisement comme celui effectué en 1983. En effet, avant l'aménagement du Rhin, les déboisements de certaines parties de la forêt du fait des crues du fleuve étaient fréquents, le secteur déboisé étant ensuite recolonisé par la forêt. Le déboisement sauvage de 1983 n'avait ainsi que répété un phénomène naturel et le site permettait aux scientifiques d'étudier le processus de recolonisation.

Par ailleurs, la richesse scientifique des forêts est reconnue par l'Etat qui s'était engagé à protéger les forêts rhénanes rélictuelles. Or, même si certains massifs forestiers avaient ponctuellement fait l'objet de mesures de protection[12], cette promesse n'avait pas été tenue, comme en témoigne le blocage, en raison d'un conflit entre protection de la nature et développement des industriels extractives, du projet de classement en réserve naturelle du delta de la Sauer, considéré comme un site rhénan d'une valeur exceptionnelle, là encore reconnue au plan international[13].

Enfin, dès le début du conflit, l'Association Fédérative Régionale pour la Protection de la Nature avait menacé d'occuper le site comme lors de la première affaire en 1974. L'Etat craint que les associations de protection de l'environnement mettent à exécution cette menace pour bloquer le projet. Le risque politique est important car, même isolé comme on pourra le voir ci-après, le mouvement associatif est soutenu par les élus écologistes. L'utilisation de la force publique contre des élus présente un risque politique non négligeable. Enfin, le Président de la République devait en décembre 1990 venir à Strasbourg pour présider une Conférence mondiale sur la forêt et il était difficile d'envisager de tenir un discours protecteur des forêts à une cinquantaine de kilomètres d'un site occupé par des mouvements écologistes pour bloquer le défrichement d'une forêt dont la valeur internationale était incontestable.

1.2.1.2 Les faiblesses au plan juridique

Dès l'annonce de l'octroi de l'autorisation de défrichement et avant même sa notification, l'Association Fédérative Régionale pour la Protection de la Nature avait saisit le Tribunal administratif de Strasbourg pour obtenir son annulation. L'issue de ce recours est incertaine mais l'administration ne peut oublier que le même Tribunal avait déjà lors du précédent conflit annulé la déclaration d'utilité publique relative à la création de la zone industrielle de Marckolsheim[14].

Le juge administratif avait par ailleurs confirmé la nécessité de prendre en compte la protection des espaces naturels rhénans remarquables en annulant l'extension d'une gravière dans le site du delta de la Sauer[15]. Compte tenu de l'importance de la forêt rhénane de Marckolsheim, notamment au plan scientifique, le Tribunal pouvait très bien estimer que le maintien de cette forêt était nécessaire à l'équilibre biologique de la région[16] et confirmer sa jurisprudence favorable à la protection de la forêt.

En outre, au delà de la procédure menée contre le défrichement, l'Association Fédérative Régionale pour la Protection de la Nature pouvait entamer une véritable guérilla juridique en attaquant systématiquement les nombreuses autres autorisations nécessaires à la réalisation du projet[17]. Comme ces recours risquaient pour le moins de retarder la réalisation du projet, l'Etat craignait un abandon du projet par l'industriel car ce dernier désirait pouvoir démarrer son entreprise dans les plus brefs délais.

1.2.2 Les faiblesses du mouvement associatif

Si la solution négociée s'explique par les faiblesses de l'Etat, ce sont surtout les points faibles du mouvement associatif qui ont permis la signature du compromis.

1.2.2.1 La solitude du mouvement associatif

Même s'il est soutenu par les élus écologistes, le mouvement associatif n'a pas la puissance nécessaire pour s'opposer au projet et notamment pour mettre sa menace d'occuper le site à exécution, car d'une part la population locale est favorable au projet et d'autre part les associations badoises de protection de l'environnement sont peu motivées par cette affaire.

Contrairement à la première affaire, où la population locale était farouchement opposée au projet d'industrialisation car elle craignait les effets de la pollution, les habitants de Marckolsheim sont favorables à l'implantation de l'usine d'acide citrique. Celle-ci ne comporte pas de risque de pollution toxique et le canton de Marckolsheim connaît des problèmes de chômage très importants. Ceci explique le succès d'une manifestation organisée en faveur du projet début septembre par des élus de tous bords politiques favorables à l'implantation de cette usine.

Par ailleurs, l'Association Fédérative Régionale pour la Protection de la Nature n'est pas soutenue par les mouvements écologistes badois qui avaient en 1974 contribué au succès de la première occupation du site. L'absence de cette solidarité transfrontalière fragilise également la position du mouvement associatif.

La fédération des associations était ainsi consciente de la difficulté d'occuper le site sans le soutien de la population locale laquelle était à l'origine du succès de la première occupation en 1974 et des mouvements écologistes allemands. Cet élément va pousser les écologistes à accepter un compromis d'autant plus qu'ils ne sont plus soutenus par les médias.

1.2.2.2 La fin du soutien des médias

Le deuxième point faible du mouvement associatif est, à partir du mois d'août, le désintérêt des médias pour l'affaire de Marckolsheim. En effet, dans les premiers jours du mois d'août 1990, les troupes de l'Irak envahissent le Koweït et c'est le début de ce qui deviendra la guerre du golfe. Les médias perçoivent immédiatement l'importance de l'événement auquel ils se consacrent presque entièrement. L'affaire de Marckolsheim passe rapidement au second plan.

Or, le succès de l'action du mouvement associatif reposait essentiellement sur la portée que lui avait donné les médias prenant fait et cause pour la protection de la forêt rhénane. Sans le soutien des médias la position du mouvement écologiste était profondément affaiblie.

Consciente de ses faiblesses, l'AFRPN va accepter un compromis qui permet l'implantation de l'usine et un défrichement partiel de la forêt, mais qui donne un élan primordial à la conservation des forêts rhénanes.

2. Les leçons de la seconde affaire de Marckolsheim

Le 11 septembre 1990, le conflit s'achève par la signature d'un document qui matérialise un point d'accord entre les promoteurs du projet et la fédération des associations de protection de l'environnement. Au delà de la signature de ce compromis et des raisons justifiant cette solution, deux enseignements majeurs peuvent être tirés de ce second conflit. Le premier porte sur les conséquences de l'absence totale de prise en compte de l'environnement lors du choix du site retenu pour le projet et qui a été à l'origine même du conflit (A), le second met en lumière l'absence de cadre juridique adéquat pour formaliser les accords négociés entre pouvoirs publics et associations de protection de l'environnement (B).

2.1. L'absence de prise en compte de l'environnement à l'amont du projet

Le conflit trouve son origine dans l'erreur qui a été commise dans le choix du site aussi bien par l'industriel que par l'Etat, en raison de l'ignorance d'une donnée pourtant fondamentale, la valeur scientifique de la forêt. Pourtant ces deux acteurs auraient pu éviter une telle erreur si les outils mis à leur disposition avaient été utilisés, à savoir l'étude d'impact et l'avis des services compétents.

2.1.1 L'étude d'impact

Introduit en France par la loi n° 76-623 relative à la protection de la nature et son décret d'application n° 77-1141 du 12 octobre 1977, le système de l'étude d'impact a été étendu à toute l'Union Européenne par la directive du 27 juin 1985. Le projet d'implantation d'une usine d'acide citrique était soumis à une telle étude car il entraînait un défrichement réalisé à des fins industrielles[18] et car l'exploitation devait faire l'objet d'une autorisation au titre de la législation des installations classées pour la protection de l'environnement[19].

Cet instrument, destiné à éclairer les populations concernées et les autorités administratives compétentes pour autoriser ou approuver un projet soumis à étude d'impact sur les conséquences de ce projet pour l'environnement est considéré par les maîtres d'ouvrage comme une simple formalité administrative à laquelle il faut obligatoirement satisfaire pour pouvoir réaliser son projet. C'est pourquoi, l'étude d'impact est en général faite juste avant le dépôt de la demande d'autorisation alors que les choix fondamentaux concernant le projet ont déjà été fixés.

Or l'étude d'impact devrait être considérée non comme un pièce purement formelle à ajouter à une demande d'approbation mais comme une procédure ou un outil permettant d'optimiser les choix en matière d'environnement. Par ailleurs l'étude d'impact est toujours envisagée dans sa globalité alors que les textes prévoient qu'elle doit contenir plusieurs parties distinctes sans pour autant exiger qu'elles soient toutes rédigées de manière simultanée. Ainsi, la première partie de l'étude d'impact doit porter sur l'état initial de l'environnement avant la réalisation du projet[20] et la logique voudrait que cette partie soit faite avant le choix définitif du site afin que le maître d'ouvrage puisse le cas échéant étudier d'autres variantes peut être moins néfastes pour l'environnement[21].

Dans l'affaire de Marckolsheim, il apparaît que lorsque l'industriel a pris en 1989 la décision de principe de s'implanter dans la zone de Marckolsheim, il ignorait totalement la valeur écologique du site qui lui était proposé ainsi que tous les aspects sociologiques qui lui étaient liés en raison de la première affaire de Marckolsheim. Or une analyse détaillée de l'état initial de l'environnement aurait sans doute permis au maître d'ouvrage de réorienter son choix, ce qui devenait plus difficile à faire lorsque, près d'une année plus tard, le conflit avec les associations de protection de l'environnement est entré dans une phase aiguë.

L'affaire de Marckolsheim montre que l'étude d'impact est également un outil mis à la disposition des maîtres d'ouvrage eux-mêmes pour optimiser leurs décisions en fonction des préoccupations d'environnement.

2.1.2 Les services spécialisés en matière d'environnement

L'absence de prise en compte de l'environnement peut aussi être constatée au niveau de l'Etat. Elle s'explique par l'organisation des services de l'Etat en matière d'environnement. Il peut sembler de prime abord étonnant que les autorités de l'Etat et particulièrement le Président de la République aient pu commettre une grossière erreur sur la valeur scientifique de la forêt rhénane située dans l'emprise du projet.

En réalité, l'origine de l'erreur vient du fait que l'Etat n'a pas eu à sa disposition l'ensemble des données du problème en raison de l'éclatement de ses services chargés de la gestion de l'environnement, notamment au niveau local..

Bien qu'il existe en France depuis 1971 un ministère chargé de l'environnement , celui-ci n'a toujours pas dans ses attributions la gestion des forêts qui est toujours dans le domaine de compétence du ministère de l'agriculture. Par conséquent, l'instruction des demandes d'autorisation de défrichement est, au plan local, assurée par la Direction Départementale de l'Agriculture et de la Forêt et non par la Direction Régionale de l'Environnement[22]. Ceci peut expliquer que l'intérêt scientifique de maintenir les espaces forestiers touchés par le projet n'ait pas été perçu à sa juste mesure. Par ailleurs, les textes qui fixent la procédure à suivre pour accorder une autorisation de défrichement n'imposent pas, même si le dossier doit comporter une étude d'impact, la consultation systématique de la Direction Régionale de l'Environnement[23]. Or ce service compétent en matière d'études d'impact et chargé de la protection des espaces naturels aurait pu, à l'occasion d'une telle consultation, mettre en évidence la valeur scientifique de la forêt et la nécessité de conserver cet espace naturel remarquable.

Le conflit de Marckolsheim illustre ainsi la nécessité pour les autorités chargées de prendre des décisions ayant des conséquences pour l'environnement d'avoir au préalable tous les éléments d'un dossier y compris et surtout ceux relatifs à l'environnement afin qu'elles ne se prononcent pas seulement sur les seules considérations économiques d'un projet d'implantation industriel.

La seconde affaire de Marckolsheim met aussi en évidence l'absence de cadre juridique adéquat pour la résolution non juridictionnelle des conflits.

2.2 L'absence de cadre juridique adéquat pour formaliser les accords négociés

Les conflits entre les associations de protection de l'environnement et les pouvoirs publics sont habituellement tranchés par le juge administratif. Ceci explique peut être l'absence dans le droit français d'un cadre juridique adapté à la résolution négociée des conflits. Le compromis de Marckolsheim illustre particulièrement cette carence du droit.

En effet, le document signé le 11 septembre 1990 pour mettre fin au conflit s'avère au plan juridique complètement atypique. Sa nature est en effet incertaine et la portée des obligations souscrites par les différentes parties au conflit particulièrement floue.

2.2.1 Une nature incertaine

Il est difficile de qualifier au plan juridique le document[24] qui formalise la fin du conflit. A priori, le nombre des signataires et la réunion d'un accord de volontés pour mettre fin au litige indique qu'il s'agit d'un contrat. Pourtant, et la terminologie utilisée n'est pas innocente, le compromis s'intitule Relevé de décisions de la réunion du 11 septembre 1990 concernant la recherche d'un lieu d'implantation en Alsace pour la société JUNGBUNZLAUER (J.B.L.).

Les signataires n'ont, semble-t-il, pas voulu se placer sur le terrain du contrat. Mais malgré l'allusion à des décisions, ce qui pourrait faire croire à une compilation d'actes unilatéraux, la nature contractuelle du document ressort du texte même du compromis[25] même si l'obligation contractée par l'AFRPN, à savoir l'acceptation de l'industrialisation et le défrichement partiel du site n'est pas clairement décrite[26].

Dès lors que le compromis a une nature contractuelle il se pose la question de savoir s'il s'agit d'un contrat de droit public ou de droit privé. La solution n'est pas aisée à dégager pour deux raisons.

La première raison tient à la diversité et au nombre des parties. Le document a été signé par des personnes publiques comme l'Etat, des collectivités locales (le département du Bas-Rhin et la Commune de Marckolsheim), un établissement public (le port autonome de Strasbourg) mais aussi par des personnes privées comme la fédération des associations de protection de l'environnement et l'industriel.

La deuxième raison concerne la diversité des engagements qui sont pris par les différentes parties lesquelles sont autant de concessions faites à la fédération des associations de protection de la nature pour qu'elle accepte le principe de l'implantation de l'usine sur le site initialement choisi.

Une première série d'engagements sont pris par l'industriel pour limiter les effets défavorables de son projet en ce qui concerne la forêt, comme la réduction de la superficie de son terrain de 22 ha ou encore la conservation d'une partie à l'état naturel[27]. Ces mesures peuvent s'analyser comme des obligations de droit privé contractées par l'industriel envers l'Association Fédérative Régionale pour la Protection de la Nature.

A l'inverse toute une série de mesures comprises dans le compromis, comme la renonciation par la Commune de Marckolsheim et le Port Autonome de Strasbourg à la poursuite de l'industrialisation du reste de la zone, doivent être rattachées au droit public. Il en est de même pour l'engagement pris par le Préfet de lancer la procédure de classement en réserve naturelle du massif forestier de Marckolsheim-Schoenau.

Force est donc de relever la nature mixte du contrat mettant fin au conflit et de s'interroger sur la portée réelle des engagements qui ont été souscrits.

2.2.2 La portée du compromis

La nature incertaine du compromis rejaillit sur la portée réelle des engagements qui ont été pris par les différentes parties même s'il est à présent admis qu'en compensation de la mise en oeuvre d'un projet detruisant un site particulier, l'Etat puisse proposer la mise en place de mesures de protection sur d'autres sites[28].

Il se pose en effet la question de l'effectivité[29] des engagements qui ont été pris et notamment des conséquences du non respect du compromis aussi bien par les pouvoirs publics que par le mouvement associatif.

En outre, il est permis de douter de la légalité de certains aspects du compromis comme la renonciation à la poursuite de l'industrialisation de la zone. En effet, ces dispositions relèvent de l'application de mesures de police et le juge administratif a rappelé que dans ce domaine l'administration doit agir par la voie de décisions unilatérales et non par la voie contractuelle[30]. Par conséquent, les dispositions d'ordre contractuel qui auraient pour objet ou pour effet d'entraver l'exercice de pouvoirs de police[31] ne peuvent être invoquées par les administrés[32].

De même, le fait que ce soit le maire de Marckolsheim qui ait seul signé l'engagement de la commune de réviser son plan d'occupation des sols permet de douter de la légalité d'une mesure qui relève de la compétence du Conseil municipal.

Force est donc de constater que la portée réelle du compromis est bien plus politique que juridique. Sa bonne ou sa mauvaise application par l'ensemble des parties peut avoir un effet non négligeable quant à la possibilité de trouver des solutions négociées aux futurs conflits en matière d'environnement.

Parallèlement, il serait utile que le législateur mette en place un cadre juridique approprié à la résolution négociée des conflits entre les pouvoirs publics et les associations de protection de l'environnement.

3. Conclusion

Indéniablement la seconde affaire de Marckolsheim et le compromis auquel elle a abouti ont été bénéfiques pour la protection de la forêt rhénane.

Paradoxalement, la position de l'Etat sur la question de la protection des forêts a été renforcée car il a affirmé à plusieurs reprises pendant le conflit et notamment lors des Etats généraux de la forêt rhénane, la nécessité et sa volonté de protéger l'ensemble des forêts rhénanes résiduelles, sans que cette position de principe soit contestée par les communes et les groupes de pression favorables à l'industrialisation de la frange rhénane.

Grâce à ce renforcement de sa position politque, l'Etat a pu faire aboutir un certain nombre de procédures de protection de forêts rhénanes, malgré les avis défavorables des communes concernées[33]. Il a ainsi pu honorer les engagements pris même si pour le mouvement associatif les procédures de protection mises en oeuvre n'étaient pas les plus adéquates[34].

La position du mouvement associatif est également renforcée dans la mesure où il apparaît non seulement comme le seul interlocuteur officiel des pouvoirs publics dans le domaine de l'environnement[35] mais encore comme un interlocuteur sensé car capable d'accepter des solutions négociées.

RELEVE DE DECISIONS DE LA REUNION
DU 11 SEPTEMBRE 1990

concernant la recherche d'un lieu d'implantation en Alsace pour la société JUNGBUNZLAUER (J.B.L.)

Les promoteurs du projet ont fait valoir l'intérêt réel de l'implantation de J.B.L. en France, en particulier pour les raisons suivantes :

- la balance commerciale serait améliorée de 500 MF/an en assurant une plus grande sécurité d'approvisionnement en acide citrique

- l'investissement de 800 millions de francs bénéficierait très largement aux entreprises de construction et aux équipementiers français ; il générerait des travaux d'entretien élevés pour les entreprises locales de sous-traitance.

- les débouchés pour la culture du blé et du maïs dans l'Est de la France seraient améliorés. Ce sera un atout supplémentaire à long terme sur le marché des céréales.

- les 180 emplois (400 à 500 à terme) profiteraient à un

secteur où le taux de chômage est le plus élevé d'Alsace ; la moitié des actifs du canton de MARCKOLSHEIM travaille à l'extérieur.

Ces considérations avaient conduit à proposer l'implantation de J.B.L. sur un terrain de 82 ha appartenant au Port Autonome de Strasbourg et situé en zone industrielle de MARCKOLSHEIM, ce qui imposait un défrichement de 50,1 ha de forêt rhénane.

Or, les reliquats des forêts alluviales rhénanes constituent les écosystèmes forestiers les plus précieux d'Europe de pair avec quelques autres massifs rélictuels sur les grands fleuves.

Le classement en zone industrielle de la forêt de MARCKOLSHEIM fut effectué à une époque où cette valeur, depuis lors très largement reconnue par la Communauté Scientifique Internationale, n'était pas encore prise en compte.

La Communauté Scientifique Internationale s'élève contre toute amputation supplémentaire des forêts alluviales des grands fleuves, vu notamment les efforts très coûteux entrepris par ailleurs dans d'autres pays pour la reconstitution de tels écosystèmes.

Aussi, devant les réactions suscitées par ce projet, il a été décidé lors des Etats généraux de la forêt rhénane le 2 août 1990 :

- de lancer un plan de protection de la forêt rhénane

- de faire rechercher des solutions par un groupe de travail présidé par le Préfet pour faciliter l'implantation de J.B.L. en Alsace

Après un examen attentif des sites envisageables en Alsace par le groupe le 8 août et le 11 septembre 1990, les participants conviennent d'écarter les sites potentiels suivants :

- HOMBOURG - Petit Landau

- NAMBSHEIM - BALGAU

- HERRLISHEIM - DRUSENHEIM

- Cité EDF à MARCKOLSHEIM

Dès lors les participants reconnaissent la nécessité de réexaminer l'implantation de J.B.L. sur la zone industrielle de MARCKOLSHEIM et de l'organiser selon les modalités suivantes

a) J.B.L. accepte de réduire la superficie de son terrain de 82 à 60 ha. J.B.L. s'engage d'autre part à conserver à l'état naturel une bande de 6,55 ha (6 ha boisés, 0,55 ha de pré) le long de la limite nord de son terrain entre la limite ouest du terrain et la pointe de la forêt domaniale, bande qui sera laissée à l'extérieur de sa clôture. Ainsi le besoin de défrichement est réduit à 27,2 ha au lieu des 50,1 initialement prévus, et la forêt domaniale préservée.

b) Le Port Autonome renonce à la poursuite de l'industrialisation sur les 172 ha restants de la partie boisée actuellement classée en zone industrielle. Ainsi le Port n'amortira les infrastructures prévues initialement pour 276 ha que sur les seuls produits de 104 ha exploités.

c) La Commune de MARCKOLSHEIM renonce pour ce qui la concerne à la poursuite de l'aménagement de zones industrielles ou artisanales le long de la façade rhénane et s'engage à réviser son plan d'occupation des sols en ce sens.

En conséquence, le Préfet de Région ne notifiera pas les autorisations de défrichement en date du 16 juillet 1990 et demandera au Ministre de l'Agriculture de délivrer de nouvelles autorisations se substituant à celles du 16 juillet et limitées à 27,2 ha.

*

D'autre part, les engagements suivants sont pris par le Port Autonome :

- il fermera la route de desserte intérieure de la forêt de MARCKOLSHEIM à hauteur de la limite des communes de MARCKOLSHEIM et de MACKENHEIM.

- il achètera à E.D.F. 16 ha de forêt sur le ban de MACKENHEIM, en vue du classement en réserve naturelle dans la mesure où E.D.F. ne souhaite pas en demander le classement.

- il reboisera une bande de terrain à l'est du Muhlbach dévié, en continuité du boisement existant en partie sud de la zone industrielle ; ce boisement sera effectué sur une longueur d'environ 800 mètres et une largeur moyenne de 30 mètres environ pour une surface de 2,3 ha.

- il conservera à l'état boisé un surface de 7 ha environ en limite ouest de la zone industrielle ; surface comprenant les 6 ha compris dans le POS de MARCKOLSHEIM et la ZERC 4 comme zone graviérable.

*

Par ailleurs, le Préfet :

- proposera au comité de pilotage pour la protection de la forêt rhénane d'étudier la reconquête progressive de écosystème des forêts alluviales du massif de MARCKOLSHEIM - SCHOENAU à l'est de la digue des hautes eaux, pour une superficie minimale de 27 ha.

- proposera également au comité de pilotage de lancer dès 1991 une étude en vue de la réalisation de l'inondabilité du massif.

- engagera dans les plus brefs délais la procédure tendant au classement en réserve naturelle du massif de MARCKOLSHEIM - SCHOENAU, y compris la forêt de MACKENHEIM et de WYHL.

Enfin, le comité de pilotage sera chargé de définir et de coordonner les mesures de protection de l'ensemble des forêts rhénanes subsistant sur la base d'un inventaire exhaustif et quel que soit leur statut juridique actuel.

*

Les participants expriment en conclusion le souhait de prévenir le retour de pareilles situations.

A cet effet, conscient de la complémentarité nécessaire entre écologie et économie, ils souhaitent que des principes soient étudiés et proposés, dans un cadre approprié, existant ou à créer, regroupant les collectivités concernées, des représentants socio-professionnels, des personnalités qualifiées et des associations intéressées à la protection de l'environnement.

Le Préfet de la Région Alsace, Préfet du Bas-Rhin

Le Port Autonome de Strasbourg

JUNGBUNZLAUER S.A.

Le Maire de MARCKOLSHEIM

A.F.R.P.N.

DEPARTEMENT du BAS-RHIN

Notes

[1] Voir par exemple le numéro spécial consacré à la protection de la nature de la Revue Saison d'Alsace, n° 42, printemps 1972, 275 pages.

[2] Pour une présentation de l'importance des associations de protection de l'environnement en Alsace et de leur fédération voir E. Joly-Sibuet, P. Lascoumes, A. Guchan, R. Léost, Conflits d'environnement et intérêts protégés par les associations de défense, Aquitaine, Alsace, Bretagne, Rhône-Alpes, Paris, Ministère de l'Environnement, mai 1988 pages 175 à 195.

[3] Sur le déroulement de la première affaire de Marckolsheim, voir Edith Wenger, L'affaire C.M.W./Marckolsheim et ses prolongements, Strasbourg, Université Robert Schuman, Mémoire de DESS de droit de l'environnement et de l'aménagement du territoire, 1980, 51 pages.

[4] Cf. Edith Wenger, Mémoire précité page 19.

[5] L'acide citrique est un agent conservateur couramment utilisé dans les industries agro-alimentaires.

[6] Pour une présentation détaillée des péripéties du conflit voir Jean-Louis English, Claude Keiflin, Les carnets secrets des chuchotements, Strasbourg, Koufra et Editions de la Nuée

Bleue, pages 85 à 112.

[7] Alain Rollat, Le Président aime-t-il les arbres d'Alsace ?, Journal Le Monde, 19 juillet 1990.

[8] Le compromis rappelle ainsi que les reliquats des forêts alluviales rhénanes constituent les écosystèmes forestiers les plus précieux d'Europe de pair avec quelques autres massifs rélictuels sur les grands fleuves.

[9] Sur les 15 000 hectares de forêts rhénanes existant en 1930, il n'en y avait plus que 7 400 hectares en 1976.

[10] La municipalité avait informé la population que les habitants pouvaient librement se procurer du bois sur le site. En quelques jours tous les arbres de valeur avaient été abattus.

[11] C'est sur la base de ces informations que le Président de la République avait refusé de s'opposer au défrichement de la forêt.

[12] Voir par exemple le décret du 19 septembre 1988 portant classement comme forêt de protection de la forêt d'Artolsheim (Bas-Rhin), J.O. du 23 septembre 1988 page 12130 ou encore le décret du 22 décembre 1989 portant classement comme forêt de protection du massif forestier de Marckolsheim (Bas-Rhin), J.O. du 2 janvier 1990.

[13] Voir la présentation détaillée de ce conflit par Edith Wenger in L'écologie et la loi, le statut juridique de l'environnement, sous la direction d'Alexandre Kiss, Paris, Editions de L'Harmattan 1989 pages 285 et suivantes.

[14] Michel Prieur, Commentaire sous Tribunal administratif de Strasbourg 6 juin 1975, Ep. Ott Hubert et autres c/ Préfet du Bas-Rhin, Revue Juridique de l'Environnement 1976 n° 1, pp. 46-51.

[15] Bernard Dyssli, Note sous Tribunal administratif de Strasbourg, 2 décembre 1982. Revue Juridique de l'Environnement 1983, n° 2, p. 118-127.

[16] Selon l'article L. 311-3 du code Forestier, l'autorisation de défrichement peut être refusée lorsque la conservation des bois

ou massifs qu'ils complètent est reconnue nécessaire à l'équilibre biologique d'une région. Sur la base de ce texte, le juge administratif peut annuler des autorisations de défrichement manifestement contraire à ce principe.

[17] La construction et l'exploitation de l'usine devait encore faire l'objet d'un permis de construire ainsi que d'une procédure autorisation d'exploitation comprenant une enquête publique au titre de la législation sur les installations classées pour la protection de l'environnement.

[18] Jusqu'en 1993, tous les défrichements réalisés à des fins autres qu'agricoles étaient soumis à étude d'impact. Depuis l'intervention d'un décret du 25 février 1993, seuls les défrichements portant sur une surface de plus de 25 hectares sont soumis à étude d'impact sans qu'il soit tenu compte du but du défrichement.

[19] La loi n° 76-663 du 19 juillet 1976 relative aux installations classées pour la protection de l'environnement soumet à contrôle de l'administration toutes sortes d'activités ou d'installations qui peuvent être à l'origine de pollutions ou de nuisances. Les activités qui présentent le plus de risques de pollution sont soumises à une procédure d'autorisation préalable comportant obligatoirement une étude d'impact et une enquête publique.

[20] En vertu de l'article 2 du décret du 12 octobre 1977 l'étude d'impact doit en premier lieu comporter une analyse de l'état initial du site et de son environnement, portant notamment sur les richesses naturelles et les espaces naturels, agricoles, forestiers, affectés par le projet.

[21] Ce qui est implicitement prévu par les textes puisque le décret de 1977 prévoit que l'étude d'impact doit présenter les raisons pour lesquelles, notamment du point de vue des préoccupations d'environnement, parmi les partis envisagés, le projet a été retenu.

[22] Jusqu'en 1991, ce service s'appelait la Délégation Régionale à l'Architecture et à l'Environnement.

[23] Dans la procédure d'autorisation d'exploiter au titre des

installations classées, la consultation de la Direction Régionale de l'Environnement n'est obligatoire que depuis juin 1994.

[24] Voir le texte intégral du compromis en annexe.

[25] Ainsi le compromis fait état de certains engagements pris par la Commune de Marckolsheim et le Port Autonome de Strasbourg.

[26] Le texte du compromis mentionne simplement que les participants (dont l'Association Fédérative Régionale pour la Protection de la Nature) reconnaissent la nécessité de réexaminer l'implantation de J.B.L. sur la zone industrielle et de l'organiser selon certaines modalités.

[27] Alors qu'à l'origine le projet emportait le défrichement d'une cinquantaine d'hectares, ce dernier est réduit de moitié.

[28] Voir sur ce point Jean Untermaier, De la compensation comme principe général du droit et de l'implantation de télésièges en site classé, Commentaire de l'arrêt du 27 novembre 1985, Commune de Chamonix-Mont-Blanc c/ Association de sauvegarde de la haute vallée de l'Arve et de la vallée de l'Arveyron, Revue Juridique de l'Environnement n° 4/1986 pages 381 à 412.

[29] Cf. Jean Untermaier, article précité, page 409.

[30] Conseil d'Etat 8 mars 1985, Association Les Amis de la Terre, AJDA 1985 page 382, Rec. page 73 Observations Jacques Moreau, AJDA 1985 page 383.

[31] En l'espèce les dispositions des schémas et plans d'urbanisme qui prévoient l'industrialisation de la zone.

[32] Tribunal administratif de Toulouse 10 juin 1987, Société Alran.

[33] Voir Corinne Léonhart, Projet de classement du massif forestier de Marckolsheim-Schoenau, Strasbourg, Université Robert Schuman, Mémoire de DESS de droit de l'environnement et de l'aménagement du territoire, 1993, 50 pages.

[34] L'Etat a utilisé la procédure de la forêt de protection,

procédure dont les textes figurent dans le code forestier et qui permet essentiellement de péréniser l'état boisé alors que les associations de protection de l'environnement auraient souhaité la mise en place de réserves naturelles qui permettent la protection et la gestion de l'ensemble de l'éco-système.

[35] On constate que le parti écologiste "Les Verts" n'a pas été associé à la signature du compromis.

Voluntary Agreements. A French Example: The Marckolsheim Affair

Summary

Marckolsheim is a small town situated on the Rhine in the middle of Alsace, around 50km to the south of Strasburg. In 1960 a large part of the Rhine valley forest around Marckolsheim was declared an industrial zone to permit the construction of a vast inland port covering almost 2,000ha (1ha = 2.4711 acres). While this ambitious project never matured, two conflicts have occurred since the 1960s over proposals to clear part of the forests to make room for industrial development.

The first conflict erupted in 1974 over the proposal to clear part of the remaining Rhine valley forest around Marckolsheim for an industrial development that involved the construction of a factory for the manufacturing of industrial lead components. Fierce opposition to the project from the local population which feared the adverse effects of pollution from the factory and the combined efforts of both environmental groups from Alsace, notably the Association Fédérative Régionale pour la Protection de la Nature (A.F.R.P.N.), and neighbouring Baden (Germany) helped to frustrate this development proposal. The decision not to go ahead with this project came after environmental groups from both France and Baden had occupied the proposed site of the project.

In the late 1980s, however, a new project emerged which involved an Austrian investor who proposed to clear almost

50ha of the forest to make room for a factory that was to produce citric acids from cereals. This time around the ensuing conflict could only be resolved through a compromise solution negotiated between the environmental associations, the developer and the authorities.

The necessity to arrive at a negotiated compromise solution had arisen because both the public authorities' and the environmental groups' position was open to challenge from the other side due to a number of weaknesses in political and legal respects.

Politically, the authorities were in a weak position because some of the highest state officials, including the President of the Republic, had committed themselves to the protection of the remaining Rhine valley forests. By the late 1980s the latter had already been reduced to 50 percent of the terrain they at one time used to cover. Furthermore, the State had also committed itself to protecting the forest's scientific value. Prior to the 1980s, however, promises in this direction had not been lived up to despite the growing international recognition of the forest's scientific value as well. Finally, the environmental associations threatened to occupy the chosen site, as they had done on the occasion of the first conflict in 1974. Such a move would have been potentially very embarrassing to the authorities, as the President of the Republic was to address soon an international conference in Strasbourg on the protection of forested areas.

Legally, the authorities' campaign to push the project through suffered from a defect in that the environmental associations had commenced proceedings in the Strasburg administrative court (Tribunal administratif) as soon as the announcement had been made that an authorization to clear part of the forest had been given. While the outcome of the these particular proceedings may have been uncertain, the administrative court had made it clear, however, in previous cases that it was quite willing to annul executive decisions where these failed to take adequate account of environmental considerations. In any case, the environmental associations were in a position to engage the authorities in protracted legal wrangles which threatened to delay the approved project by a considerable amount of time. The investor, however, had made it clear that he wished to begin operating his facility as quickly as possible.

The environmental association's position suffered from serious weaknesses as well, though. To begin with, it could not count on large measure of support within the local population which was largely in favour of the project as it would bring in badly needed jobs in an area plagued by high unemployment. Moreover, the Association Fédérative Régionale pour la Protection de la Nature this time could not rely on the same measure of support from its counterparts across the river. The A.F.R.P.N.'s position was further weakened in August 1990 when Saddam Hussein invaded Kuwait. Follwing the Iraqi invasion of Kuwait the national media immediately lost interest in the story and the association ran the risk of losing support among the larger national public. Hence, a negotiated solution had to be found.

Two lessons can be drawn from the outcome of the dispute.

The first revolves round the near total absence of environmental considerations in private and public decision-making concerning the proposed development and its site. The developer and the authorities could have avoided the conflict, at least in part, if a more sensible use had been made of the available EIA procedures and if the developer had not viewed these as a mere formality to rubber-stamp his and the authorities' decision as to an appropriate site for the project. For under the French EIA legislation the first part of an impact study is to be drawn up before any decision has been made as to the concrete site of the proposal. This first part of the study is to focus exclusively on the original state of the environment around the proposed site and, depending on the evaluation of the environment in its original state, is to leave room for an alternative siting decision. It would appear that in the present case this first step in the compilation of an EIA had been undertaken far too late in the investor's internal decision-making process, and consequently, proposed site's outstanding environmental and ecological value. The unfolding of events in this affair has demonstrated that EIA procedures are a tool that is available to developers in their own interest as well to optimize their decision-making in accordance with environmental considerations.

The authorities' decision-making in relation to the authorization to clear part of the forest also showed a marked lack of awareness of the area's outstanding environmental value. The problem here turned out to be that authorisations for clearing forest lands continue to be under the jurisdiction of the Ministry of Agriculture rather than the Ministry of the Environment. The decision to grant an authorization to clear the forest also revealed procedural *lacunae* in that the Ministry of Agriculture's offices are not necessarily under an obligation to consult first with the Ministry of Environment where the necessary expertise to evaluate the true environmental and ecological value of the concerned forest lands would have been available.

The second lesson that can be drawn from the outcome of the second conflict surrounding the Marckolsheim forests is the lack of an appropriate legislative framework within which agreements between the authorities, the investors and the environmental associations can be negotiated. For the legal value and status of the document eventually signed by the developer, the authorities, and the environmental associations on 11 September 1990 remains doubtful. While promises and assurances given by the developer to the environmental association, notably an undertaking to reduce the proposed site by 22ha, could be interpreted as a contract under private law, commitments made by the authorities not to licence any other project for the industrialization of the area under the original zoning ordinances would appear to be of doubtful validity. For the administrative courts have made it clear that decisions in this area concern the public police powers which can only be exercised unilaterally by the authorities and cannot be "contracted out".

In conclusion one has to say that the agreed compromise has benefited the remaining Rhine valley forest and contributed to its protection.

Paradoxically, the position of the state and its authorities emerged reinforced from the conflict. For in the course of the dispute, the authorities repeatedly confirmed their commitment to protecting the remaining forests without receiving any objections from those who continued to be in favour of further industrial developments in the area.

The position of the environmental association emerged strengthened form the conflict as well. Not only had they been perceived by the public as the state's only official interlocutor on environmental matters. They had also come to be seen as a sensible interlocutor capable of accepting compromise solutions.

Authors

Gerrit Betlem, lawyer, Centre for Enforcement of European Law, University of Utrecht, Utrecht, the Netherlands

Luuk Boerema, lawyer, Werkgroep Eemsmond, Groningen, the Netherlands

James Cameron, barrister, director of the Foundation for International Environmental Law and Development (FIELD, Department of Law, University of London, London, UK. James Cameron was Junior Counsel for Greenpeace in the Thorp case.

Yves Corriveau, lawyer, Quebec Environmental Law Centre, Montreal, Canada

Sven Deimann, research associate. Institute for Public and Environmental Law, University of Frankfurt, Frankfurt, Germany

Bernard Dyssli, director of the Institut de Franco-Allemand de Recherche sur l'Environnement, Strasbourg, France

Carol A Hatton, planning officer, WWF UK, Godalming, UK

Ulf Kjellerup, research assistant, EIA Centre, Roskilde University, Roskilde, Denmark

Ludwig Krämer, lawyer, Commission of the EC, Brussels, Belgium

Sanford Lewis, lawyer, director of the Good Neighborhood Project for Sustainable Industries, Waverly MA, USA

Marie-José Littmann-Martin, director of the Centre du Droit de l'Environnement, professor at the Université Robert Schuman, Strasbourg, France

Stefano Nespor, lawyer, Milano, Italy

Zurab Nogaideli, President of the Environmental Committee, Parliament of the Republic of Georgia, Tbilisi, Georgia

Thomas Ormond, lawyer, official with the administration of the State of Hesse, Darmstadt, Germany

Dumitra Popescu, professor of law, Institute for Legal Research, Romanian Academy of Science, Bucharest, Romania

Y.S. Shemshuchenko, director of the Institute of State and Law, Ukrainian Academy of Sciences, Kiev, the Ukraine

Paul L. Stein, judge, Land and Environment Court of New South Wales, Sydney, Australia

Todd True, lawyer, Sierra Club Legal Defense Fund, Seattle CA, USA. He and his colleagues in the Northwest Office represent the environmental litigants in the cases discussed in this paper.

Sandra Walker, lawyer in a private practice, Toronto, Ontario, Canada. Formerly she was employed by the Ontario Ministry of Environment and Energy as Senior Policy Analyst in the Environmental Bill of Rights Office.

INDEX